KANJI PICT·O·GRAPHIX

To Hyang
I'll never forget

KANJI

PICT·O·GRAPHIX

OVER 1,000 JAPANESE KANJI AND KANA MNEMONICS

Michael Rowley

Stone Bridge Press
Berkeley, California

■ ACKNOWLEDGMENTS

My wife, Kang Hyang Kil, has helped me with every facet of this book for the past three years; giving insights into meaning of characters, critiquing my drawings and page designs, and constructing layouts on the computer. I dedicate this book to her for all her sacrifices and inspiration. I'd also like to thank my brother Chris Rowley for helping put the manuscript on disk, my parents for their help and encouragement, and my publisher, Peter Goodman, for his patience and skill.—*M.R.*

Kanji definitions are taken from *A Guide to Remembering Japanese Characters* by Kenneth G. Henshall (Tokyo, Japan, and Rutland, Vermont: Charles E. Tuttle Co., Inc., 1988) with permission of the publisher.

This book was produced on an Apple Macintosh II computer. Illustrations were drawn by hand, scanned into the computer, and redrawn using Adobe Illustrator, Streamline, and Photoshop. The pages, including the text and illustrations, were laid out in Adobe Illustrator and then imported into QuarkXPress. QuarkXPress was also used for the front- and backmatter. Macrons and underlines for the Roman characters were made with Altsys Fontographer. The kanji were set on a Toshiba Dynabook laptop computer and output on a Compugraphic phototypesetter in Tokyo, and were placed both electronically in QuarkXPress and by hand. Final output was done on a Linotronic 330.

Book design by Michael Rowley, Eye Cue Design.

25 24 23 22 21 20

Published by Stone Bridge Press, P.O. Box 8208, Berkeley, CA 94707.

Printed in the United States of America.

Library of Congress Cataloging-in-Publication Data
Rowley, Michael.
Kanji pict-o-graphix: over 1,000 Japanese kanji and kana mnemonics / Michael Rowley.
p. cm.
Includes index.
ISBN 978-0-9628137-0-2
1. Chinese characters—Japan—Glossaries, vocabularies, etc. 2. Japanese language—Glossaries, vocabularies, etc. I. Title.
PL677.6.R69 1991
495.6'82421—dc20 91-23153
CIP

Contents

Introduction

How do you study the written Japanese characters known as kanji? If you are a child in a Japanese school, you write each kanji hundreds of times at your desk. After a while, by sheer persistence, it sticks in your memory. If you are not a Japanese schoolchild, you probably do what I did. You stare at each kanji and make up a story in your head that you can mentally "attach" to the kanji to help you recall its meaning when you meet it again in the future. This kind of mental memory aid is called a "mnemonic" device. In this book I provide mnemonic devices in the form of text and pictures for over 1,000 kanji, or about half of all the kanji in general use in Japanese newspapers and other printed material.

Kanji developed from pictures used by the Chinese several thousand years ago to represent the world around them. Some types of kanji have retained their pictographic forms and look very much like the objects they represent. The group of kanji called **pictographs** are stylized representations of actual physical objects:

川	山	門
river 55	*mountain* 167	*gate* 1101

Symbols use logical designs to indicate more abstract notions:

上	下	中
over 942	*under* 943	*middle* 950

Ideographs put two pictographs or symbols together to create a related idea:

日	+	月	=	明
sun 1		*moon* 14		*bright* 8

The above three types of kanji are fairly easy to remember. The group of kanji called **phono-ideographs**, however, are more challenging. These kanji combine an element that gives a clue to pronunciation with an element that hints at the "subject matter" of the kanji. Most kanji—perhaps 80%—fall into this category. The theme element, called a radical, may itself be a stand-alone kanji or some graphic variant of one. TREE 126, for example, is a character by itself. Used as a radical it usually indicates something made of wood or relating to trees:

木	柳	材
tree 126	*willow* 128	*timber* 152

The right-hand elements here give a clue to pronunciation. The problem is that they may have little or nothing to do with the character's meaning. This makes creating a mnemonic for them much more difficult. But even pictographic forms have often been simplified and stylized over the centuries. The kanji STOP 1205, for instance, has changed greatly from its original depiction of a footprint:

■ HOW TO USE THIS BOOK

The organization of this book differs from that used in most kanji-learning books for Westerners, where characters appear in order of frequency or in the order used in Japanese schools. Since the whole point of mnemonics is to create associations, I have grouped my kanji thematically with their cousins and near cousins in sound, meaning, or appearance. There is no formal pedagogical basis for my organization. My goal was simply to discover graphic and mnemonic affinities, thus bringing kanji together that are normally very distant from each other in dictionaries as well as people's minds.

My kanji selections do include several that are not on the list of kanji approved for general use by the Japanese Ministry of Education. They are here because they were visually interesting to me. By the same token, several common kanji have been excluded because frankly I couldn't come up with a satisfactory visual or textual mnemonic. For a comprehensive, graduated course in kanji, see Kenneth G. Henshall's very fine book, *A Guide to Remembering Japanese Characters* (Charles E. Tuttle, 1988). I have relied heavily on Henshall's book, which was especially useful for its kanji definitions and its descriptions of kanji elements and origins. For simplicity and economy of space, I have occasionally made modifications to Mr. Henshall's listings.

You may find it easier to learn the complex kanji if you begin with the stand-alone characters and the other elements used as radicals. Many of these basic kanji and kanji elements are presented here alongside the large-format illustrations. Flip through the book and concentrate on these characters first.

The smaller entries on each two-page spread often incorporate the basic elements presented in the large-format illustrations. A few character entries appear without an illustration. Illustrations of the elements that appear in these characters can be found using the schematics and cross-reference numbers at the bottom of each entry.

■ GUIDE TO THE ENTRIES

The standard kanji entries in this book include the following information:

1. Meaning in English. For the most part the kanji definitions are drawn from Henshall's book. Definitions that treat the whole kanji as a semantic form are somewhat misleading and imprecise, however. The meaning of any kanji is best gleaned from the many words it is used to represent. When the entry kanji is used in Japanese only as an element within other kanji, the definition is enclosed in quotation marks.

2. Reference number. A sequence number used in the index and in kanji cross-references.

3. Kanji character. A plain typeset form was selected for each entry character to make the association with the visual mnemonic more clear. This form is commonly encountered in printed materials. (Kanji written by hand sometimes look very different from their typographic forms.)

4. *On* (borrowed Chinese) reading. Always in upper case. These pronunciations (*on-yomi*) derive from those used in China when the kanji was first brought to Japan. The Japanese adapted the Chinese sounds to their own speech. The same character may have been imported several times each time with a different reading, thus producing the multiple readings in use today.

5. *Kun* (Japanese) reading. Always in lower case. These pronunciations (*kun-yomi*) represent native Japanese words "fitted" to the imported kanji. Most Japanese verbs and adjectives are *kun* readings. Underlined letters represent verbal or adjectival inflections that are not a part of the kanji's actual reading.

6. Visual mnemonic. I have taken many liberties in creating the pictures that go with the kanji. Sometimes I have tried to preserve the historical etymology of the character; elsewhere I have abandoned it in favor of something that, to my eyes, made more sense. I usually used the identical drawing to represent the same kanji element in different visual mnemonics, but not always. I have, for example, taken creative license with the element MOUTH 566 (also used to express "opening," or "enclosed"), drawing it instead as a tomato in CULTIVATE 246 and a box in DOUBLE 631. I have also

口 *mouth 566* 培 *cultivate 246* 倍 *double 631*

willfully visually "confused" certain elements that Japanese teachers are always insisting must *never* be confused. One example: the interchanging of SOIL 101 and WARRIOR 753. The schematic of elements (see number 8, below) identifies the correct form.

土 *soil 101* 士 *warrior 753*

7. Text mnemonic. Keyed to the visual mnemonic. The keywords are in boldface type.

8. Schematic of elements. Each box indicates the position of one of the main elements in the kanji. The element may be a radical, or it may be another kanji (if it is another kanji, its shape as an element may be compressed or slightly altered). The schematic boxes are not used when the entry kanji is a stand-alone kanji or is a radical or element with no other use except as a combining form. And again, sometimes I have had to concoct and interpret elements when none, according to Henshall and others, may actually exist. While the schematic of elements is a helpful reference aid, keep in mind that it is a guideline only.

9. Element meaning. Refers to the first definition given for the kanji or radical used as an element in the entry kanji. I have tried to use the meaning of the element in the visual and text mnemonics.

10. Cross-reference number. Refers to the sequential reference number of the element used in the entry kanji.

11. Notes reference number. Some characters have elements whose meanings are archaic or that correspond to no stand-alone character or radical in Japanese, such as the right side of PLACE 28. Other characters, like COCOON 307, are too complex graphically to describe with a simple schematic:

場 *place 28* 繭 *cocoon 307*

Comments on such complex elements appear in a numbered Notes section at the back of the book. These comments are referenced by "n–000" instead of a cross-reference number. Again, much of the information here derives from Henshall's book, which describes the kanji elements in detail.

THE SYLLABARIES

In addition to kanji, Japanese uses two phonetic syllabaries, hiragana and katakana. Each syllabary of forty-six characters represents the same sounds. The cursive hiragana are used to write words not normally written in kanji and for verb endings and parts of speech. The angular katakana are used for emphasis and to write words and names not of Japanese or Chinese origin.

GOODBYE

さ sa
よ yo
う (u)
な na
ら ra

(hiragana)

MCDONALD'S

マ ma
ク ku
ド do
ナ na
ル ru
ド do

(katakana)

か
な

A (hiragana)

あ 

Ah! I see the letter "A".

A (katakana)

ア 

Ah! I see the letter "A".

KA (hiragana)

か 

Cut the sausage.

KA (katakana)

カ 

Cut the sausage.

I (hiragana)

い 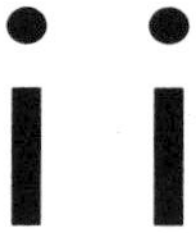

Hawa**ii**.

I (katakana)

イ 

Eat with chopsticks.

KI (hiragana)

き 

Key.

KI (katakana)

キ 

Key.

U (hiragana)

う 

Uhh!

U (katakana)

ウ 

Uhh!

KU (hiragana)

く 

Koo-koo bird.

KU (katakana)

ク 

Co**coo**n.

E (hiragana)

え 

Exotic bird.

E (katakana)

エ 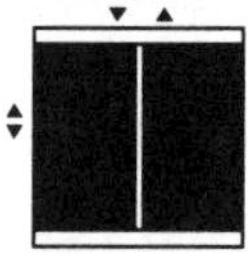

Elevator doors.

KE (hiragana)

け 

Keg.

KE (katakana)

ケ 

A tilted letter "**K**".

O (hiragana)

お 

Olive.

O (katakana)

オ 

On and Off Switch.

KO (hiragana)

こ 

Coin.

KO (katakana)

コ 

A street **co**rner.

SA (hiragana)

さ

Sob.

SA (katakana)

サ

Sod.

TA (hiragana)

た

ta

ta

TA (katakana)

タ

Tomahawk.

SHI (hiragana)

し

She has flowing hair.

SHI (katakana)

シ

She has a funny smile.

CHI (hiragana)

ち

AAAA**CHI**OOOO!

CHI (katakana)

チ

Cheer.

SU (hiragana)

す

Soon the sprout will bloom.

SU (katakana)

ス

Suit hanger.

TSU (hiragana)

つ

I**t's** a snake.

TSU (katakana)

ツ

Balls and ba**ts**.

SE (hiragana)

せ

Say.

SE (katakana)

セ

Say.

TE (hiragana)

て

Ten

Ten.

TE (katakana)

テ

Telephone pole.

SO (hiragana)

そ

Sew a zigzag stitch.

SO (katakana)

ソ

Sew a stitch.

TO (hiragana)

と

A thorn in my **toe**.

TO (katakana)

ト

toe

The "t" in **toe**.

NA (hiragana)

な

Knot.

NA (katakana)

ナ

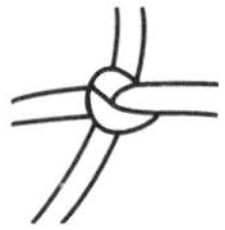

Knot.

HA (hiragana)

は

Ha, ha, ha.

HA (katakana)

ハ

Break it in **ha**lf.

NI (hiragana)

に

Knee.

NI (katakana)

ニ

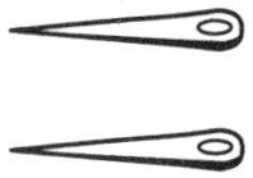

Two **nee**dles.

HI (hiragana)

ひ

Hee, hee, hee.

HI (katakana)

ヒ

He's sitting down.

NU (hiragana)

ぬ

Noodle held by chopsticks.

NU (katakana)

ヌ

Violence is in the **new**s.

FU (hiragana)

ふ

Who?

FU (katakana)

フ

Who?

NE (hiragana)

ね

Net a big fish.

NE (katakana)

ネ

I **ne**ver go to church.

HE (hiragana)

へ

This way to **he**aven.

HE (katakana)

ヘ

This way to **he**aven.

NO (hiragana)

の

NO Smoking.

NO (katakana)

ノ

NO Smoking.

HO (hiragana)

ほ

Half a **who**le note.

HO (katakana)

ホ

Holy cross.

MA (hiragana)

ま

A baby cries,"**Ma**ma."

MA (katakana)

マ

Mama's breast.

MI (hiragana)

み

Me, I'm 21.

MI (katakana)

ミ

Do, re, **mi**.

MU (hiragana)

む

A cow says, "**Moo**."

MU (katakana)

ム

A cow says, "**Moo**."

ME (hiragana)

め

Me is Japanese for "eye."

ME (katakana)

メ

Mexico.

MO (hiragana)

も

Catch **mo'** fish with this.

MO (katakana)

モ

Catch **mo'** fish with this.

YA (hiragana)

や

Yak.

YA (katakana)

ヤ

Yak.

YU (hiragana)

ゆ

Trying to make a **U**-turn.

YU (katakana)

ユ

You are number one.

YO (hiragana)

よ

Yo-yo.

YO (katakana)

ヨ

Yodel.

ya yu yo

ya	yu	yo
ゃ	ゅ	ょ
Yak.	**U**-turn.	**Yo**-yo.

*These kana written small turn **ki**, **shi**, **chi**, **ni**, **hi**, **mi**, **ri**, into **kya**, **sha**, **cha**, **nya**, **hya**, **mya**, **rya**; **kyu**, **shu**, **chu**, **nyu**, **hyu**, **myu**, **ryu**; and **kyo**, **sho**, **cho**, **nyo**, **hyo**, **myo**, **ryo**.*

DOUBLERS

う

*The kana **U** is used to double the O and U vowel sounds of other kana: ko→ kō, ku→ kū, etc.*

DOUBLERS

っ

*Certain consonants are doubled when preceded by a smaller, silent **tsu**, as in:*

ざっし
zasshi

RA

ら

Roger the rabbit.

RA

ラ

Rocket.

WA

わ

Wasp.

WA

ワ

Wow, his head's knocked off!

RI

り

Reeds.

RI

リ

Reeds.

(W)O

を

The cowboy said, "**Whoa**."

(W)O

ヲ

An arr**ow** head.

RU

る

Three **ru**bies.

RU

ル

Leg and tail of kanga**roo**.

N

ん

The sound of "**n**".

N

ン

Nicks and cuts.

RE

れ

Rain and lightning.

RE

レ

Rain shoe.

NONVOICED SOUNDS

ぱ

(Soda) ***p**op sound.*

*This mark changes the pronunciations of **ha**, **hi**, **fu**, **he**, and **ho** to popping sounds: **pa**, **pi**, **pu**, **pe**, and **po**.*

RO

ろ

Three rubies **ro**lled away.

RO

ロ

Rotate a nut.

VOICED SOUNDS

ば

*Vocal cord vi**b**rations.*

*This mark changes the pronunciations of all the kana in the series beginning **ka**, **sa**, **ta**, and **ha** to vibrating sounds: **ga**, **za**, **da**, and **ba**.*

KANJI COMPOUNDS

Each kanji has meaning by itself. Kanji also can be combined in kanji compounds, or *jukugo*, to form new meanings, much as root words, prefixes, and suffixes are combined in English. The compound meaning "world," shown at right, is composed of **SE** 1081, meaning WORLD, and **KAI** 203, meaning BOUNDARY. Other combinations include:

JAPAN

日本

NI *sun* 1 — **HON** *origin* 125

FEBRUARY

二月

NI *two* 898 — **GATSU** *month* 14

FOREIGNER

外人

GAI *outside* 13 — **JIN** *person* 363

EXIT

出口

de *emerge* 955 — **guchi** *opening* 566

STUDENT

学生

GAKU *study* 839 — **SEI** *gain* 214

LETTER

手紙

te *hand* 579 — **gami** *paper* 974

世界

The Sun

日 SUN, DAY 1

NICHI, JITSU
hi, -ka

The **sun** rises each **day**.

PROSPEROUS, GOOD, CLEAR 2

昌

SHŌ

As **clear** as a day with two suns.

sun 1 sun 1

CRYSTAL, CLEAR, BRIGHT 3

晶

SHŌ

As **bright** as a day with three suns.

sun 1 sun 1 sun 1

CLEAR, BRIGHT 4

晃

KŌ

The sun and a candle shine **clear** and **bright** light.

sun 1 shine 869

REFLECT, SHINE 5

映

EI
utsuru/su, haeru

The sun **shines** outward from its center.

sun 1 center 955

DAMP, MOIST, HUMID 6

湿

SHITSU
shimeru/su

The sun evaporates water, making the air **humid**.

water 66 sun 1 wet n–6

WARM 7

温

ON
atatakai/meru

The sun **warms** water in a tray.

water 66 sun 1 dish 265

CLEAR, BRIGHT 8

明

MEI, MYŌ
akarui, akeru

As **bright** as the sun and moon together.

sun 1 moon 14

EVENING 11

夕

SEKI
yū

In the **evening**, the moon rises …

MORNING, COURT 9

朝

CHŌ
asa

The **morning** is shared by the sun and the moon.

rise n–9 moon 14

NIGHT 12

夜

YA
yo, yoru

… making a nice view at **night**.

shelter 1147 person 362 evening 11

DARK, GLOOMY 10

暗

AN
kurai

Gloomy people see the **dark** shadow instead of the sun.

sun 1 stand 627 sun 1

OUTSIDE, OTHER, UNDO 13

外

GAI, GE
soto, hoka, hazusu

He went **outside** and **undid** his pants when nature called.

evening 11 crack n–13

The Moon

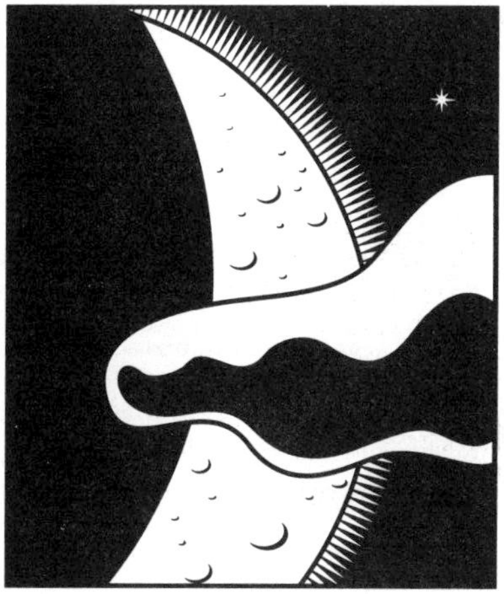

月 MOON 14

GATSU, GETSU
tsuki

A crescent **moon** in the clouds.

The Day

MORNING, DAWN 15

旦

TAN

From **dawn** …

sun 1 one 897

NOON, DAYTIME 16

昼

CHŪ
hiru

… til **noon**, we measure the land.

measure 884 dawn 15

DAY OF THE WEEK 18

曜

YŌ

The **days of the week** fly by.

sun 1 winged bird n–18

EVENING, LATE 17

晩

BAN

We can only escape the sun's heat in **late evening**.

sun 1 escape 1167

EARLY, PROMPT, FAST 19

早

SŌ
hayai

The sun rises through the grass **early** in the morning.

sun 1 grass n–19

DAWN, LIGHT, EVENT 20

暁

GYŌ
akatsuki

Three stars were seen at **dawn**.

sun 1 clear n–20

OLD, PAST 21

旧

KYŪ

One day is **past** …

high n–21 · sun 1

BRIGHT, LIGHT 24

昭

SHŌ

The **bright light** of the sun glints off the sword.

sun 1 · sword 1023 · opening 566

SUNNY, MALE, POSITIVE 27

陽

YŌ
hi

On the **sunny** side of the hill …

hill 1094 · sun 1 · rays n–26

CHILD 22

児

JI, NI
ko

… and one more **child** is born.

past 21 · kneeling n–22

ILLUMINATE, SHINE 25

照

SHŌ
teru/rasu

The sword is **illuminated** by the sun above and fire below.

bright 24 · fire 82

PLACE 28

場

JŌ
ba

… is a **place** in the soil …

soil 102 · sun 1 · rays n–26

EASY, CHANGE, DIVINATION 23

易

EKI, I
yasui, yasashii

Life is **easy** in the sunshine.

sun 1 · big-eyed lizard n–23

RAISE, FRY 26

揚

YŌ
ageru/garu

Raise your hand in the **frying** hot sun.

hand 000 · sun 1 · rays n–26

HOT WATER, HOT SPRING 29

湯

TŌ
yu

… where **hot water springs** up.

water 66 · sun 1 · rays n–26

Time

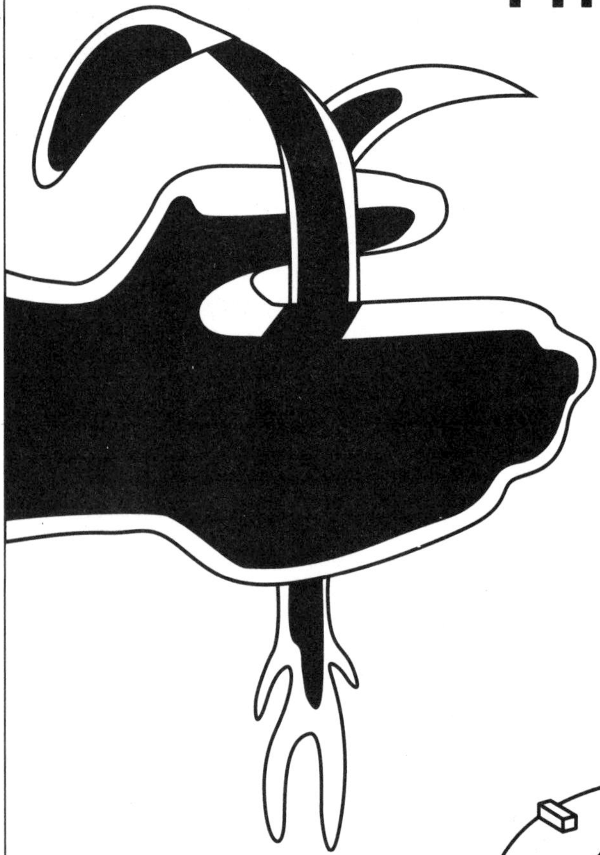

NOON 32

午

GO

It's **noon**—straight up.

YEAR 31

年

NEN
toshi

We plant rice every **year**.

LONG TIME, LASTING 33

久

KYŪ, KU
hisa<u>shii</u>

I've been waiting a **long time**.

NOW 30

今

KON, KIN
ima

What time is it **now**?

RECITE 34

吟

GIN

I will now **recite** …

◧ mouth 566 ◨ now 30

THOUGHT, CONCERN 35

念

NEN

… my heartfelt **thoughts**.

⬒ now 30 ⬓ heart 499

SEASON, YOUNG 36

季

KI

A child as **young** and green as a new **season's** rice plants.

rice plant 231 child 447

TEN-DAY PERIOD 37

旬

JUN

Ten days of sunshine in June.

wrap 949 sun 1

PERMIT, FORGIVE 38

許

KYO
yurusu, moto

Permit me to speak at noon.

speak 840 noon 37

GRIEF, SADNESS 39

愁

SHŪ
urei/eru

I've got the autumn **blues**.

autumn 41 heart 499

SUMMER 40

夏

KA, GE
natsu

Inescapable **summer** heat.

mask n–40 slow progress 1218

AUTUMN 41

秋

SHŪ
aki

Rice stalks turn the fiery colors of **autumn**.

rice plant 231 fire 83

WINTER 42

冬

TŌ
fuyu

Winter snow and ice impede my progress.

slow progress 1218 ice 94

SPRING 43

春

SHUN
haru

Cherry trees bloom in the **spring** sun.

branches n–43 sun 1

Wind, Rain, & Clouds

WIND, STYLE 44

風

FŪ
kaze

A boat is tossed by the **wind**.

RAIN 45

雨

U
ame, ama–

Drops of **rain** come …

CLOUD 46

雲

UN
kumo

… and **clouds** swirl …

rain 45 cloud 54

CLOUD, DIM, MAR 47

曇

DON
kumoru

... and **dim** the light of day.

sun 1 — cloud 46

THUNDER, LIGHTNING 48

雷

RAI
kaminari

Lightning flashes and **thunder** echoes in the field.

rain 45 — field 201

ELECTRICITY 49

電

DEN

An **electrical** field travels down the wire.

rain 45 — lightning n–49

SHAKE, TREMBLE 50

震

SHIN
furuu/eru

I **shake** and **tremble** at the foot of a cliff.

rain 45 — tremble n–50

DEW, REVEAL, SMALL, RUSSIA 51

露

RO, RŌ
tsuyu

Dew is on the **Russian** road.

rain 45 — road 1214

CONVEY, TRANSMIT 52

伝

DEN
tsutaeru/waru

People **transmit** clouds of contagious diseases.

person 362 — cloud 54

ATMOSPHERE 53

雰

FUN

Rain is part of the **atmosphere**.

rain 45 — divide n–53

"CLOUD" 54

云

As an element this means ***cloud****. Alone, it is a rarely used character meaning "speak." See 840.*

Water

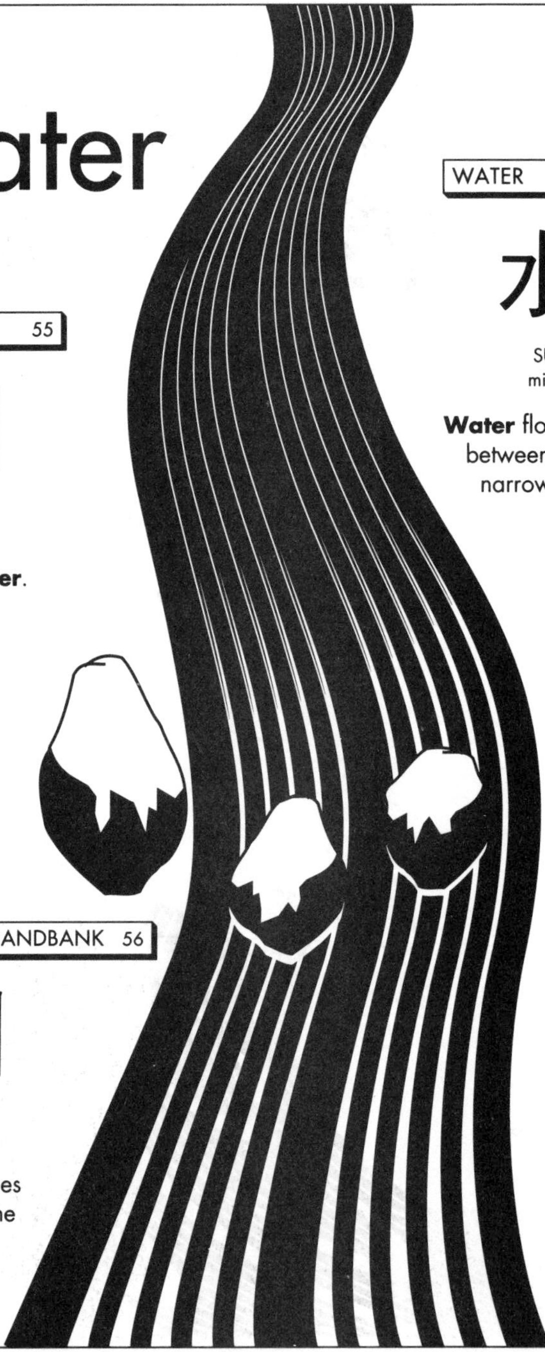

RIVER 55

川

SEN
kawa

A flowing **river**.

PROVINCE, SANDBANK 56

州

SHŪ
su

Stepping stones lead across the river to the **sandbank**.

WATER 57

水

SUI
mizu

Water flows between the narrow banks.

FLOW, STREAM 58

流

RYŪ, RU
nagareru/su

A person **flows** down**stream**.

water 66 · person n–58 · river 55

FACTION 59

派

HA

Rivulets **diverge** from the mainstream.

water 66 · river 55

CALAMITY 60

災

SAI
wazawai

A **calamity** of flood and fire.

river 55 · fire 83

OPEN SEA, SOAR 61

沖

CHŪ
oki

A ship in the middle of the **open sea**.

water 66 | middle 954

HARBOR, PORT 64

港

KŌ
minato

Together, two people come to the **harbor** to see their reflection.

water 66 | together 388 | self 450

BAY, GULF 65

湾

WAN

Sittin' on the dock of the **bay**.

water 66 | red n–65 | pull 817

DEEP WATER, ABYSS 62

淵

EN
fuchi

Deep water engulfs the trees.

water 66 | planks n–62

"WATER" 66

氵

*This is the radical for **water**.*

SEA 67

海

KAI
umi

The **sea** is the mother of life.

water 66 | person 363 | mother 446

CAVE, PENETRATE 63

洞

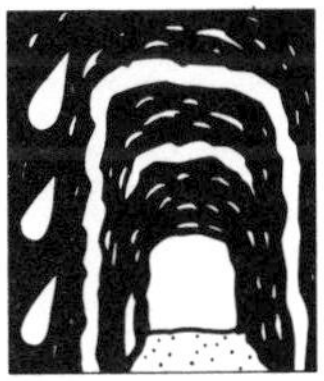

DŌ
hora

Water **penetrates** the **cave**.

water 66 | same 889

Wash

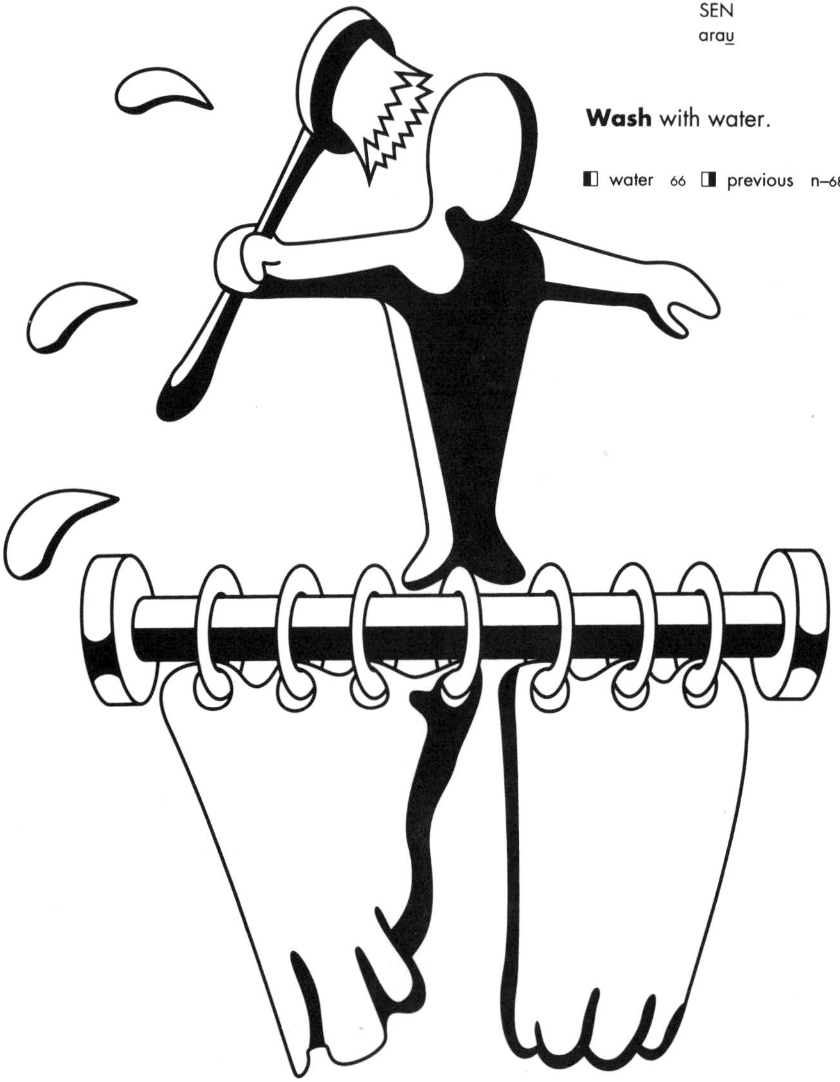

WASH, INVESTIGATE 68

洗

SEN
arau

Wash with water.

◧ water 66 ◨ previous n–68

STEAM, VAPOR 69

汽

KI

Swirling **steam**.

◧ water 66 ◨ steam n–69

DIRT, DISHONOR 70

汚

○
kegareru/su/rawashii,
yogoreru/su, kitanai

Tears cannot wash the **dirt** of your **dishonor**.

◧ water 66 ◨ stagnant n–70

BATHE 71

浴

YOKU
abiru

Bathe in a valley of water.

◧ water 66 ◨ valley 168

SHALLOW, LIGHT 72

浅

SEN
asai

Splash in the **shallow** water.

water 66 halberds 801

FLOAT, FLEETING 75

浮

FU
uku/kabu/kaberu

A hand lets a child **float** in the water.

water 66 hand 611 child 447

BOIL, GUSH 78

沸

FUTSU
waku/kasu

A **gushing** fountain of **boiling** water.

water 66 emerge n–78

DRY, DEFENSE 73

干

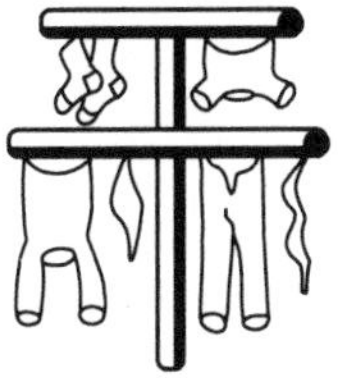

KAN
horu, hiru

Clothes **dry** on the line.

DEPEND ON, DUE TO, REASON 76

由

YU, YŪ
yoshi

Depending on where you place the drill in the field …

SOURCE, ORIGIN 79

源

GEN
minamoto

The spring is our **source** of water.

water 66 origin 81

SWEAT 74

汗

KAN
ase, asebamu

This sweater makes me **sweat**.

water 66 dry 72

OIL 77

油

YU
abura

… you may have gushing **oil**.

water 66 depend on 76

SPRING 80

泉

SEN
izumi

A **spring** …

white 45 water 57

PLAIN, ORIGIN 81

原

GEN
hara

… **originates** from the **plain**.

cliff n–81 spring 80

Fire

"FIRE" 82

灬 *This is a radical for **fire**.*

FIRE 83

火

KA
hi

A camp **fire**.

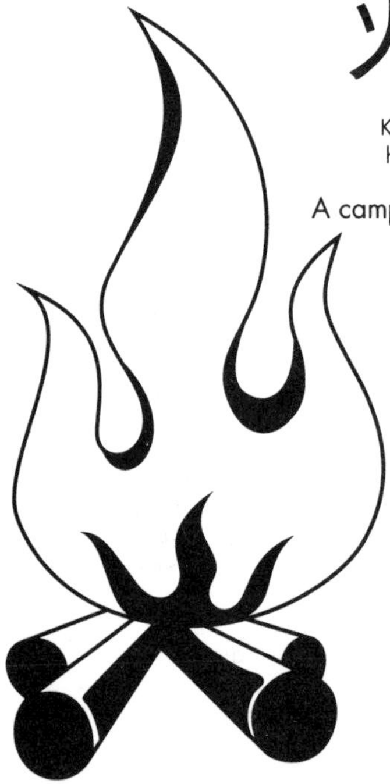

LIGHT, LAMP 84

灯

TŌ
hi

Light the **lamp** with fire.

◧ fire 83 ◨ exact 1089

BURN, ROAST 85

焼

SHŌ
yaku/keru

Roast barbeque.

◧ fire 83 ◨ high n–20

FLAME 86

炎

EN
honō

The **flames** of two fires …

⬒ fire 83 ⬓ fire 83

PALE, LIGHT, FAINT 87

淡

TAN
awai

… become **faint** because of the rain.

◧ water 66 ◨ flame 86

THREATEN, MENACE 88

嚇

KAKU
odosu/kasu

Two samurai screamed when **threatened** by **menacing** flames.

◧ mouth 566 ◨ red (x2) n–65

VIOLENCE, EXPOSE 89

暴

BŌ, BAKU
abareru/ku

Exposed to the **violent** heat of the sun …

⬒ sun 1 ⬓ offer n–89

BURST, EXPLODE 90

爆

BAKU

… a firecracker **explodes** in a **burst** of fire.

◧ fire 83 ◨ violence 89

Ice

EAST 91

東

TŌ
higashi

The sun rises through the trees in the **east**.

tree 126 sun 1

FREEZE 92

凍

TŌ
kōru, kogoeru

It's **freezing** in the east.

ice 94 east 91

ICE 94

氷

HYŌ
kōri

A penguin looks through cracks in the **ice**.

water 66 crack n–94

"ICE" 95

冫

*This element means **ice**.*

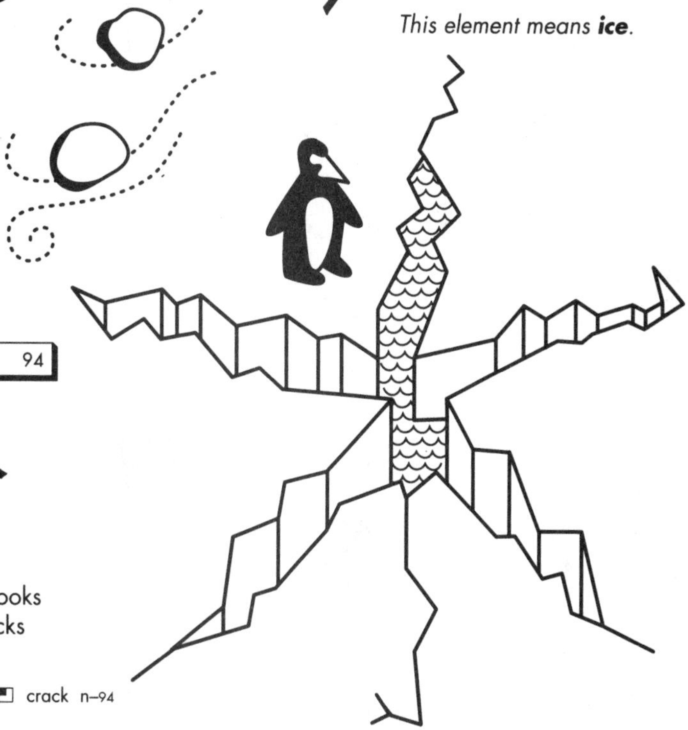

COLD 93

寒

KAN
samui

When it's **cold**, the shrubs have no leaves.

roof 1144 plants n–93 ice 94

SNOW 96

雪

SETSU
yuki

Snow: rain you can hold in your hand.

rain 45 hand n–597

FROST 97

霜

SŌ
shimo

I can see the **frost** forming on the tree.

rain 45 tree 126 eye 538

AREA, LIMITS 98

域

IKI

Hal draws up the **area's** boundaries.

◧ soil 101 ◨ halberd 801

SLOPE 99

坂

HAN
saka

A man puts his hand against the **sloping** cliff.

◧ soil 101 ◨ against 957

EMBANKMENT 100

堤

TEI
tsutsumi

The sun shines on the **embankment** of soil.

◧ soil 101 ◨ sun 1 ◨ leg 617

Soil

EARTH, SOIL, GROUND 101

土

DO, TO
tsuchi

A plant grows in the **soil**.

GROUND, LAND 102

地

CHI, JI

Creatures live in the **ground**.

◧ soil 101
◨ creature n–102

MINE, PIT, HOLE 103

坑

KŌ

Miners work in a **hole** deep in the earth.

◧ soil 101 ◨ shelter 1147 ◨ desk 157

RESIST, OPPOSE 104

抗

KŌ

The hands **oppose** management.

◧ hand 660 ◨ shelter 1147 ◨ desk 157

Metal

GOLD, MONEY, METAL 105

金

KIN, KON
kane, kana

Two **gold** nuggets in the soil.

MIRROR 106

鏡

KYŌ
kagami

He stands in front of the metal **mirror**.

metal 105 · stand 627 · scene n–106

CHAIN, LINK 107

鎖

SA
kusari

A little metal **chain**.

metal 105 · little 926 · money 708

FISH, LURE, CHANGE 108

釣

CHŌ
tsuri/ru

A metal **fish lure**.

metal 105 · ladle 265

NEEDLE, POINTER 109

針

SHIN
hari

The metal **needle points** ten degrees north.

metal 105 · ten 906

COIN 110

銭

SEN
zeni

Hal flips a metal **coin**.

metal 105 · halberd 801

TURF, LAWN 111

芝

SHI
shiba

A path winds through the **lawn**.

grass 126 path n–111

STALK, STEM 112

茎

KEI
kuki

A hand cuts the grassy **stalks** from the soil.

grass 124 hand 600 soil 101

CHRYSANTHEMUM 113

菊

KIKU

A **chrysanthemum** in the grass, with rice-colored petals.

grass 124 rice 217

WORK, DUTIES 114

勤

KIN
tsutomeru

My **duty** is to **work** in the garden.

grass 124 flower 119 power 745

GROW THICKLY 115

茂

MO
shigeru

Hal makes the grass **grow thickly**.

grass 124 halberd 801

FLOWER 116

花

KA
hana

The plants change into **flowers**.

grass 124 change 374

ART, SKILL, PLANT 117

芸

GEI

Planting is a **skill** and an **art**.

grass 124 speak n–117

FLOWER, SHOWY, CHINA 118

華

KA, GE
hana

A **Chinese flower** grows among the grass.

grass 124 flower n–118

FRAGRANT, SWEET SMELL 119

芳

HŌ
kanbashii

This person takes in the **sweet smell** of the grass.

grass 124 person 386

Bamboo & Grass

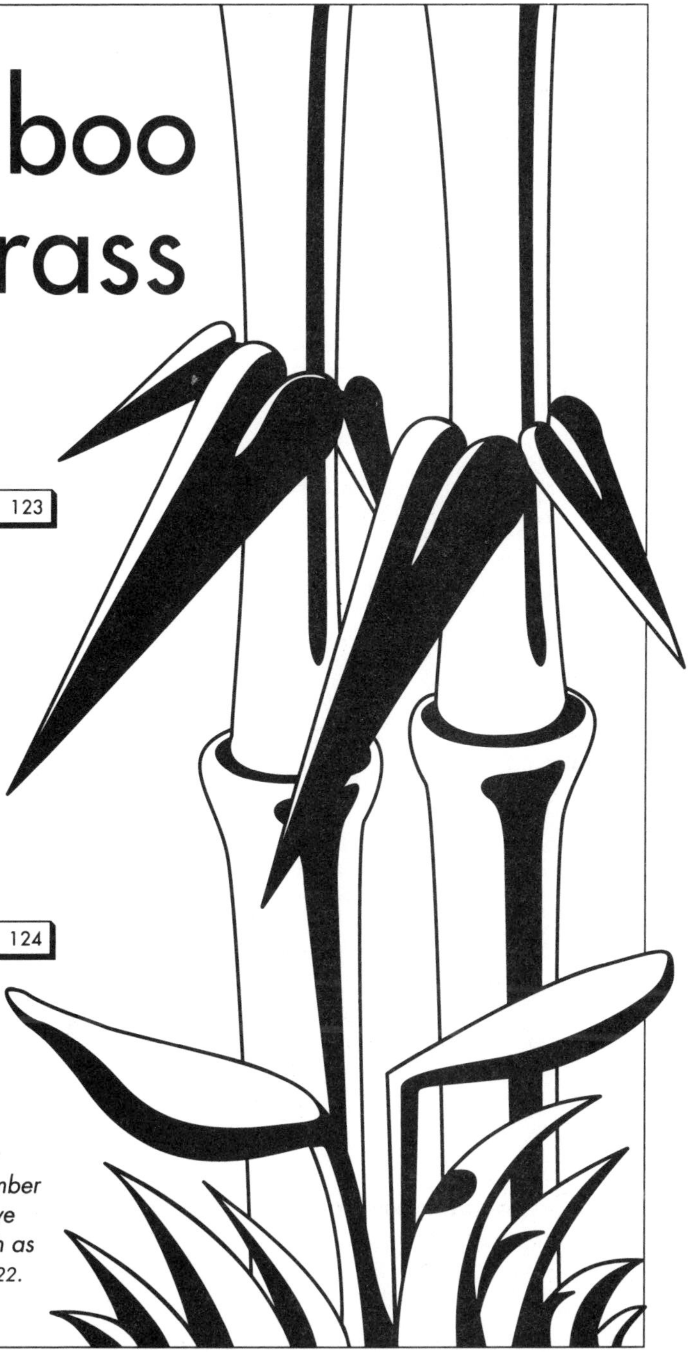

TUBE, CYLINDER 120

筒

TŌ
tsutsu

Cylindrical bamboo **tubes** …

bamboo 123   same 889

PIPE, CONTROL 121

管

KAN
kuda

… are used as **pipes** in the officials' building.

bamboo 123   official 467

RECKON, COUNT 122

算

SAN

Two hands **count** with a bamboo abacus.

bamboo 123   eye 538   hands n–122

BAMBOO 123

竹

CHIKU
take

Bamboo reeds.

"GRASS" 124

艹

This is the radical for ***grass****, though a number of other elements have the same shape, such as* hands *in character* 122.

Trees

本 ROOT, ORIGIN, BOOK 125

HON
moto

The **roots** of a tree are cylindrical.

tree 126 roots n–125

*Character 125 is also used after numbers to indicated that the things being counted are **cylindical**.*

TREE, WOOD 126

木

BOKU, MOKU,
ki, ko-

A **tree** with spreading branches.

GLORY, FLOURISH, SHINE 127

栄

EI
sakaeru, haeru

Blossoms **flourish** on the tree.

shine n–127 tree 126

WILLOW, WILLOWY 128

柳

RYŪ
yanagi

A **willow** tree.

tree 126 flow n–128

GATHER 129

集

SHŪ
atsumeru/maru

Birds **gather** in a tree.

bird 319 tree 126

NEST 130

巣

SŌ
su

Three birds **nest** in a fruit tree.

basket n–130 fruit 126

BALANCE 131

権

KEN, GON

A heron **balances** in a tree.

tree 126 heron 331

TAKE, GATHER 132

採

SAI
toru

Hands **take** acorns from the tree.

hand 580 · hand 611 · tree 126

EXTREME, POLE 133

極

KYOKU, GOKU
kiwameru

Magnetic **poles** are at the **extreme** ends of earth.

tree 126 · extreme n–133

BODY 134

体

TAI, TEI
karada

The **body** is the "root" of a person.

person 362 · root 125

LEAF 135

葉

YŌ
ha

Plants and trees generate **leaves**.

grass 124 · generation 100 · tree 126

PLANTING 136

栽

SAI

Hal **plants** a tree in the soil.

soil 101 · tree 126 · halberd 801

REST 138

休

KYŪ
yasumu

A vacationer **rests** by a tree.

person 362 · tree 126

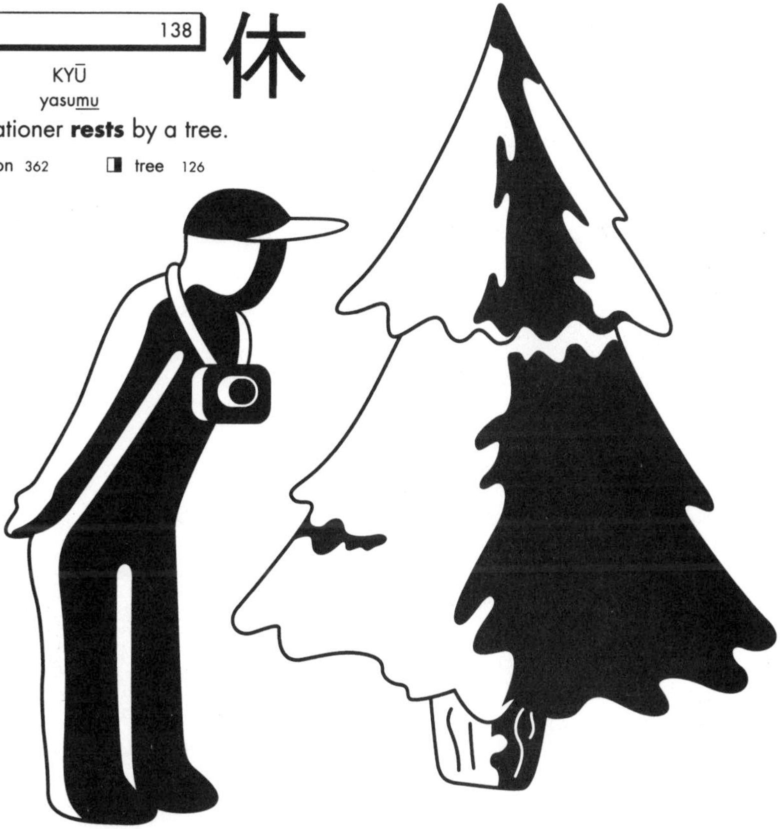

PLANT 137

植

SHOKU
ueru

Plant a tree in the soil.

tree 126 · upright n–137

DIVIDE, ANALYZE 139

析

SEKI

Divide a tree to **analyze** it.

tree 126 ax 1072

FIREWOOD, KINDLING 140

薪

SHIN
takigi, maki

I cut the tree into **kindling**.

grass 124 needle 1006 ax 1072

SHEET, COUNTER 141

枚

MAI

Slice the tree into **sheets**.

tree 126 strike 802

林 FOREST 142

RIN
hayashi

Two trees make a **forest**.

tree 126 tree 126

IMMATURE, NOT YET 144

未

MI
mada

This tree is **immature**.

END, TIP 145

末

MATSU, BATSU
sue

This tree has a big **tip**.

森 WOODS 143

SHIN
mori

Three trees mean **woods**.

tree 126 tree 126 tree 126

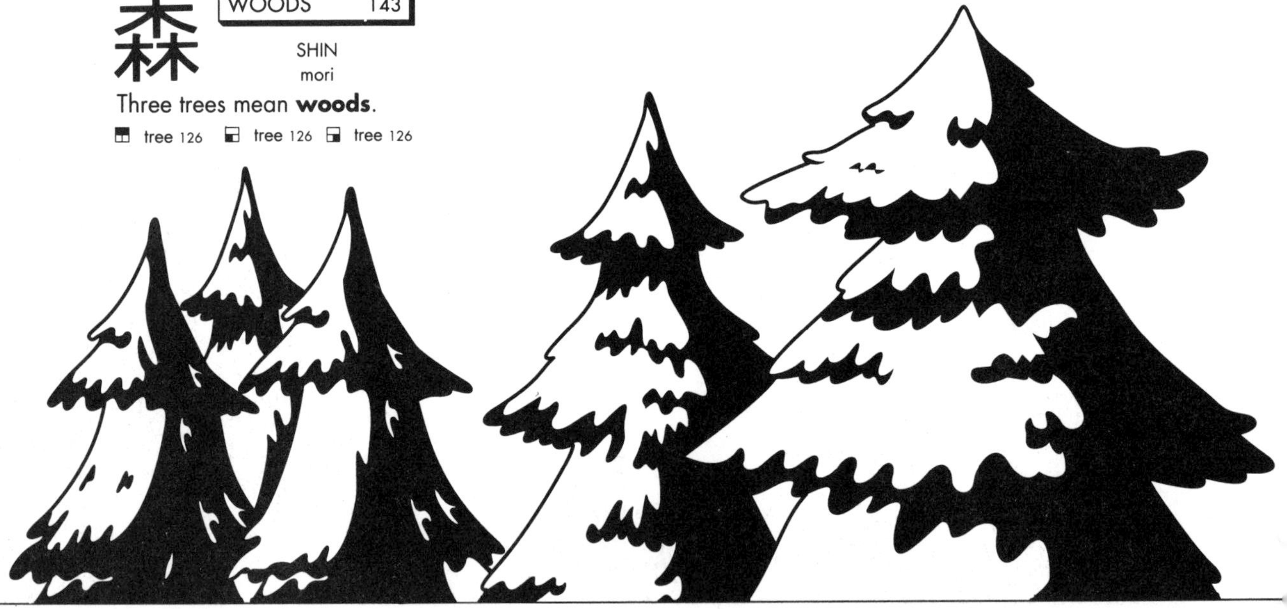

LIMBS 146

肢

SHI

The **limbs** are like branches of flesh.

flesh 267 · branch 148

DRUM 147

鼓

KO
tsuzumi

Beat the **drum** with a branch.

soil 101 · miniature 245 · branch 148

BRANCH, SUPPORT 148

支

SHI
sasaeru

A hand holds up a **branch**.

(TREE) BRANCH 151

枝

SHI
eda, e

A **branch** from a tree.

tree 126 · branch 148

KILL 149

殺

SATSU, SETSU
korosu

Kill the trees.

tree 126 · hand w/ax 792

BRANCH OFF 150

岐

KI

Mountain trails **branch off**.

mountain 167 · branch 148

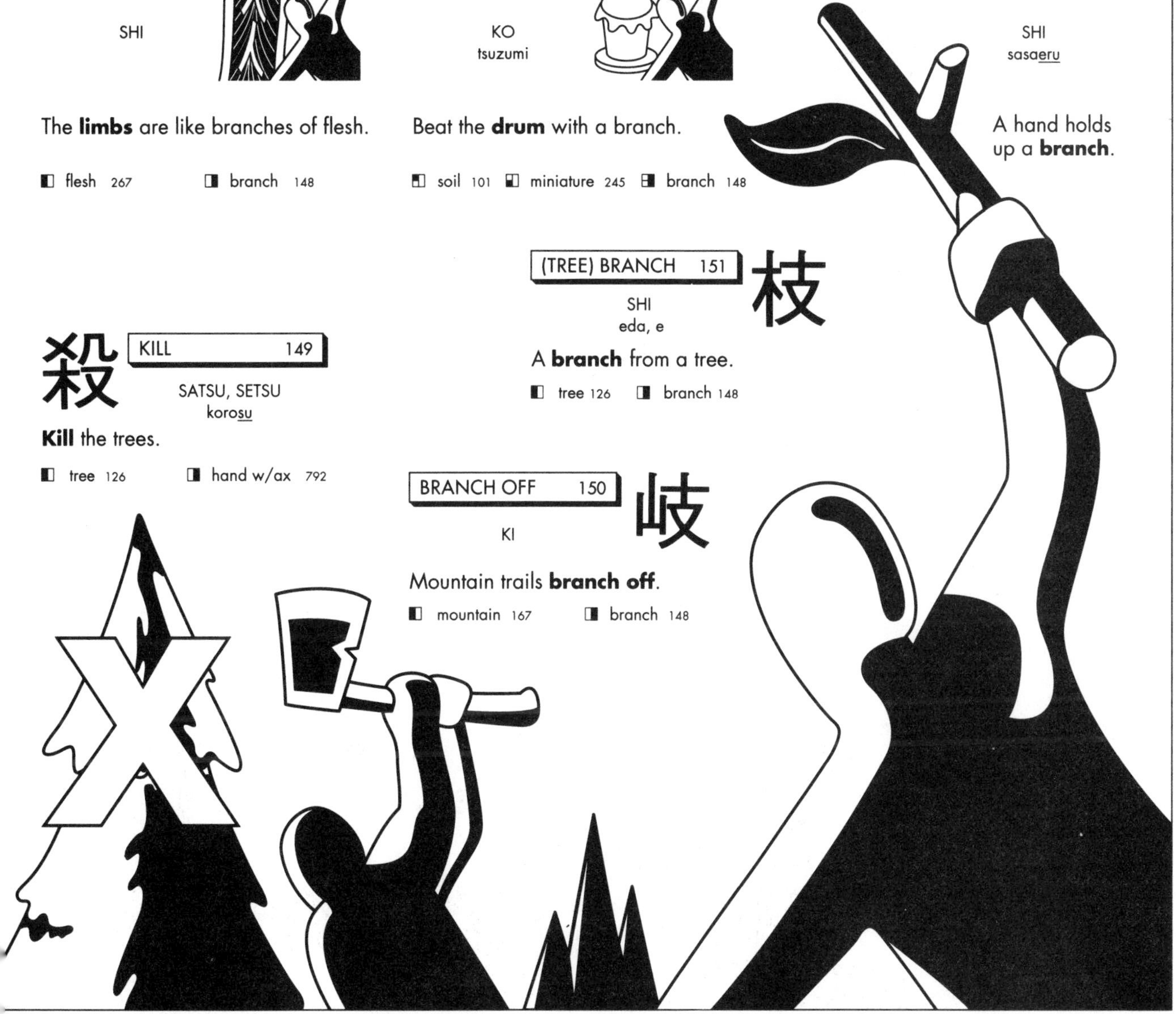

Timber

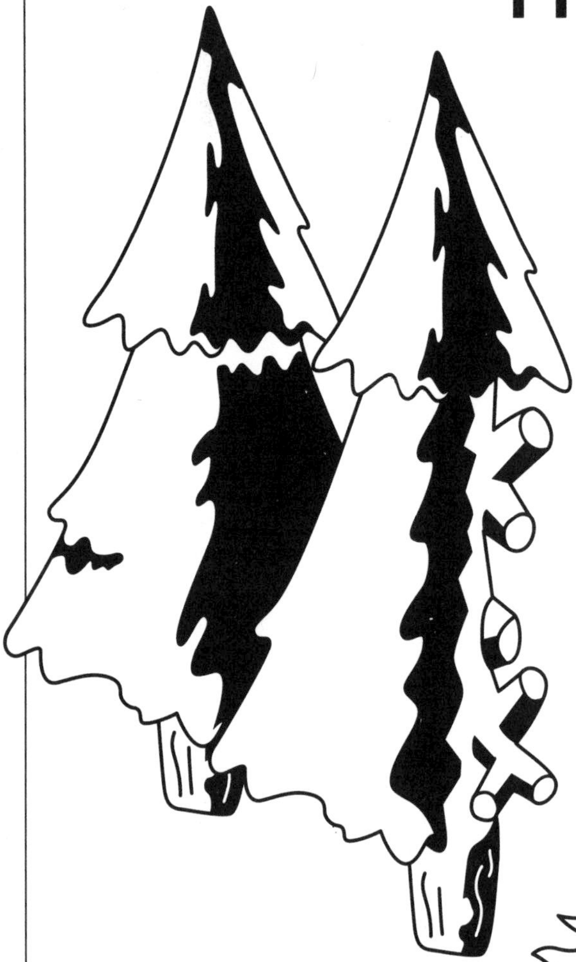

TIMBER, RESOURCE 152

材

ZAI

People have a talent for making trees into **timber**.

◧ tree 126 ◨ talent 871

BUNDLE, SHEAF 153

束

SOKU
taba, taba<u>neru</u>, tsuka, tsuka<u>neru</u>

Bundled tree branches.

◘ tree 126 ◙ opening 566

WEALTH, ASSETS 154

財

ZAI, SAI

A talent for turning **assets** into **wealth**.

◧ money 708 ◨ talent 871

DEVICE 155

械

KAI

Hal made a wooden **device**.

◧ tree 126 ◨ command 793

BOARD, PLATE 156

板

HAN, BAN
ita

Trees are cut into **boards**.

◧ tree 126 ◨ against 957

DESK, TABLE 157

机

KI
tsukue

A wooden **table**.

tree 126 · desk n–157

BOOKSHELF, ARCHIVES 158

档

TŌ

Three books sit atop a wooden **bookshelf**.

tree 126 · apply 595

SHELF, TRELLIS 159

棚

tana

It took two months to build these wooden **shelves**.

tree 126 · month (X2) 14

FENCE 160

柵

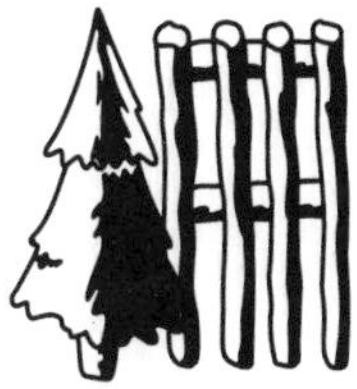

SAKU
shigarami

I read a book on making **fences**.

tree 126 · book 868

COLUMN, PILLAR 161

柱

CHŪ
hashira

A tree is cut into a **pillar** for the master's house.

tree 126 · master 734

POLE, BAR, CLUB 162

棒

BŌ

A wooden **club**.

tree 126 · respectful 703

BOX 163

箱

hako

A **box** made of bamboo and wood.

bamboo 123 · tree 126 · eye 538

LACQUER, VARNISH 164

漆

SHITSU
urushi

Varnish resins ooze like water from a tree.

water 66 · tree 126 · water 57

ARRANGE 165

整

SEI
totonou/eru

Correctly **arrange** the bundle of sticks.

bundle 153 · strike 802 · correct 826

CUT BRANCHES 166

柮

TOTSU

Leave nothing but **cut branches**.

tree 126 · leave 956

Mountains & Valleys

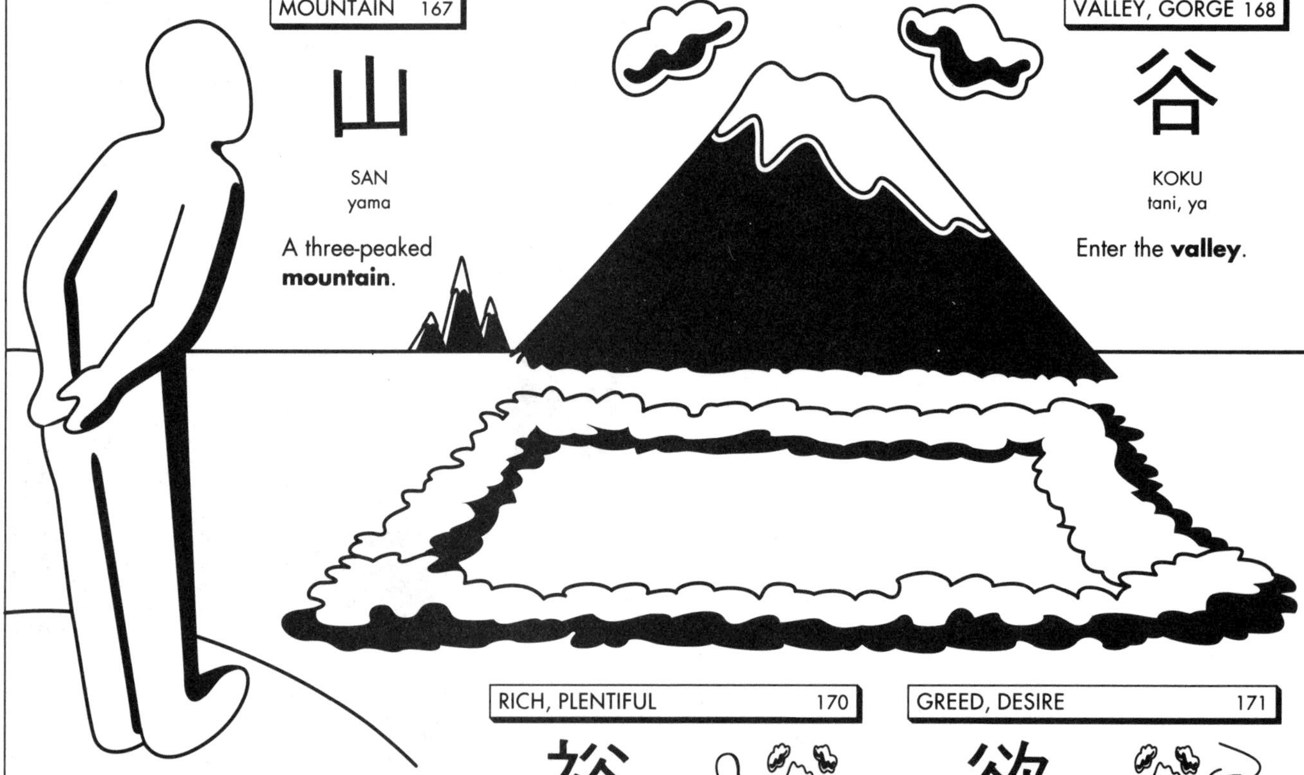

MOUNTAIN 167

山

SAN
yama

A three-peaked **mountain**.

VALLEY, GORGE 168

谷

KOKU
tani, ya

Enter the **valley**.

WORDLY, VULGAR, CUSTOM 169

俗

ZOKU

Having left the valley of **vulgar customs**, this person became **worldly**.

◧ person 362 ◨ valley 168

RICH, PLENTIFUL 170

裕

YŪ
yuta<u>ka</u>

Clothes are **plentiful** in the **rich** valley.

◧ clothes n–170 ◨ valley 168

GREED, DESIRE 171

欲

YOKU
ho<u>shii</u>

So **greedy** he could eat the valley.

◧ valley 168 ◨ gaping mouth 553

DARK, OBSCURE, LONELY 172

幽

YŪ
kasuka

Two **dark** and **lonely** paths thread into the mountain.

mountain 167 thread (x 2) n–172

PASS, CREST, CRISIS 173

峠

tōge

The **pass** runs above and below the mountain.

mountain 167 up 942 down 943

CRUMBLE, COLLAPSE 174

崩

HŌ
kuzureru/su

The mountain will **crumble** in two months.

mountain 167 month (x2) 14

PEAK, TOP 175

峰

HŌ
mine

He made slow progress to the **top** of the mountain.

mountain 167 slow progress n–175

RAVINE, GORGE 176

峡

KYŌ

A **ravine** between mountain peaks.

mountain 167 insert n–176

EXTREMITY, EDGE, UPRIGHT 177

端

TAN
hashi, hata, ha

A person stands **upright** on the **edge** of a cliff.

stand 627 mountain 167 plant n–177

CAPE, STEEP 178

崎

KI
saki

A **steep** mountain.

mountain 167 strange 179

STRANGE, ODD 179

奇

KI

How **strange** to step off the cliff.

big 913 opening 566

DRAW NEAR, VISIT 180

寄

KI
yoru/seru

A **visitor** approaches our house.

roof 1144 strange 179

Stones

ASSIST, HELP 181

助

JO
tasukeru/karu

With a little **help** we can …

◧ cairn 182 ◨ power 1023

FURTHERMORE, BESIDES 182

且

SHO, SO
katsu

… pile the stones **beside** or on top of each other …

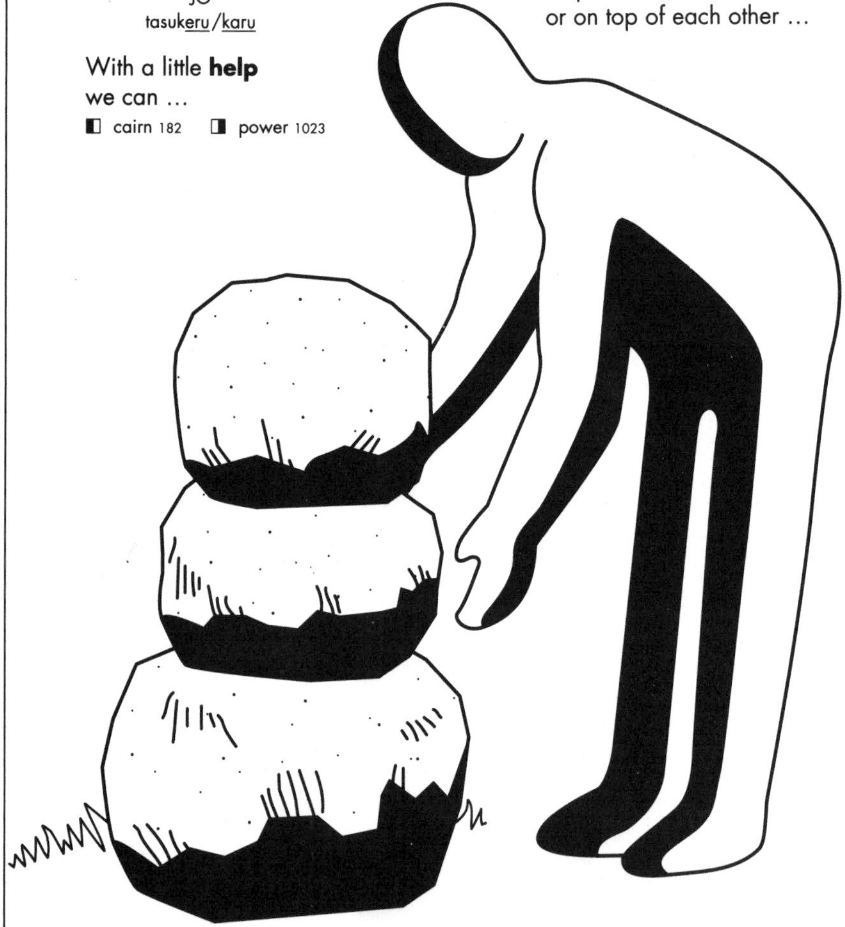

GROUP, ASSEMBLE 183

組

SO
kumi, kumu

… and **assemble** them with string …

◧ thread 964 ◨ cairn 182

OBSTRUCT, PREVENT, IMPEDE 184

阻

SO
habamu

… to **obstruct** the hill and **impede** our enemies ….

◧ hill 1094 ◨ cairn 182

ANCESTOR 185

祖

SO

… who took the lives of our **ancestors**.

◧ religion 696 ◨ cairn 182

RECLAIM, CLEAR, RUB 186

拓

TAKU

A hand **reclaims** the land by **clearing** it of stones.

hand 580 stone 190

ROCK, CRAG 189

岩

GAN
iwa

A **crag** is a stone outcropping on a mountain.

mountain 167
stone 190

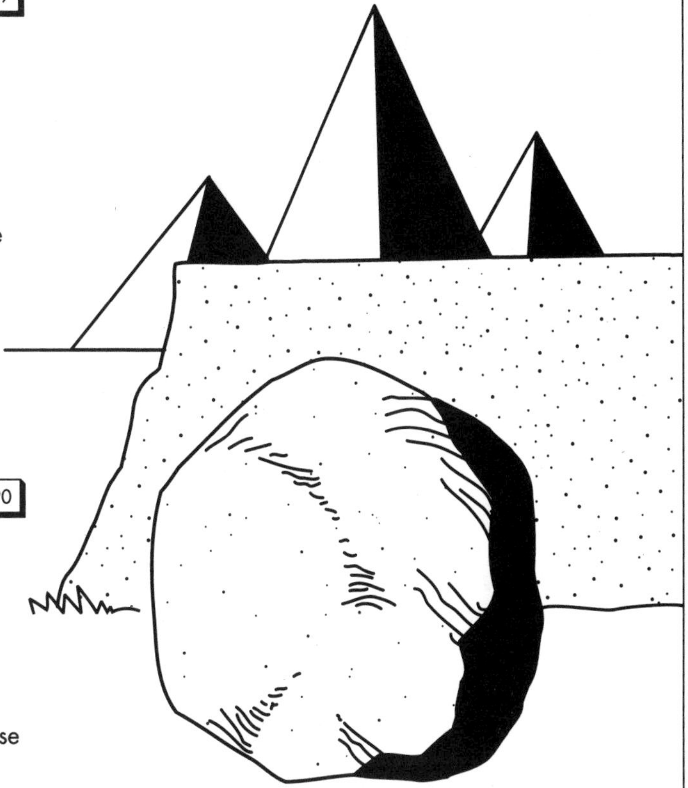

HONE, REFINE 187

研

KEN
togu

The plow is **honed** on a stone.

stone 190 uniformity n–187

STONE, ROCK 190

石

SEKI, SHAKU
ishi

A **rock** at the base of a cliff.

MAGNET, PORCELAIN 188

磁

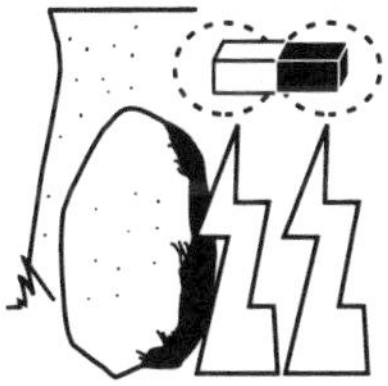

JI

A **magnet** is a stone with magical threads of force.

stone 182 occult (x2) n–172

CHARCOAL, COAL 191

炭

TAN
sumi

Charcoal comes from the mountain.

mountain 167 fire 83

ASHES 192

灰

KAI
hai

Ashes at the foot of the cliff.

cliff n–81 fire 83

SAND, GRAVEL 193

砂

SA, SHA
suna

Sand is small stones.

stone 190 little 926

Cave

INVESTIGATE, EXAMINE 194

究

KYŪ

Examine nine caves.

hole 194 nine 905

HOLE, CAVE 195

穴

KETSU
ana

The **cave** sheltered eight people.

roof 1144
eight 904

SEARCH, PROBE 198

探

TAN
saguru, sagasu

By hand, we **probed** behind a tree to **search** for a cave opening.

hand 580 hole 194 tree 126

THRUST, LUNGE, PROTRUDE 199

突

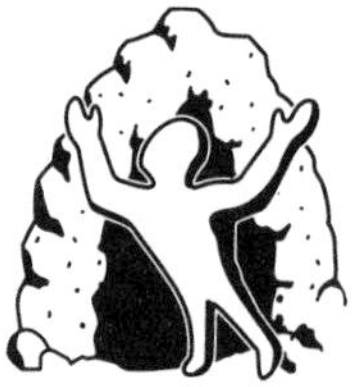

TOTSU
tsuku

Big John **lunged** from the cave.

hole 194 big 913

SKY, EMPTY 196

空

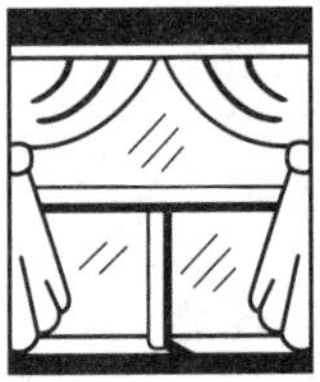

KŪ
sora, kara, aku

The **empty sky**, seen through a window in a cave.

hole 194 construction 1054

KILN, OVEN 197

窯

YŌ
kama

Fire fine pottery in the **kiln**.

hole 194 fine 290 fire 82

EXTREME, SUFFER 200

窮

KYŪ
kiwamaru/meru

A body pulled from the cave showed **extreme suffering**.

hole 194 body 459 pull 817

2 — FOOD

食物

READINGS

A single kanji can have multiple sounds or readings. Kanji were borrowed from China and used both for their phonetic values (the *on-yomi*, shown in capital letters), which shifted over time, and for words of native Japanese origin (the *kun-yomi*, shown in lowercase letters). Which reading to use for a character depends on context and what characters it is grouped with.

FOOD

食	物
tabe	**mono**
eat 232	*thing* 277

SIGHTSEEING

見	物
KEN	**BUTSU**
see 543	*thing* 277

DINE

食	事
SHOKU	**JI**
eat 232	*act* 590

SPLENDID

見	事
mi	**goto**
see 543	*thing* 590

ONE O'CLOCK

一	時
ICHI	**JI**
one 897	*time* 691

BRIEF

一	時
i(t)	**toki**
one 897	*time* 691

Field & Plant

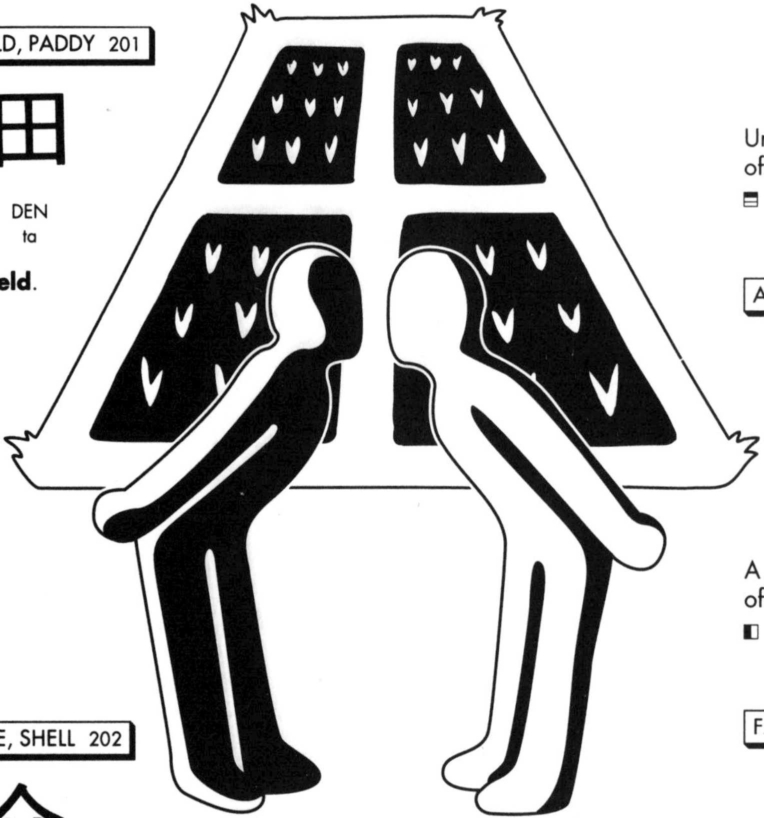

RICE FIELD, PADDY 201

田

DEN
ta

A **rice field**.

MEDIATE, SHELL 202

介

KAI

Two people **mediate** over …

person n–202
person n–202

AREA, BOUNDARY 203

界

KAI

… the **boundaries** of the field.

field 201 mediate 202

WEALTH, RICHES 204

富

FU, FŪ
tomi, tomu

Under whose roof will go the **riches** of the field?

roof 1144 opening 566 field 201

ABBREVIATE, OUTLINE 205

略

RYAKU

A surveyor walks around the **outline** of each field.

field 201 each 1209

FARM, DRY FIELD 206

畑

hata, hatake

The paddy is burned dry and made into a **field**.

fire 83 field 201

RIDGE, EDGE 207

畔

HAN
aze

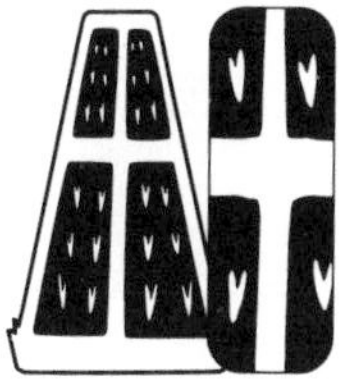

The **ridges** divide the paddy and hold in water.

field 201 · half 907

POISON 210

毒

DOKU

Mom ate a **poisonous** plant!

grow 214 · mother 446

BIRTH, PRODUCE 213

産

SAN
umu

My garden **produces** plants.

stand 627
grow 214

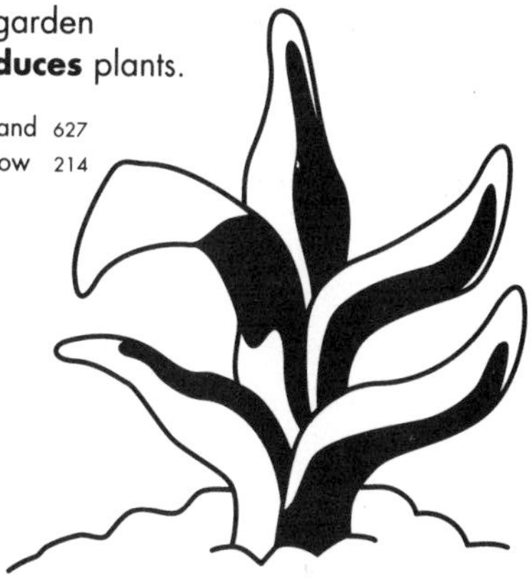

SEEDLING, SAPLING, SHOOT 208

苗

BYŌ, MYŌ
nae, nawa

Seedlings shoot up from the field.

grass 124 · field 201

BARLEY, WHEAT 211

麦

BAKU
mugi

Check on the growth of the **wheat**.

grow 214 · slow progress 1218

LIFE, BIRTH, GROW 214

生

SEI, SHŌ
nama, ikiru, umu, umareru, haeru

A **life**-giving plant.

TATAMI MAT, SIZE, FOLD, REPEAT 209

畳

JŌ
tatami, tatamu

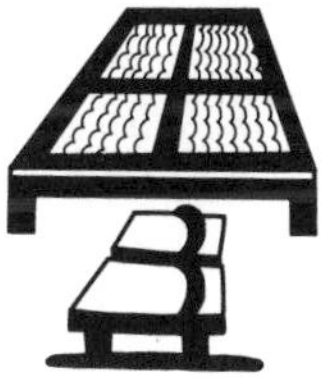

Shoes are for the field, not the **tatami**.

field 201 · besides 182

TILL, PLOW 212

耕

KŌ
tagayasu

A **plow tills** the soil well.

plow n–212 · well n–212

SACRIFICE 215

牲

SEI

A cow's life is **sacrificed**.

cow 275 · life 214

STAR 216

星

SEI, SHŌ
hoshi

The sun: a life-giving **star**.

sun 1 · life 214

Rice

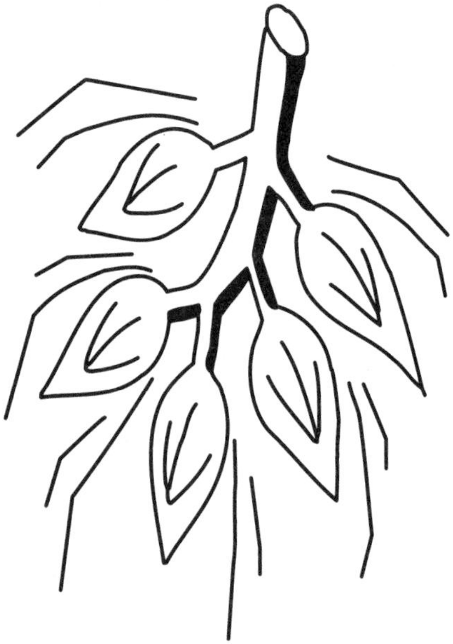

米 **RICE, AMERICA 217**

SEI, MAI
kome

Japan won't buy **American rice**.

GRAIN, PARTICLE 218

粒

RYŪ
tsubu

In Japan, rice is bought at **grain** stands.

rice 217 — stand 627

PROVISIONS, FOOD 219

糧

RYŌ, RŌ
kate

The town's daily **food** is rice.

rice 217 — quantity n–219

NEIGHBOR, ADJOIN 220

隣

RIN
tonari

I'll borrow rice from my **neighbor** on the **adjoining** hill.

hill 1094 — rice 217 — stop n–220

MATERIALS, MEASURE, CHARGE 221

料

RYŌ

A ladle is used to **measure** the rice.

rice 217 — measure 886

POWDER 222

粉

FUN
kona, ko

Chop the rice into **powder**.

rice 217 — divide 1025

稼 **WORK, EARN MONEY 223**

KA
kase<u>gu</u>

Earning money to bring home rice.

rice plant 231 — home 281

香 **FRAGRANCE, INCENSE 224**

KŌ, KA
kao<u>ru</u>/<u>ri</u>

The **fragrant** rice dries in the sun.

rice plant 231 — sun 1

GRAIN, CEREALS 225

穀

KOKU

Hands wield axes to harvest the **grains** from the soil.

soil 101 · rice plant 231 · hand w/ax 792

PRODUCT, PILE 228

積

SEKI
tsumu/moru

Our rice **products** earn a **pile** of money.

rice plant 231 · grow 214 · money 708

COURSE, SECTION 229

科

KA

Sort the grains of rice in a **sectioned** box.

rice plant 231 · measure 886

PROFIT, GAIN, EFFECT 226

利

RI
kiku

We **profit** by cutting grain …

rice plant 231 · knife 1037

HARVEST 230

穫

KAKU

At **harvest** time we feast on fowl.

rice plant 231 · bird 319 · hand 600

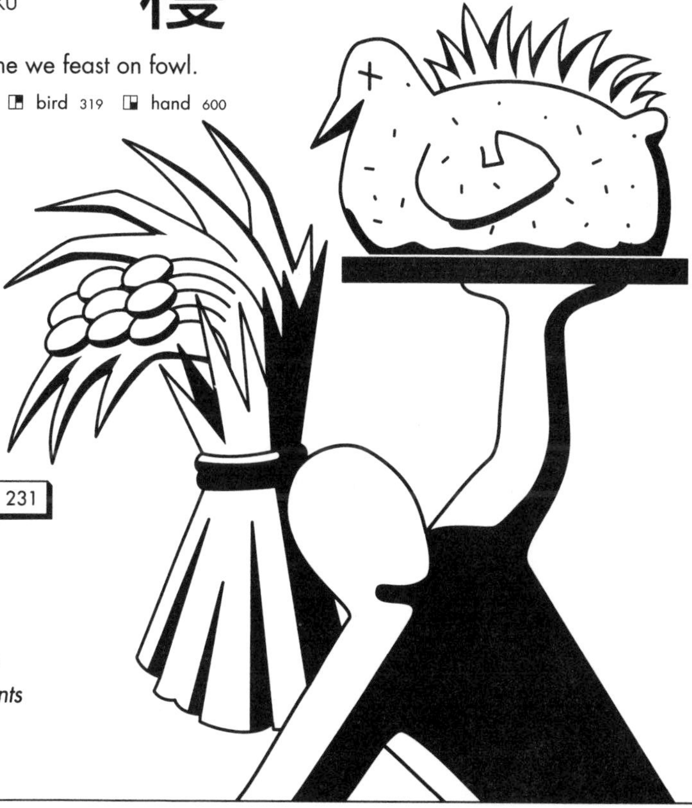

ORDER, STIPEND 227

秩

CHITSU

… but lose the grain to workers' **stipends**.

rice plant 231 · lose 577

"RICE PLANT" 231

禾

*This **rice plant** radical represents "grain."*

Eat

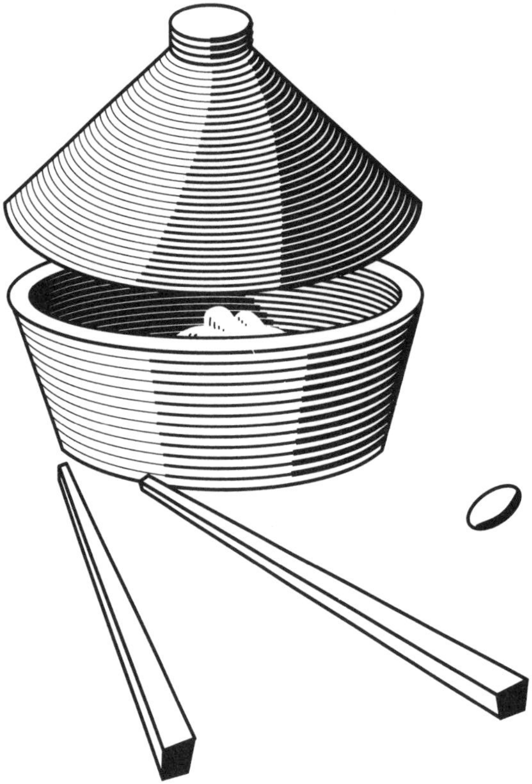

FOOD, EAT 232

食

SHOKU
taberu, kuu

Eat a bowl of **food**.

DRINK, SWALLOW 236

飲

IN
nomu

A mouth opens wide to **drink**.

eat 232 — gaping mouth 553

COOKED RICE, FOOD 237

飯

HAN
meshi

Cooked rice eaten in a cupped hand.

eat 232 — turning hand n–237

LARGE BUILDING, HALL 233

館

KAN

Keep eating and you'll have to keep your butt in a **large building**.

food 323 — roof 1144 — buttocks 466

STARVE 234

餓

GA
ueru

A **starving** body eats itself.

eat 232 — self 450

STARVE, HUNGER 235

飢

KI
ueru

Food on the table makes me **hungry**.

food 232 — table 157

REAR, SUPPORT 238

養

YŌ
yashinau

I **support** myself by **rearing** sheep.

sheep 290 — eat 232

SECTION, LESSON 239

課

KA

Her speech **lesson** bears fruit.

speak 840 — fruit 240

FRUIT, RESULT, CARRY OUT 240

果

KA
hate, hatasu

Fruit from the trees in the field.

field 201 tree 126

JUICE, SOUP, LIQUID 243

汁

JŪ
shiru

Ten parts water makes a good **soup**.

water 66 ten 906

CULTIVATE, GROW 246

培

BAI
tsuchikau

I **grew** a mouth-watering tomato.

soil 101 stand 627 mouth 566

VEGETABLE 241

菜

SAI
na

Vegetables grow between the grass and the trees.

grass 124 hand 609 tree 126

SALT 244

塩

EN
shio

I put Earth **salt** on my dish of eggs.

soil 101 opening 566 dish 265

COMPENSATE 247

賠

BAI

I was **compensated** with money …

money 708 stand 627 mouth 566

EGG, ROE 242

卵

RAN
tamago

Two **eggs**.

BEANS, MINIATURE 245

豆

TŌ, ZU
mame

A **tiny** bowl of **beans**.

DIVIDE, CUT UP 248

剖

BŌ

… when my tomato was **cut up**.

stand 627 mouth 566 knife 1037

Wine

"WINE" 249

酉

*A **wine** jar.*

ALCOHOL, SAKÉ 250

酒

SHU
sake, saka

Pour out the **saké**.

water 66 · wine 249

DRUNK, DIZZY 251

酔

SUI
you

I get **drunk** after nine or ten bottles.

wine 249 · nine 903 · ten 906

DISTRIBUTE 254

配

HAI
kubaru

I'll **distribute** the wine personally.

wine 249 · me 445

SEVERE, CRUEL, HARSH 255

酷

KOKU

The wine has a **severe**, **harsh** taste.

wine 249 · grow 214 · mouth 566

FERMENT, YEAST 252

酵

KŌ

The young wine needs yeast to **ferment**.

wine 249 · piety 403

CURD, DAIRY PRODUCE 253

酪

RAKU

Jars of **dairy products** are left on each doorstep.

wine 249 · each 1209

BOTTLE, JUG, JAR 256

瓶

BIN
kame

A **bottle** and a **jug**.

pair n–256 · vessel n–256

GAIN, PROFIT, BENEFIT 257

益

EKI, YAKU
masu

In a **profitable** year my dish overflows.

⬒ water n–257 ⬓ dish 261

Tray

DISH, BOWL, PLATE, TRAY 261

sara

皿

A **bowl** on a **tray**.

TRAY, BON FESTIVAL 258

盆

BON

A **tray** is used for cutting.

⬒ divide 1025 ⬓ dish 261

STEAL 262

盗

TŌ
nusumu

I cry over what'll be **stolen** next—my dish!

⬒ next 553 ⬓ dish 261

SERVE WINE, LADLE, SCOOP 264

酌

SHAKU
kumu

Serve wine with a **ladle**.

◧ wine jar 249 ◨ ladle 265

酬 REWARD, TOAST 259

SHŪ

Drink a **toast** to the state.

◧ wine 249 ◨ state 56

盤 TRAY, BOWL, PLATE 260

BAN

Carry the **tray**.

⬒ carry 1182 ⬓ dish 261

LIQUID MEASURE 263

升

SHŌ
masu

Measure ten spoonfuls of **liquid**.

◧ person 362 ◨ ten 906

LADLE, MEASURE 265

勺

SHAKU

Measure liquid with a **ladle**.

Meat

肉 **MEAT, FLESH 266**

NIKU

This **meaty** steak serves two people.

"FLESH, MEAT" 267 月

*This radical can mean either **flesh** 266 or **moon** 14 depending on the character it's in.*

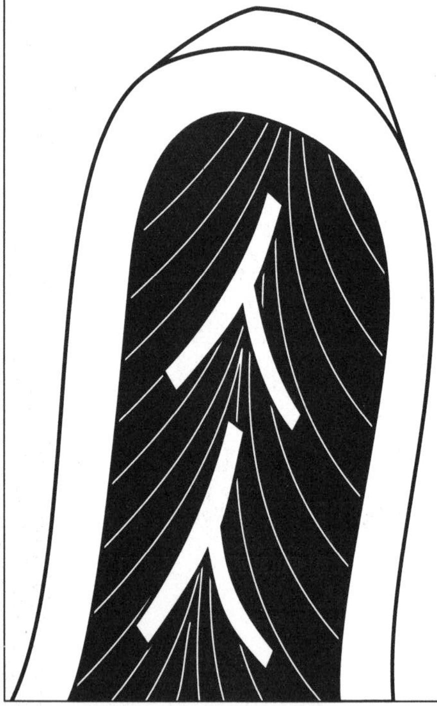

BE LIKE, BE LUCKY 268

肖

SHŌ
ayakaru

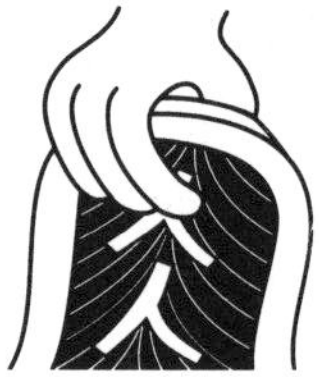

You'll **be lucky** if you get a little meat.

little 926 — meat 267

PARE, REDUCE 269

削

SAKU
kezuru

Pare the little piece of meat.

little 926 — meat 267 — knife 1037

EXTINGUISH, VANISH, CONSUME 270

消

SHŌ
kesu, kieru

A little water **extinguishes** the burning meat.

water 66 — little 926 — meat 267

FAT, GREASE 271

脂

SHI
abura, yani

The **fat** of the meat …

meat 267 — tasty 272

SWEET, PRESUME UPON 272

甘

KAN
amai/eru/yakasu

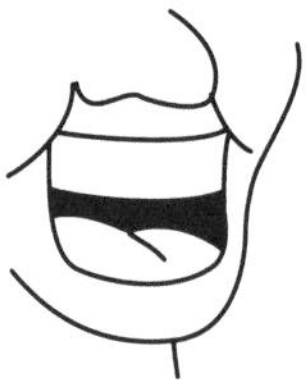

…is **sweet**.

旨 **TASTY, GOOD, GIST 273**

SHI
mune, umai

I spoon **tasty** things into my mouth.

spoon n–273 — mouth n–273

肪 **FAT 274**

BŌ

Trim the **fat** off the sides of the meat.

meat 267 — side 386

INTERESTING WORDS

"Fire-flower" burns a picture in your mind, while "flowering fire" is much more playful than the English "fireworks." Words like "interesting" and "genius" make you wonder how they came to be. Compounds like "adult" and "tomorrow" have assigned readings that can't be guessed at from their kanji. *Dōbutsu,* "animal," at right, literally means "move thing."

FIREWORKS		SPARK	
花	火	火	花
hana	**bi**	**hi**	**bana**
flower 116	*fire* 83	*fire* 83	*flower* 116

INTERESTING		GENIUS	
面	白	鬼	才
omo	**shiroi**	**KI**	**SAI**
face 469	*white* 936	*devil* 645	*talent* 871

ADULT		TOMORROW	
大	人	明	日
otona		**asu**	
big 913	*person* 363	*bright* 8	*sun* 1

動物

Cow, Pig, & Sheep

牛

COW 275

GYŪ
ushi

This is the **cow** with the crumpled horn.

PASTURE 276

牧

BOKU
maki

Drive the cow to **pasture**.

cow 275 strike 802

THING 277

物

BUTSU, MOTSU
mono

To get milk you pull on the cow's **thing**.

cow 275 thing n–277

UNRAVEL, EXPLAIN, SOLVE 278

解

KAI, GE
toku

A cow's horn **explains** a lot about its life.

horn 280 knife 1023 cow 275

豕

"PIG" 279

*This means **pig** when used as an element.*

HORN, ANGLE, CORNER 280

角

KAKU
tsuno, kado

A **horn** bends at an **angle**.

HOUSE, SPECIALIST 281

家

KA, KE
ie, ya

A sty is a **house** for pigs.

roof 1144 pig 279

PIG, HOG 285

豚

TON
buta

We use a **pig** for its meat.

meat 267 pig 279

CHASE, PURSUE 289

逐

CHIKU
ou

In **pursuit** of a pig.

move 1153 pig 279

GROUP, FLOCK 282

群

GUN
mura, mure/reru

The lord of the sheep attends his **flock**.

lord 417 sheep 290

GOOD FORTUNE, OMEN 286

祥

SHŌ

A sheep is sacrificed on the altar to bring **good fortune**.

altar 696 sheep 290

SHEEP, FINE, PRAISEWORTHY 290

羊

YŌ
hitsuji

Sheep are **fine** assets.

FRESH, VIVID, CLEAR 283

鮮

SEN
azayaka

Fine **fresh** fish.

fish 354 sheep 290

BEAUTIFUL, FINE 287

美

BI
utsukushii

Big **beautiful** sheep.

sheep 290 big 913

DETAILED 284

詳

SHŌ
kuwashii

His was a **detailed** speech on sheep.

word 840 sheep 290

ARRIVE, WEAR 288

着

CHAKU
tsuku, kiru

I like to **wear** wool myself.

sheep 290 self 542

Horse

HORSE 291

馬

BA
uma, ma

A **horse** lies on its side.

*This tends to look more like a **horse**, if you picture it on its side.*

STOP, STAY 292

駐

CHŪ

A horse **stays** by his master.

◧ horse 291 ◨ master 734

NOISE, DISTURBANCE 293

騒

SŌ
sawagu/gashii

The horse is **disturbed** by a snake.

◧ horse 291 ◳ strike 802 ◲ snake 311

SURPRISE 294

驚

KYŌ
odoroku/kasu

Surprise a horse with a stick and it will respect you.

⬒ respect 295 ⬓ horse 291

RESPECT 295

敬

KEI
uyamau

I'll beat some **respect** into you.

◧ humility n–295 ◨ strike 802

WARN, REPROACH 296

警

KEI

He **warned** me of the hand with the stick.

⬒ respect 295 ⬓ speak 840

EXAMINE 297

験

KEN

A good scout **examines** his horse …

◧ horse 291 ◨ all n–297

SWORD, BAYONET 298

剣

KEN
tsurugi

… checks his **sword** …

◧ all n–297 ◨ sword 1023

INVESTIGATE 299

検

KEN

… and **investigates** behind trees …

◧ tree 126 ◨ all n–297

STEEP, SEVERE, PERILOUS 300

険

KEN
kewashii

… before making camp in the **steep** and **perilous** hills.

◧ hill 1094 ◨ all n–297

STATION 301

駅

EKI

Load the horse at the **station**.

◧ horse 291 ◨ measure 884

RIDER 302

騎

KI

A strange **rider** mounts …

◧ horse 291 ◨ strange 179

PACK HORSE, POOR QUALITY 303

駄

DA

… but the **poor pack horse** keels under the weight of the fat man.

◧ horse 291 ◨ fat 914

Bugs

INSECT, WORM 304

虫

CHŪ
mushi

A **bug**.

FIREFLY 305

蛍

KEI
hotaru

Firefly: a radiant insect.

fire n–305 insect 304

MOSQUITO 306

蚊

ka

A textbook case of **mosquito** bites.

insect 304 text 834

COCOON 307

繭

KEN
mayu

In the grass, an insect made a **cocoon** of thread.

grass 124 thread 964 insect 304

BARBARIAN 308

蛮

BAN

His **barbaric** smell is attracting bugs.

red 929 insect 304

IMPURE, TURBID, VOICED 309

濁

DAKU
nigoru/su

Use a net to rid the **impure** water of insects.

water 66 net 987 insect 304

TOUCH, FEEL, CONTACT 310

触

SHOKU
fureru, sawaru

An insect's hornlike antennae: "**feelers**."

horn 280 insect 304

Snakes & Birds

"SNAKE" 311

虫

***Insect** 304 originally came from a drawing of a snake and in some kanji carries the meaning **snake**.*

SNAKE, SERPENT 312

蛇

JA, DA
hebi

He fell when bit by a **snake**.

◧ snake 311 ◨ roof 1144 ◨ person n–312

BIRD 314

鳥

CHŌ
tori

A **bird** in a nest …

NON-HUMAN CRY 315

鳴

MEI
naku/ru

… **cries** out.

◧ mouth 566 ◨ bird 314

STRONG 313

強

KYŌ, GŌ
tsuyoi

A **strong** snake can pull with its tail.

◧ pull 817 ◨ snake 311

ISLAND 316

島

TŌ
shima

A bird flies above the **island** mountains.

◧ mountain 167 ◨ bird 314

CRANE, STORK 317

鶴

KAKU
tsuru

The **crane** is next to another bird.

◧ heron 331 ◨ bird 314

Plumage

SEPARATE, LEAVE 318

離

RI
hanareru/su

Only birds can **leave** from the cliffs that **separate** us.

oriole n–318 · bird 319

"BIRD" 319

隹

*Used only as a part of other characters, this means **bird**.*

SCORCH 320

焦

SHŌ
kogeru/gasu,
aseru, jireru

Scorched foul.

bird 319 · fire 82

BE EXCITED, STIR 321

奮

FUN
furuu

A big scarecrow **stirs** up and **excites** the bird in the field.

big 913 · bird 319 · field 201

SNATCH, CAPTIVATE 322

奪

DATSU
ubau

A big bird is **snatched** by the man with the gun.

big 913 · bird 319 · inch 759

WASH, RINSE 323

濯

TAKU

A bird **washing** its wings.

water 66 wings 330 bird 319

FLY, JUMP 327

飛

HI
tobu

Birds **fly** south.

WING 324

翼

YOKU
tsubasa

She wears a strange mask and **wings**.

wings 330 strange 335

NEXT (TIME) 328

翌

YOKU

"See you **next** time, I've gotta fly."

wings 330 stand 627

FLAP, CHANGE 329

翻

HON
hirugaeru/su

A bird **flapping** its wings over the rice field.

rice 231 field 201 wings 330

異 DIFFER, STRANGE 325

I
kotonaru

A **strange**, masked girl.

field 201 together 383

習 LEARN, TRAIN 326

SHŪ
narau

White wings mean you need **training**.

wings 330 white 936

FEATHER, WING 330

羽

U
ha, hane

Wing feathers.

Heron

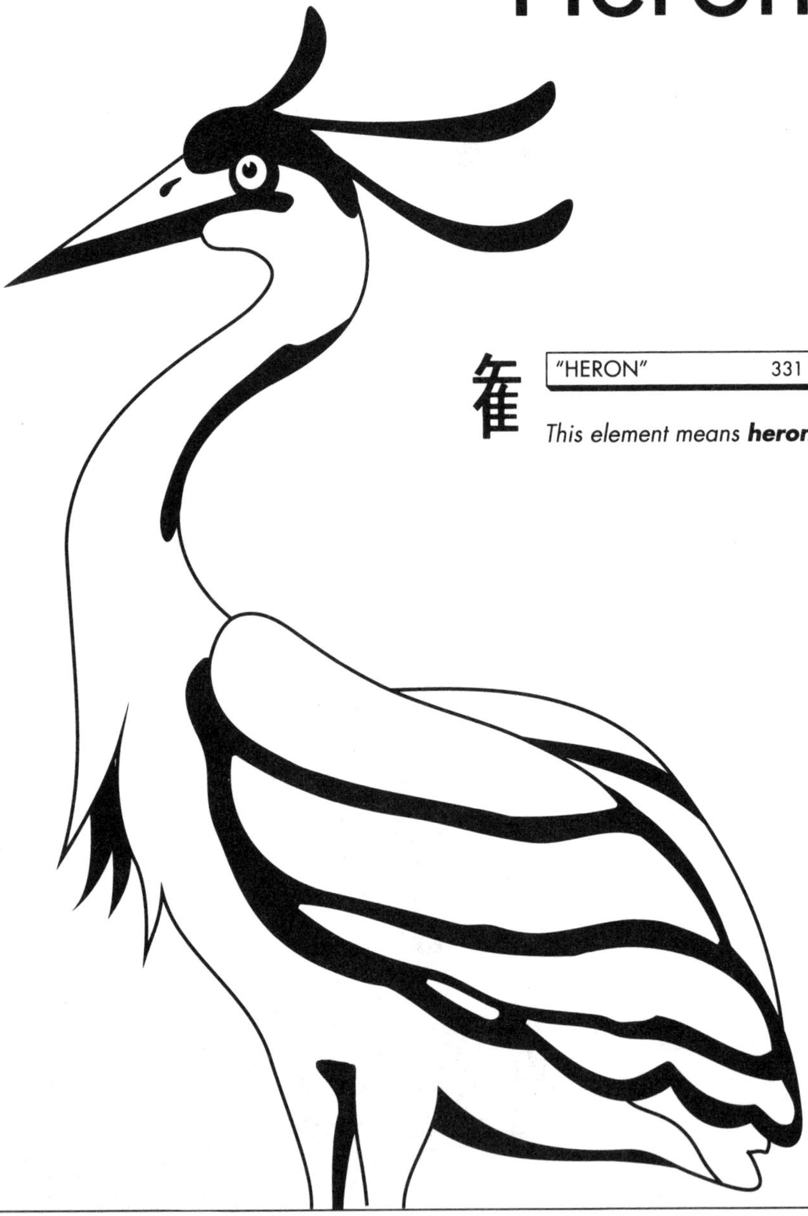

隹

"HERON" 331

This element means ***heron****.*

WATCH, OBSERVE 332

観

KAN

Bird **watching**.

◧ heron 331 ◨ watch 543

ENCOURAGE, ADVISE 333

勧

KAN
susu<u>meru</u>

Encourage heron preservation.

◧ heron 331 ◨ power 745

REJOICE, MERRY 334

歓

KAN
yoroko<u>bu</u>

Rejoice and sing like a bird.

◧ heron 331 ◨ gaping mouth 553

Dog

DOG 335

犬

KEN
inu

A big, spotted **dog**.

spot n–335 big 913

BEAST, ANIMAL 336

獣

JŪ
ke(du)mono

The mask of a **beast**.

protect n–336 dog 338

FIERCE, RAGING, BRAVE 337

猛

MŌ

The child **bravely** touches the **fierce** dog's dish.

dog 338 child 447 dish 261

HUNTING 341

猟

RYŌ

They go **hunting** for birds ...

dog 45 leap n–341

CATCH, SEIZE, GET 342

獲

KAKU
eru, toru

... usually **catching** one in the grass.

dog 338
grass 124 + bird 319
hand 580

"DOG" 338

犭

*This element means **dog**.*

PROTECT 339

守

SHU, SU
mamoru

A man **protects** the house ...

roof 1144
inch 759

HUNT 340

狩

SHU
kari/ru

... and **hunts** with his dog.

dog 338
protect 335

Forest Animals

DEER	343

鹿

ROKU
shika

A **deer** with antlers.

BEAUTIFUL	344

麗

REI
uruwa<u>shii</u>

A pair of eyes admires the **beautiful** deer.

group n–344 deer 343

ELEPHANT	345

象

ZŌ, SHŌ

A big-eared **elephant**.

DRAMA, INTENSE	346

劇

GEKI

A tiger vs. a pig with swordplay is an **intense drama**.

tiger 353 pig 279 sword 1023

CRUELTY, OPPRESS 347

虐

GYAKU
shiitageru

The tiger's **cruel**, **oppressive** paw …

tiger 353 | hand n–347

PLAY, FROLIC, JOKE 350

戯

GI
tawamureru

The circus tiger **plays** around the fire.

tiger 353 | play n–350 | halberd 801

SKIN 351

膚

FU
hada

A tiger rips open a man's **skin** and eats his guts.

tiger 353 | stomach n–351

CAPTIVE, PRISONER OF WAR 348

虜

RYO
toriko

… guards the **prisoner of war** …

tiger 353 | man 419

TIGER 352

虎

KO
tora

A **tiger** with gaping jaws.

tiger 353
tiger n–352

"TIGER" 353

虍

*This element means **tiger**.*

FEAR, ANXIETY 349

虞

GU
osore

… and this gives the prisoner's wife **anxiety**.

tiger 353 | give 834

Sea Creatures

FISH 354

魚

GYO
uo, sakana

I caught four **fish** …

FISHING 355

漁

GYO, RYŌ

… salt-water **fishing**.

◧ water 66 ◨ fish 354

DRAGON 358

竜

RYŪ, RYŌ
tatsu

A roaring **dragon**.

ATTACK 359

襲

SHŪ
osou

The dragon **attacks** by burning clothing.

⬒ dragon n–359 ⬓ clothing 1021

TORTOISE, TURTLE 356

亀

KI
kame

The **turtle** wears a shell.

SHELL, ARMOR, HIGH, 1ST 357

甲

KŌ, KAN
kōra

A turtle's **shell** is its **armor**.

WATERFALL 360

滝

taki

The **waterfall** roars like a dragon.

◧ water 66 ◨ dragon 358

WHALE 361

鯨

GEI
kujira

The **whale** is a capital fish!

◧ fish 354 ◨ capital 1077

REPEATING KANJI

A word for "people" in Japanese is *hitobito*, shown at right. The upper kanji is **hito** 363, PERSON. The lower character is a graphic device similar to ditto marks (") in English, indicating that the previous character is repeated. Sometimes, the pronunciation of the second character is changed slightly to make it easier to say.

SOMETIMES

時々

toki **doki**

time 691 (X2)

GRAND

堂々

DŌ **DŌ**

hall 1130 (X2)

VARIOUS

色々

iro **iro**

colors 927 (X2)

WE

我々

ware **ware**

self 794 (X2)

INCREASINGLY

益々

masu **masu**

gain 257 (X2)

A LITTLE BIT

少々

SHŌ **SHŌ**

few 925 (X2)

人

々

People

"PERSON" 362

亻

This is the radical for ***person****.*

PERSON 363

人

JIN, NIN
hito

A **person** taking a step.

MEET 364

会

KAI, E
a<u>u</u>

I'll **meet** a personal friend on a cloudy day.

⬒ person 363 ⬓ cloud 54

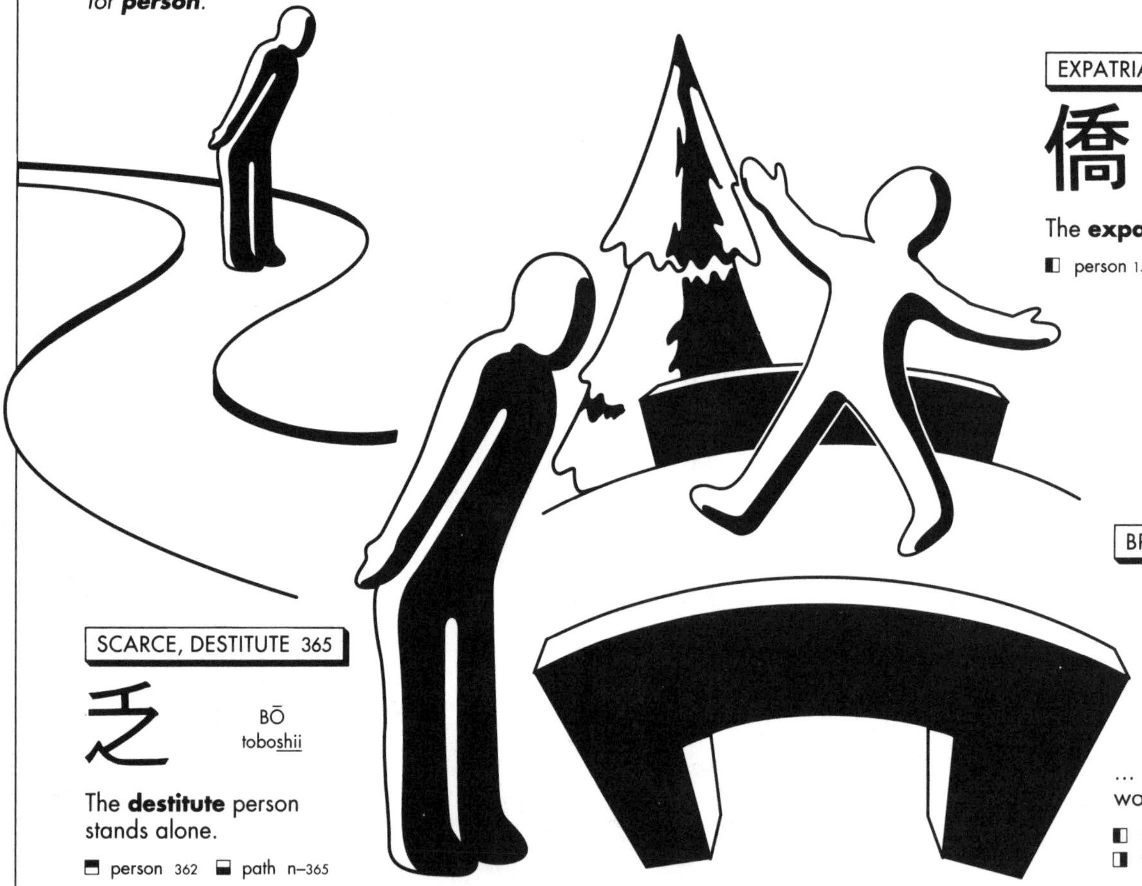

EXPATRIATE 366

僑

KYŌ

The **expatriate** ...

◧ person 157 ◨ tower n–366

SCARCE, DESTITUTE 365

乏

BŌ
tobo<u>shii</u>

The **destitute** person stands alone.

⬒ person 362 ⬓ path n–365

BRIDGE 367

橋

KYŌ
hashi

... crossed the wooden **bridge**.

◧ tree 157
◨ tower n–366

BENEVOLENT, HUMANITY 368

仁

JIN, NI

This **benevolent** person cares for two people.

person 362, two 898

SUBMIT, FOLLOW, LIE DOWN 369

伏

FUKU
fu<u>su</u>/<u>seru</u>

The dog **lies** down before its master.

person 362, dog 335

RANK, EXTENT 370

位

I
kurai

A person of lower **rank** bows to a person of higher standing.

person 362, stand 627

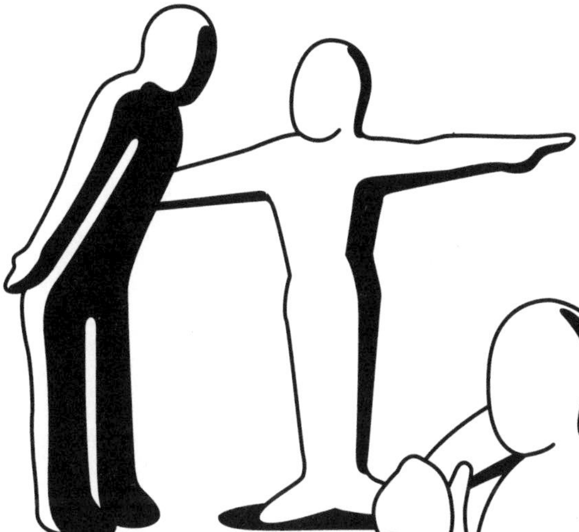

LOAD, BURDEN 371

KA
ni

荷

What is that person's **load**? Grass?

tree 157, what? n–371

SERVE, WORK, DO 372

仕

SHI, JI
tsuka<u>eru</u>

This person **serves** the samurai.

person 362, samurai 753

REACH, EXTEND 373

KYŪ
oyo<u>bi</u>/<u>bu</u>/<u>bosu</u>

及

Reach out and **extend** an open hand.

person 362, hand n–373

CHANGE 374

化

KA, KE
bak<u>eru</u>

A young person **changes** into a seated old man.

◧ person 362 ◨ fallen person n–374

PRINCIPLES, ETHICS 375

倫

RIN

People in Washington have big **principles** and few **ethics**.

◧ person 362 ◨ order n–375

REPLACE, GENERATION, FEE 376

代

DAI, TAI
ka<u>waru</u>/<u>eru</u>, yo

Every **generation** must pay its dues.

◧ person 362 ◨ halberd 801

HERMIT, WIZARD 377

仙

SEN

A **hermit** lives in the mountains.

◧ person 362 ◨ mountain 167

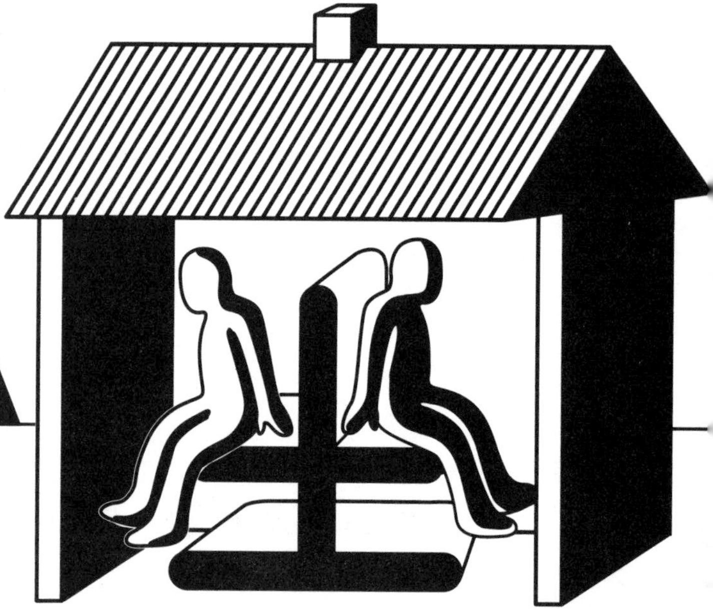

SEAT, SIT, GATHER 378

座

ZA
suwa<u>ru</u>

Two people **sit** on the ground floor.

◧ building 1143 ◨ soil + person (x2) 101

RELATIONSHIP 379

仲

CHŪ
naka

I'm in the middle of a personal **relationship**.

◧ person 362 ◨ middle 954

ASSIST, ASSISTANT 380

佐

SA

"Lefty" here is my **assistant**.

◧ person 362 ◨ left 601

ATTEND (UPON) 381

侍

JI
samurai, haberu

The samurai **attends** this temple.

◧ person 362 ◨ temple 685

OFFER, ATTENDANT 382

供

KYŌ, KU
tomo, sonaeru

The **attendant** greets ...

◧ person 362 ◨ together 383

EQUIP, PREPARE 384

備

BI
sonaeru/waru

I am **prepared** for the cliff dwellers.

◧ person 362 ◨ use n–384

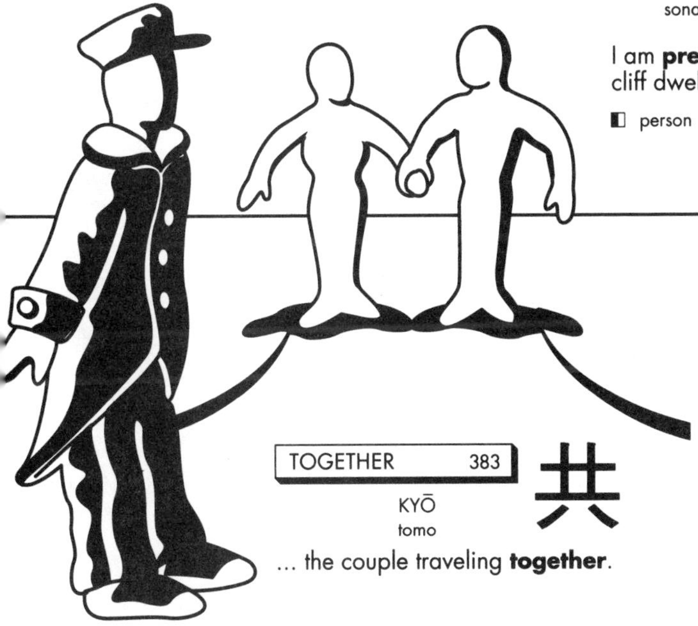

TOGETHER 383

共

KYŌ
tomo

... the couple traveling **together**.

USE 385

用

YŌ
mochiiru

I'll **use** this fence to keep them out.

Person

PERSON, SIDE, WAY, DIRECTION, SQUARE 386

方

HŌ
kata

The **person** points in that **direction**.

RELEASE, EMIT 389

放

HŌ
hanasu/tsu

This person was **released** after being beaten.

person 386 | strike 802

SIDE, BESIDES 390

傍

BŌ
katawara

Put it **beside** that standing person.

person 362 | stand 627 | person 386

FLAG 387

旗

KI
hata

A person waves a **flag**.

flag n–387 | device n–387

PERFORM, CHARITY 388

施

SHI, SE
hodokosu

A drama is **performed** for charity.

flag n–387 | creature n–102

VISIT, INQUIRE 391

訪

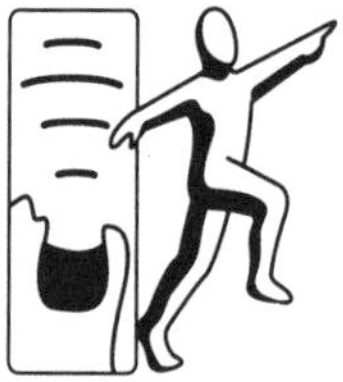

HŌ
otozureru, tazuneru

I asked him directions during my **visit**.

speak 840 | person 386

Populace

LOW 392

低

TEI
hikui

A person comforts a family member who is **low**.

person 362 family 396 one 897

TO REACH, RESIST, OPPOSE 393

抵

TEI

A hand reaches out for a **resistant** family member.

hand 580 family 396 one 897

PEOPLE, POPULACE 395

民

MIN
tami

There are no **people** with big heads …

CLAN, FAMILY, MR 396

氏

SHI
uji

… in my **family**.

COMPARE, RATIO 394

比

HI
kuraberu

Twins are always **compared**.

sitting person n–374 sitting person n–374

MULTITUDE, BUG, DESCENDANTS 397

昆

KON

A **multitude** of **descendants** sit under the sun.

sun 394 compare 394

RESIDENCE, MANSION 398

邸

TEI

My family **resides** in a **mansion**.

family 396 one 897 hill 1094

CRITICIZE, STRIKE, PASS 399

批

HI

A hand **strikes** out at the sit-in.

hand 580 compare 394

People's Burdens

INDUSTRIOUS 400

孜

SHI

If you're not **industrious**, I'll beat you with a stick.

child 447 strike 802

GOVERNMENT OFFICE, SIGN 401

署

SHO

The big eye of **government** watches the ever-burdened people.

net 987 person 408

"BURDENS" 402

耂

This element means ***burdens****.*

教 TEACH 404

KYŌ
oshi<u>eru</u>

I'll **teach** piety to you with this stick.

piety 403 strike 802

孝 FILIAL PIETY 403

KŌ

The burden a child bears: **filial piety**.

burden 402 child 447

HOT (WEATHER) 405

暑

SHO
atsui

Carrying a heavy burden in the sun makes you **hot**.

sun 1 person 408

COOK, BOIL 406

煮

SHA
niru/eru/yasu

A burdensome bag of victuals is **cooked** in the fire.

person 408 fire 82

TORTURE, HIT 407

拷

GŌ

He is beaten and **tortured** for being inconsiderate.

hand 580 consider 409

PERSON 408

者

SHA
mono

Every **person** has burdens to carry.

burden 402 sun 1

CONSIDER 409

考

KŌ
kangaeru

I sometimes stop to **consider** …

AGED MAN, TO GROW OLD 410

老

RŌ
oi, oiru

… if these burdens will crush me as I **grow old**.

Woman & Man

女 WOMAN 411

JO, NYŌ, NYO
onna, me

This **woman** ...

姦 NOISY, IMMORAL 412

KAN
kashima<u>shii</u>

... tends to be **noisy** in groups.

woman 411 · woman 411 · woman 411

PLEASURE, AMUSEMENT 413

娯

GO

She takes **pleasure** in giving advice ...

woman 411 · give 835

BEGIN, FIRST 414

始

SHI
hajimeru/maru

... but is the **first** to open her mouth ...

woman 411 · self 411 · mouth 566

FIGURE, SHAPE 415

姿

SHI
sugata

... and cry over her **figure**.

next 555 · woman 411

MAKE FUN OF, TEASE, RIDICULE 416

嬲

JŌ
nabu<u>ru</u>

Two women **tease** a man from both sides.

woman (x2) 411   man 419

Many characters containing the elements for "woman" and "man" reflect the times in which they were created.

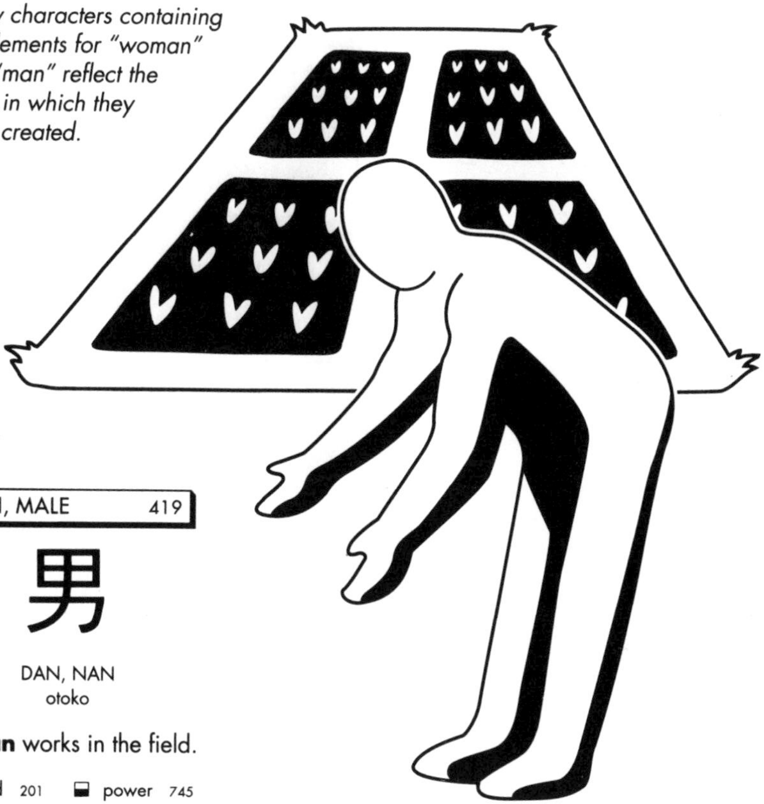

LORD, YOU, MR. 417

君

KUN
kimi

A **tycoon** with a cigar.

hand w/stick n–417   mouth 566

MAN, MALE 419

男

DAN, NAN
otoko

A **man** works in the field.

field 201   power 745

MALE, POWERFUL 418

雄

YŪ
osu, o-

Falconry is a sport for **powerful males**.

elbow n–418   bird 319

MANLY, STRONG 420

壮

SŌ

The samurai shows his **strength**.

big n– 420   samurai 753

VILLA, MANOR, MAJESTIC 421

荘

SŌ, SHŌ

The samurai strikes a **majestic** pose on the lawn of his **villa**.

grass 124   manly 420

Marriage

MARRIAGE 422

姻

IN

If you're too dependent, **marriage** will box you in.

- woman 66
- depend n–422

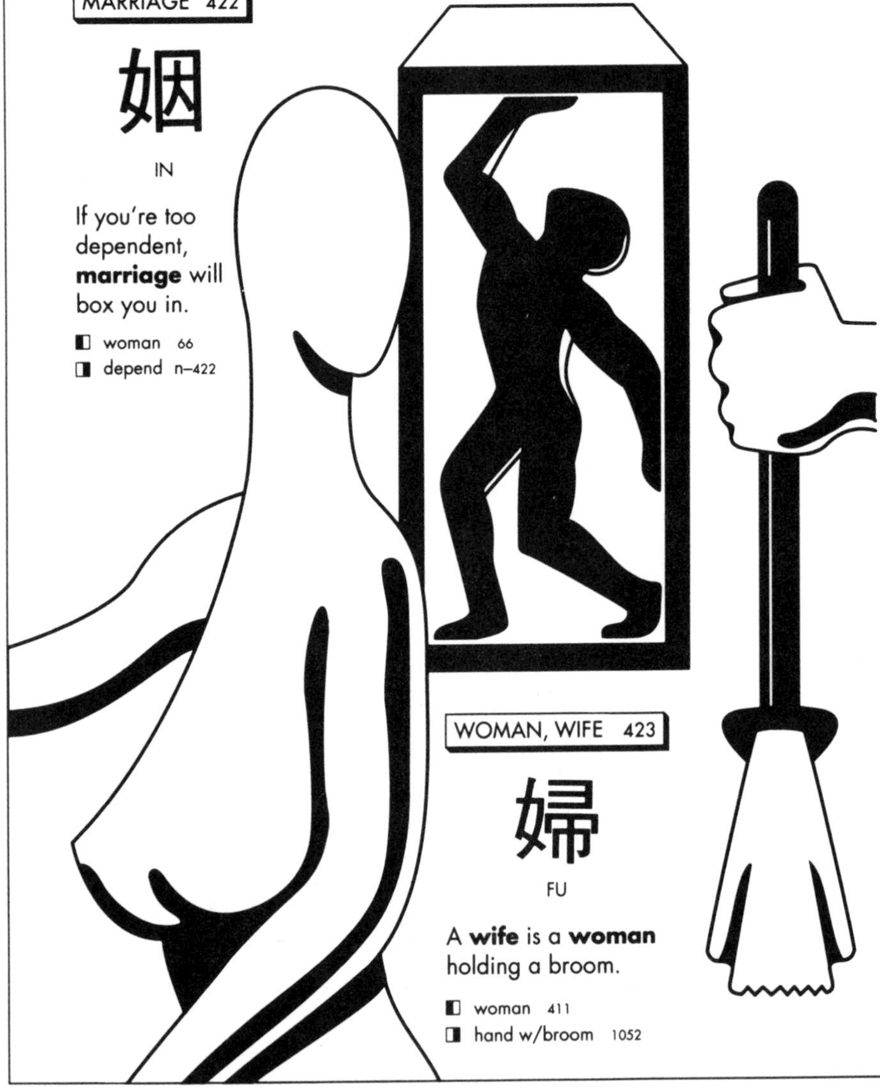

WOMAN, WIFE 423

婦

FU

A **wife** is a **woman** holding a broom.

- woman 411
- hand w/broom 1052

WIFE 424

妻

SAI
tsuma

The **wife** is handed a broom.

- woman 411
- hand w/broom 1052

CONTACT, JOIN 425

接

SETSU
tsugu

His hand reaches out to **join** hers.

- hand 1052
- stand 627
- woman 411

MISTRESS 426

妾

SHŌ
mekake

A man stands by his **mistress**.

- stand 627
- woman 411

EXQUISITE, ODD 427

妙

MYŌ

This woman is a little **odd**.

- woman 411
- little 924

MARRY, BRIDE 428

嫁

KA
yome, totsugu

The house of the **bride** looks like a pigsty.

woman 411 house 281

RESTFUL, EASE, CHEAP 429

安

AN
yasui/maru

A woman under the roof makes for **cheap** labor.

roof 1144 woman 411

BANQUET 430

宴

EN
utage

The woman gave us everything under the sun at the **banquet**.

roof 1144 sun 1 woman 411

PEACE, SETTLED 431

妥

DA

A woman's hand brings **peace**.

hand 580 woman 411

AUTHORITY, THREATEN 432

威

I
odosu

The woman **threatens** Hal's **authority**.

halberd 801 woman 411

MARRIAGE 433

婚

KON

A person sits on a hopechest next to a woman, waiting for **marriage**.

woman 411 family 396 sun 1

HUSBAND, MAN 434

夫

FU, FŪ
otto

Her **husband** wears a hairpin.

HELP, SUPPORT 435

扶

FU

A husband lends a **helping** hand.

hand 580 husband 434

STANDARD, MEASURE 436

規

KI

Look to the husband as the **standard**.

husband 434 watch 543

Family

FATHER 437

父

FU
chichi

A **father** picks up his child.

ELDER SISTER 440

姉

SHI
ane

My **older sister** lives in the city.

woman 411 city 1084

YOUNGER SISTER 441

妹

MAI
imōto

My immature **younger sister** lives in the country.

woman 411 immature 144

ELDER BROTHER 438

兄

KEI, KYŌ
ani

An **elder brother** is a mouth on two legs.

mouth 566 legs n–438

YOUNGER BROTHER 439

弟

TEI, DAI, DE
otōto

My snot-nosed **younger brother**.

CLAN, FAMILY 442

族

ZOKU

A **family's** coat of arms is displayed on a flag.

flag n–387 arrow 818

EACH, EVERY 443

毎

MAI
-goto

Every person has a mother.

person 363 mother 446

MOTHER 446

母

BO
haha

A woman's nipples become dark during **motherhood**.

DESCENDANTS, GRANDCHILDREN 444

孫

SON
mago

The **grandchild** is my **descendant.**

child 363 lineage 977

CHILD 447

子

SHI, SU
ko

A **child** …

BREASTS, MILK 449

乳

NYŪ
chichi, chi

A woman holds a child to her **breast**.

hand 609 child 447 breast n–449

I, ME, SELF, YOU 445

己

KO, KI
onore

I, **myself**, kneel before **you**.

LIKE, GOOD, FINE 448

好

KŌ
suku, konomu/mashii

… **likes** to be held by a woman.

woman 411 child 447

Self

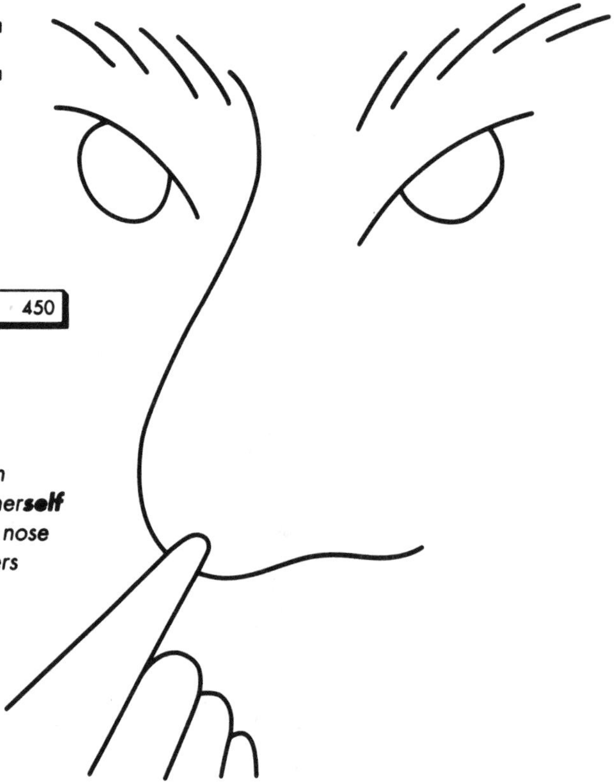

"SELF" 450

厶

*In Japan, a person indicates him- or her**self** by pointing to the nose the way Westerners point to the chest.*

STAND, PLATFORM 455

台

DAI, TAI

He's sitting on the **platform** by himself.

self 450 · mouth 566

SPLIT 456

八

*This element means **splitting** or **dividing**.*

WOMB 451

胎

TAI

Wombs are flesh-launching platforms.

flesh 267 · platform 455

ACCUSE, SUE 453

訟

SHŌ

I **sued** him for his public **accusation**.

speak 840 · public 457

PUBLIC, FAIR, LORD 457

公

KŌ

ōyake

Split open the self and make it **public**.

split 456 · self 450

DISCUSSION 452

議

GI

We had a righteous **discussion**.

speak 849 · righteousness 794

I, PRIVATE, PERSONAL 454

私

SHI

wata(ku)shi

I keep a **personal** supply of rice.

rice plant 231 · self 450

PINE 458

松

SHŌ

matsu

The **pine** tree is in public parks.

tree 126 · public 457

LOOK-ALIKE KANJI

In a writing system that uses more than 2,000 characters it is not surprising that some characters look very similar. (Imagine the difficulty of Chinese: one dictionary lists more than 48,000 characters.) The kanji **karada** 134, BODY, at right can easily be mistaken for **yasumi** 138, REST. Note the horizontal line within the right-hand element of BODY.

BODY 134	REST 138	SUBMIT 369
体	休	伏
karada	**yasumi**	**fuseru**
COME 1219	TIP 145	NOT YET 144
来	末	未
kuru	**sue**	**mada**
BIG 913	FAT 914	DOG 335
大	太	犬
ōkii	**futoi**	**inu**

体

Body

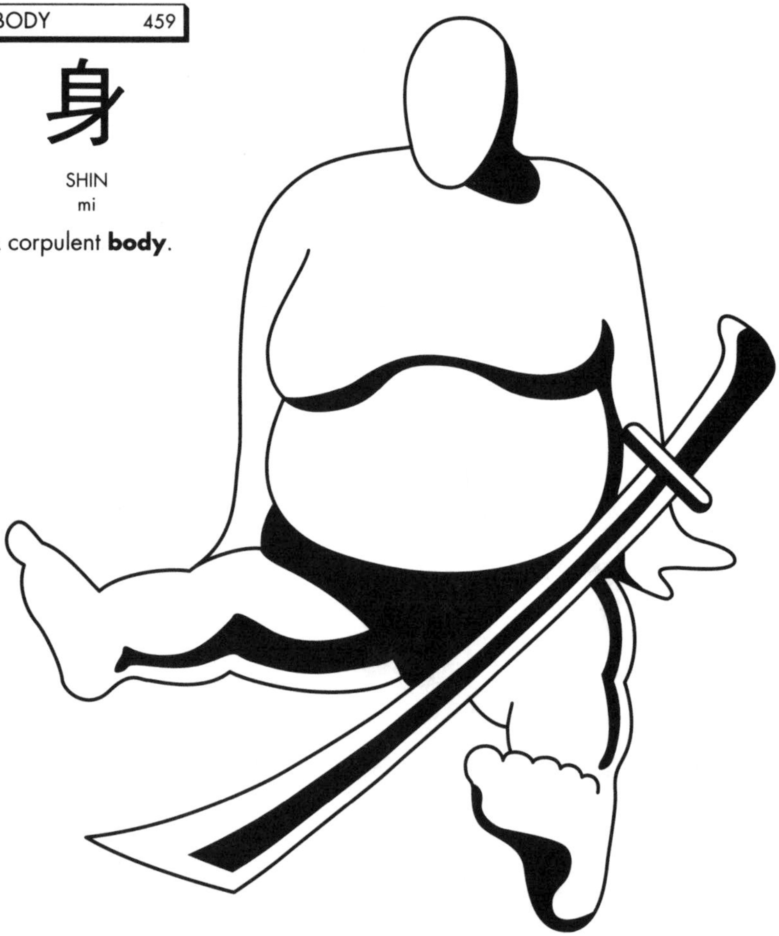

BODY 459

身

SHIN
mi

A corpulent **body**.

"BODY" 460

尸

*This element can mean **body**, and sometimes appears as a miscopying of* DOOR 1113.

URINE 461

尿

NYŌ

Urine drops from a bent-over body.

body 460 · water 57

BRAIN 462

脳

NŌ

An evil **brain** thinks only of the flesh.

flesh 267 · hand 611 · evil 647

"BUTTOCKS" 463

巴

*This element means **buttocks**.*

TAKE, GRASP, BUNDLE 464

把

HA
toru, -wa

A hand **grasps** a buttocks.

hand 580 | buttocks 463

FATTEN, ENRICH 465

肥

HI
koeru/yasu

A **fattened**, fleshy buttocks.

flesh 267 | buttocks 463

"BUTTOCKS" 466

𠂤

*This element also means **buttocks**.*

GOVERNMENT, OFFICIAL 467

官

KAN

Government officials in the House are asses.

roof 1144 | buttocks 466

ARM, ABILITY, ELBOW 468

肱

KŌ
hiji

A fleshy **arm**.

flesh 267 | elbow n–418

FACE, ASPECT, MASK 469

面

MEN
omote, omo, tsura

A **mask** covers his **face**.

NOSE 470

鼻

BI
hana

A pig sticks its **nose** in a field of grass.

self 542 | field 201 | grass 124

LAUGH, SMILE 471

笑

SHŌ
warau, emu

A moustache and a big **smile**.

bamboo 123 | big 913

Flesh & Bone

BONE 472

骨

KOTSU
hone

A **bone** protrudes from the flesh.

vertebrae 474 flesh 267

SKIN, TEXTURE, GRAIN 473

肌

KI
hada

The **skin** covers the flesh.

flesh 267 desk n–157

"VERTEBRA" 474

*This element means **vertebra**.*

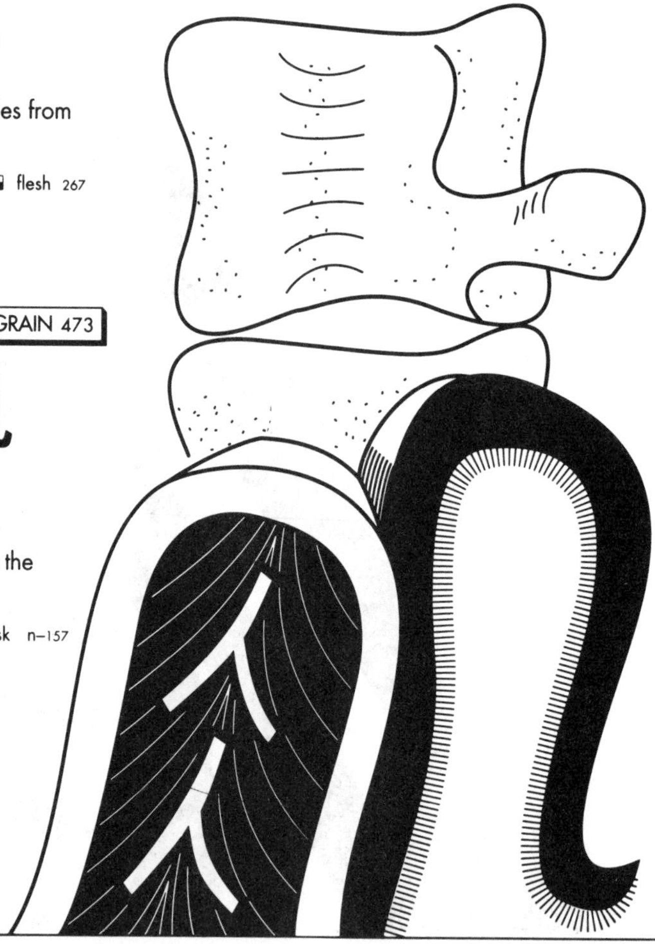

TORSO, TRUNK, BODY 475

胴

DŌ

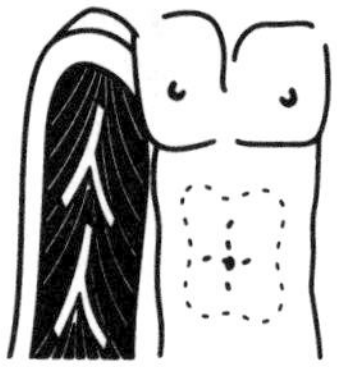

He has the same fleshy **torso** as always.

flesh 267 same 889

INTESTINE 476

腸

CHŌ
harawata

The meat I ate wasn't easy on my **intestines**.

flesh 267 sun 1 rays n–26

SLIP, SLIDE, SMOOTH 477

滑

KATSU
sube<u>ru</u>, name<u>raka</u>

A wet, **slippery** bone.

water 66 bone 472

CHEST, BREAST, HEART 478

胸

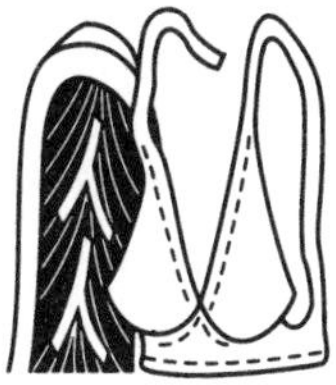

KYŌ
mune, muna

A cross-your-**heart** bra supports fleshy **breasts**.

flesh 267 lungs n–478

VEIN, PULSE 482

脈

MYAKU

Veins are little streams in the flesh.

flesh 267 river 55

BACK, STATURE, DEFY 483

背

HAI
se, sei, somuku/keru

Two professors sit **back** to back and **defy** each other.

north n–483 flesh 267

PLACENTA, WOMB 479

胞

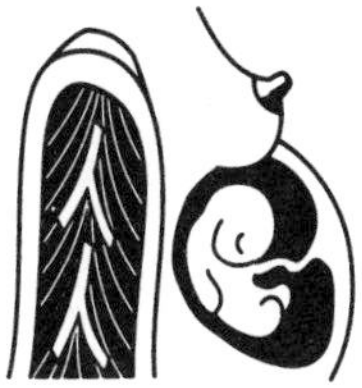

HŌ

The flesh of the **womb** protects the child.

flesh 267 protect 944

SHOULDER 484

肩

KEN
kata

Like a door on a hinge, the arm swings from the **shoulder**.

door 1113 flesh 267

MUSCLE, SINEW 480

筋

KIN
suji

Muscles as **sinewy** as bamboo.

bamboo 123 flesh 267 power 745

SWELL, BULGE 481

脹

CHŌ
fukuramu/reru

Long, **bulging** muscles.

flesh 267 long 915

Skin

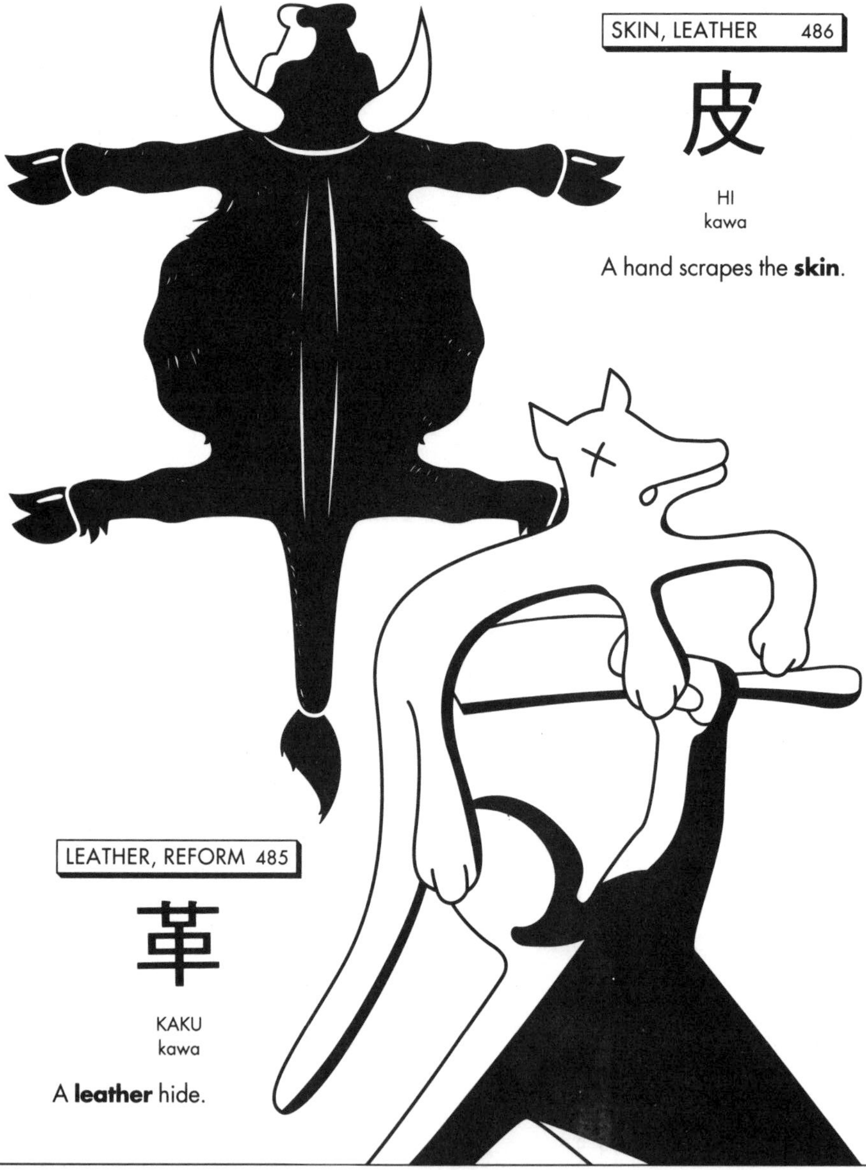

SKIN, LEATHER 486

皮

HI
kawa

A hand scrapes the **skin**.

LEATHER, REFORM 485

革

KAKU
kawa

A **leather** hide.

OPEN, DISCLOSE 487

披

HI

A hand pulls back the skin to **disclose** the innards.

◧ hand 580 ◨ skin 486

SHOE 488

靴

KA
kutsu

Change your old leather **shoes**.

◧ leather 485 ◨ change 374

破 BREAK, TEAR 489

HA
yaburu/reru

I **broke** open my skin on a rock.

◧ rock 190 ◨ skin 486

疲 TIRE, EXHAUSTION 490

HI
tsukareru

So **tired**, only skin holds me together.

◻ sick 655 ◼ skin 486

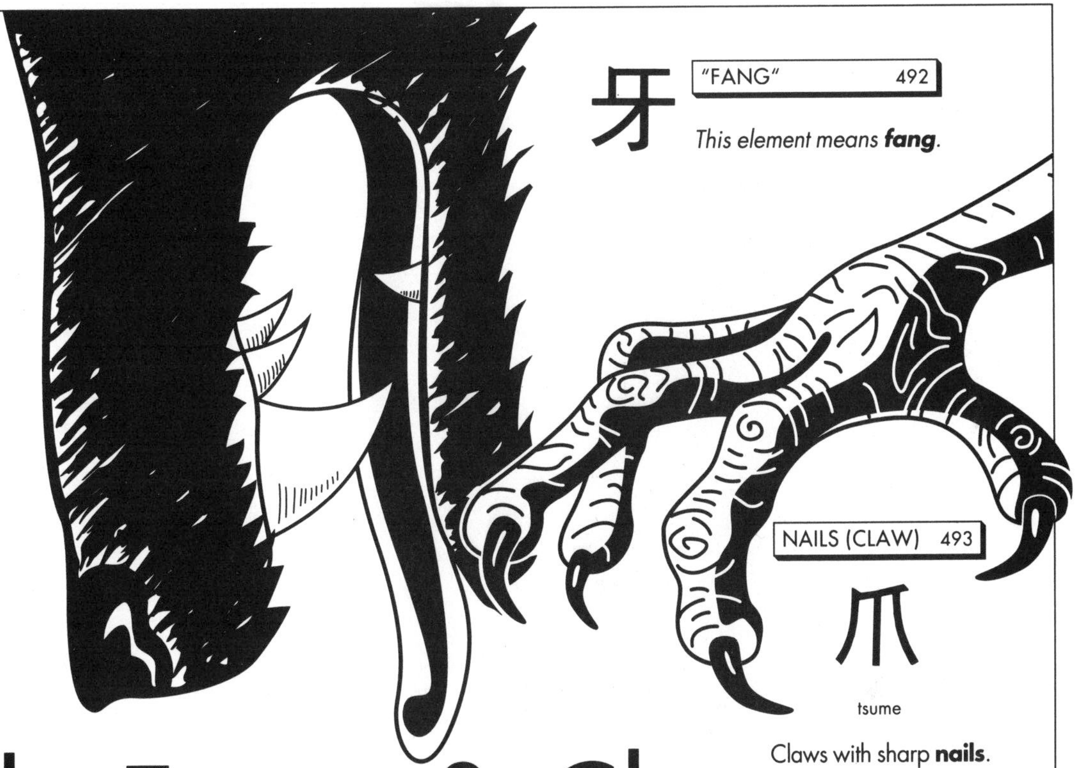

TOOTH 491

歯

SHI
ha

Bits of rice get stuck in your **teeth**.

⬒ stop 1205 ⬓ rice 217

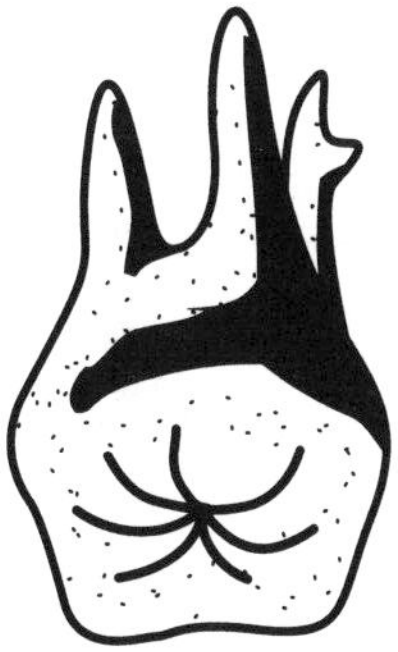

牙 "FANG" 492

This element means ***fang****.*

NAILS (CLAW) 493

爪

tsume

Claws with sharp **nails**.

Tooth, Fang, & Claw

AGE 494

齢

REI

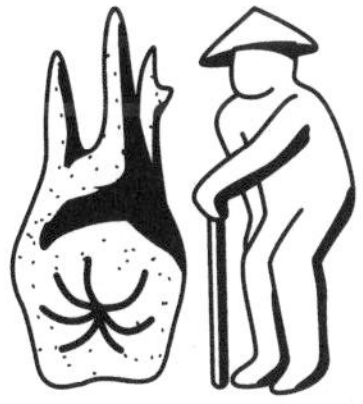

The **aged** man ordered some new teeth.

◧ tooth 491 ◨ order n–494

ELEGANCE, TASTE 495

雅

GA

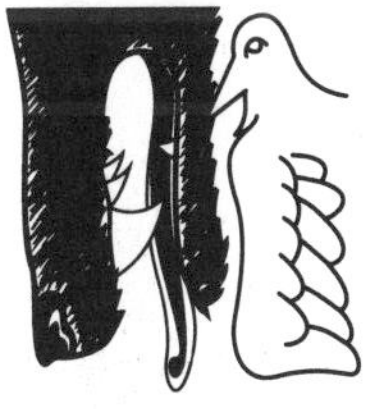

Sink your fangs into a **tasty** bird.

◧ fang 492 ◨ bird 319

PINCH, GRASP 496

抓

SŌ
tsuma<u>mu</u>,
tsune<u>ru</u>

Hands that **pinch**, claws that **grasp**.

◧ hand 580 ◨ claw 493

Heart

泌

FLOW, SECRETE 497

HITSU, HI

Blood **flows** from a stabbed heart.

◧ water 66 ◨ necessarily n–497

"HEART" 498

忄

*This form of the **heart** radical looks like bood rushing through one's veins. It often suggests feelings.*

HEART, MIND, CORE, FEELINGS 499

心

SHIN
kokoro

My **feelings** come from the **core** of my **heart**.

PLEASANT, CHEERFUL 500

快

KAI
kokoroyo<u>i</u>

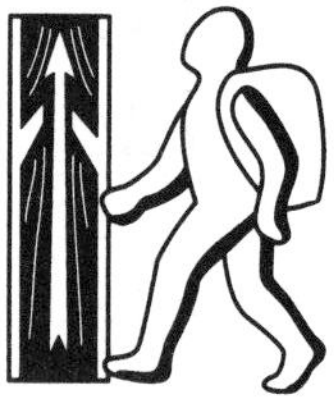

I started out on a **pleasant** hike.

◧ heart 498 ◨ pull apart n–500

DECIDE, SETTLE, COLLAPSE 501

決

KETSU
ki<u>maru</u>/<u>meru</u>

After a while I **decided** to **settle** down before I **collapsed**.

◧ water 66 ◨ pull apart n–500

SUDDEN, EMERGENCY, HURRY 502

急

KYŪ
iso<u>gu</u>, se<u>ku</u>

Suddenly, I grasped my heart. It was an **emergency**.

⊟ crouch n–502 ⊟ hand 597 ⊟ heart 499

SUSPICIOUS, WEIRD, MYSTERY 503

怪

KAI, KE
ayashii/shimu

It's a **mystery** who stabbed the samurai.

heart 499 hand 600 soil 101

BLOOD 506

血

KETSU
chi

He's **bloody**.

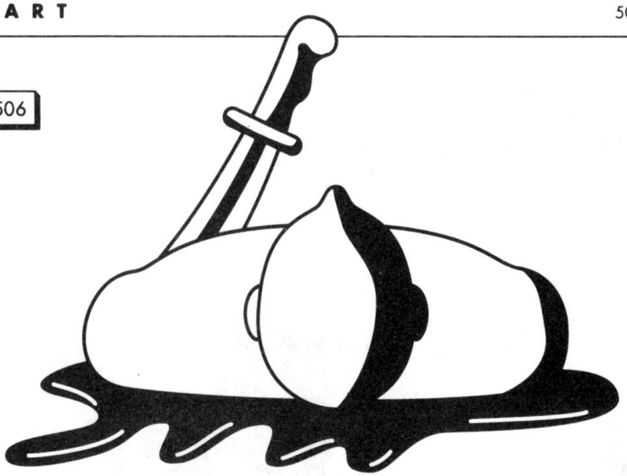

SAD 504

悲

HI
kanashii/shimu

My heart is not happy, but **sad**.

opposite 960 heart 498

GRIEVE, MOURN 507

悼

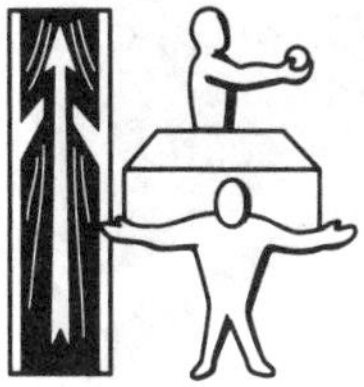

TŌ
itamu

Our hearts will **grieve** and **mourn** the deceased.

heart 498 table 508

ENDURE, STEALTH 510

忍

NIN
shinobu

Can you **endure** a blade in your heart?

blade 1024 heart 499

FEAR, AFRAID 505

怖

FU
kowai

Fear spread through our hearts.

heart 499 spread 1008

TABLE, EXCEL, HIGH 508

卓

TAKU

Set the **table** for the wake.

up 942 sun 1 ten 906

SEX, NATURE 509

性

SEI, SHŌ
saga

It's his **nature** to express his feelings.

heart 499 life 214

WILL, INTENT 511

志

SHI
kokorozashi, kokorozasu

His heart has the **will** of a samurai.

samurai 753 heart 499

RECORD, JOURNAL 512

誌

SHI

The samurai **recorded** his speech.

speak 840 samurai 753 heart 499

Love

LOVE, BELOVED 513

恋

REN
koi, koishii

His heart's filled with **love**.

red 65 heart 498

LOVE 516

愛

AI

Unless you uncover your heart, **love's** progress is slow.

hand 609 heart 499 progress n–516

THINK 517

思

SHI
omou

Thinking involves both the heart and brain.

field 201 heart 499

ANXIOUS, DISEASE, BE ILL 514

患

KAN
wazurau

He is so **anxious** his heart is tied in knots.

pierce n–514 heart 499

LOYALTY, DEVOTION 515

忠

CHŪ

My **loyalty** comes straight from the middle of my heart.

middle 954 heart 499

JOY 518

悦

ETSU

Shout for **joy**.

heart 498 brother 438

Hate

ANGER, RAGE 519

怒

DO
ikaru, okoru

His heart filled with **rage** ...

slave 520 heart 499

SLAVE, SERVANT, GUY 520

奴

DO
yatsu, yakko

... he beats the **slave** woman.

woman 520 hand 600

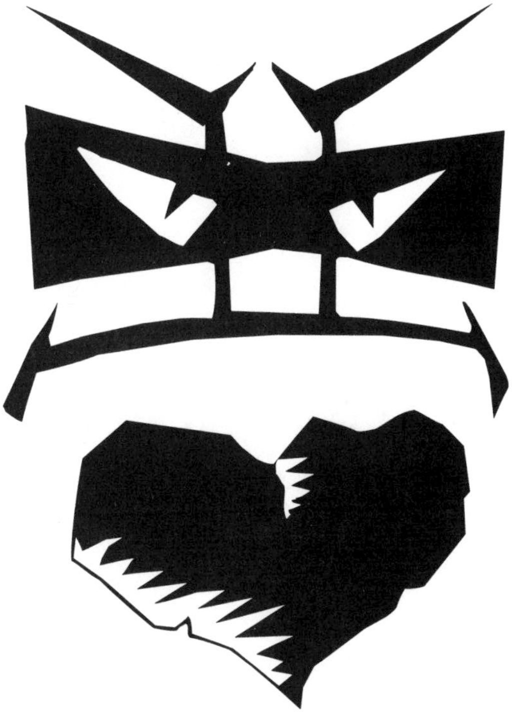

BAD, HATE 522

悪

AKU, O
warui

A **bad** heart, full of hatred.

Asia 1082 heart 499

COMPOSED, DISTANT 521

悠

YŪ

Composed, a person behind a wall watches the beating from a **distance**.

person 362 strike 802 heart 499

INDIGNANT, ANGRY 523

憤

FUN
ikidōru

The crowd becomes **angry** about money.

heart 498 ten (x3) 906 money 708

ANGRY, IN ILL HUMOR 524

怫

FUTSU

The blood of his heart boils and gushes with **anger**.

heart 498 boil n–78

Head, Neck, & Hair

"HEAD" (PAGE) 525

頁

KETSU
pēji

*As an element, this means **head**. It is a rarely used character meaning **page**.*

TROUBLE, PAIN TORMENT 526

煩

HAN, BON
wazurau/washii

I am **tormented** by a fire in my head.

◧ fire 83 ◨ head 525

SEQUENCE, COMPLIANCE 527

順

JUN

The **sequence**: shampoo head, rinse in river.

◧ river 55 ◨ head 525

頂 RECEIVE, TOP 528

CHŌ
itadaki, itadaku

I got a nail in the **top** of my head.

◧ exact 1089 ◨ head 525

頭 HEAD, TOP, START 529

TŌ, ZU
atama, kashira

That's using your bean, er, **head**!

◧ bean 245 ◨ head 525

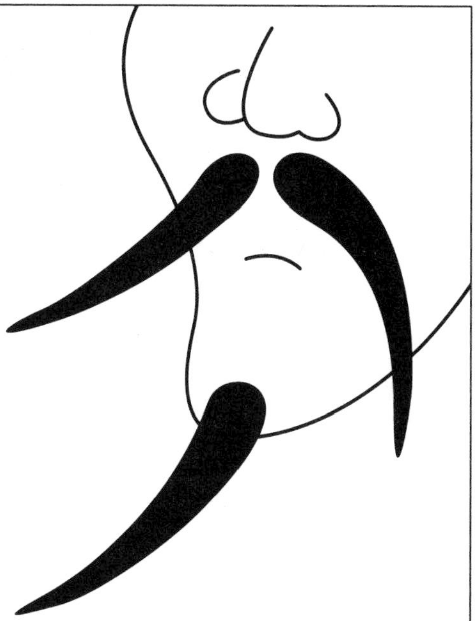

JAW, CHIN 530

顎

GAKU
ago

His **jaw** hangs from his head.

◧ jaw n–530 ◨ head 530

NECK 531

首

SHU
kubi

A **neck** X-ray.

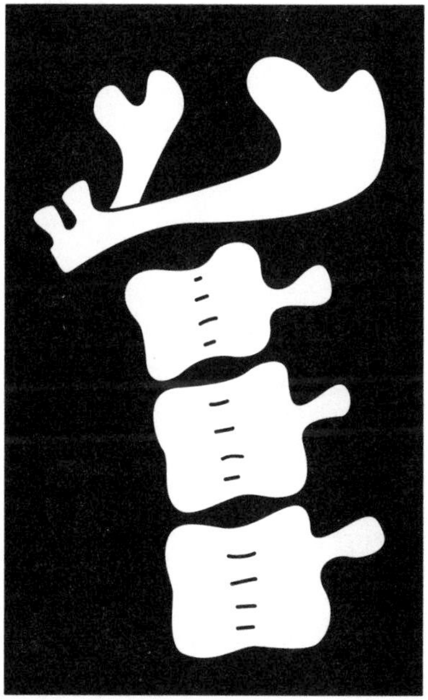

HAIR 532

毛

MŌ
ke

Hair in a comb.

TAIL 533

尾

BI
o

A **tail** is often a tuft of hair.

◻ body 460 ◼ hair 532

WAY, ROAD 534

道

DŌ, TŌ
michi

Which **way** in this neck of the woods?

◻ move 1153 ◼ neck 525

GUIDE, LEAD 535

導

DŌ
michibiku

Lead the way, inch by inch.

⬒ way 534 ⬓ inch 534

"HAIR" (DELICATE) 536

彡

This element means ***hair****, delicate, or attractive.*

HAIR (OF THE HEAD) 537

髪

HATSU
kami

Long **hair** is a girl's best friend.

◻ long 915 ◻ hair 536 ◼ friend 599

Eye

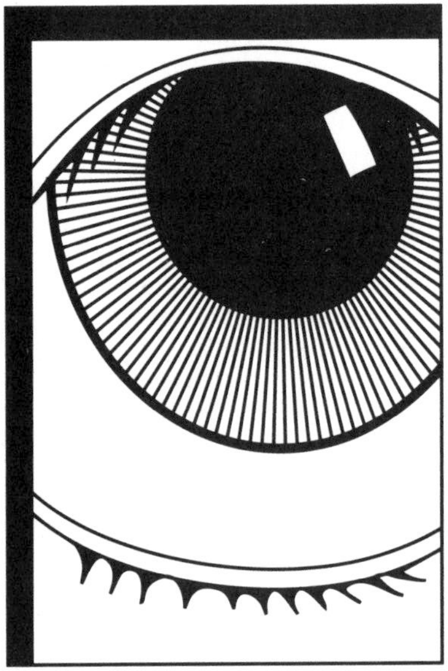

目

EYE 538

MOKU, BOKU
me, ma-

An **eye** looks through a keyhole.

WATCH, TO LOOK AT 539

看

KAN
miru

I shade my eye to **look**.

hand 579 | eye 538

SLEEP, FALL ASLEEP, SLEEPY 540

眠

MIN
nemui/ri/ru

The eyes of the people are **sleepy**.

eye 538 | people 395

MINISTRY, OMIT, EXAMINE 541

省

SEI, SHŌ
habuku, kaerimiru

The **ministry's examination** will **omit** a few things.

few 924 | eye 538

SELF 542

自

JI, SHI
mizukara

The eye is the window to your **self**.

nose n–542 | eye 538

LOOK, SEE, SHOW 543

見

KEN
miru/seru/eru

Looking on your hands and knees.

eye 538 | bent legs n–543

SEE, LOOK, REGARD 544

視

SHI
miru

Get on your hands and knees when **looking** upon the altar.

altar 696 | look 543

Ear

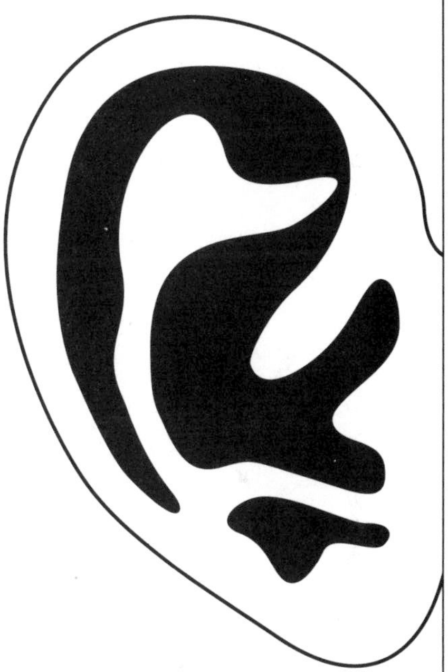

REMEMBER, WAKE	545

覚

KAKU
oboeru, sameru/masu

I **remember waking** to see the sun shine over the roof.

learn n–543 look 543

SEE, LOOK	546

覧

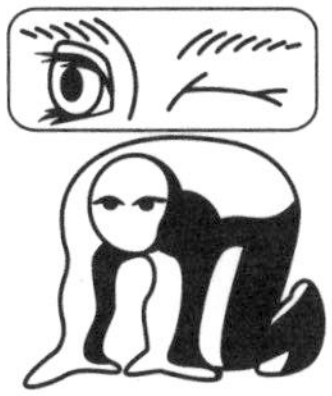

RAN

A watchful eye **looks** over the subjects.

subject n–546 person n–546 look 543

INTIMATE, PARENT	547

親

SHIN
shitashii/shimu
oya

Your **parents** keep a sharp eye on you.

needle 1006 look 543

SHAME, ASHAMED	548

恥

CHI
haji, hajiru/zukashii

My heart pumps blood to my ears when I'm **ashamed**.

ear 551 heart 499

LISTEN (CAREFULLY)	549

聴

CHŌ
kiku

Use your ears, eyes, and heart to **listen carefully**.

ear 551 net 987 heart 499

SAINT, SAGE, SACRED	550

聖

SEI
hijiri

A **sage** is a leader who listens to what his people have to say.

ear 551 mouth 566 king 743

耳

EAR	551

JI
mimi

Here's an **ear**.

Mouth

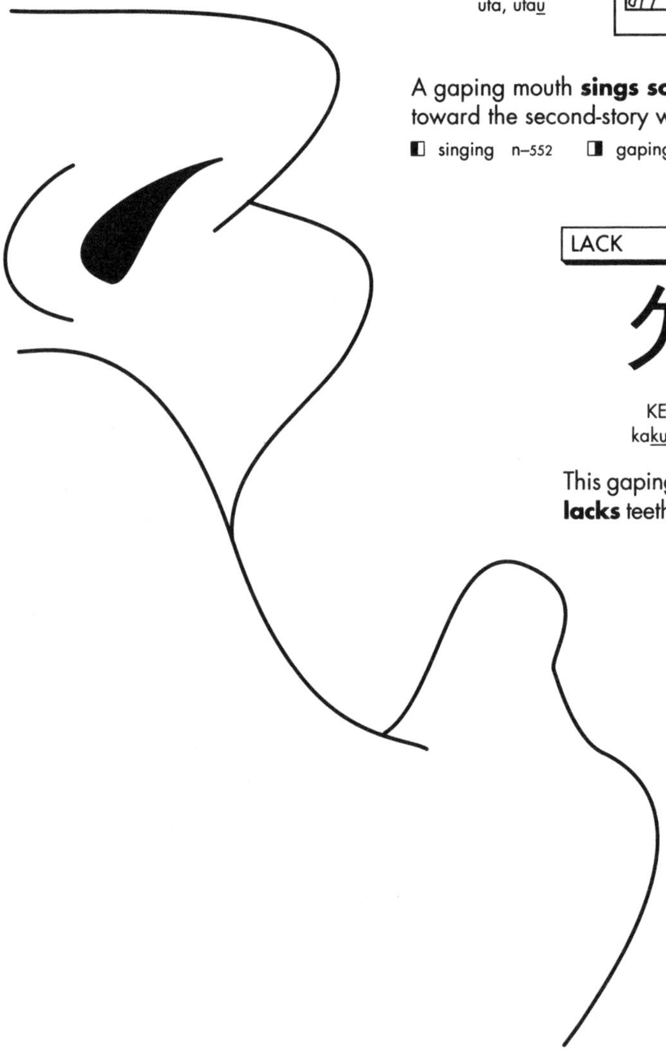

SING, SONG 552

歌

KA
uta, utau

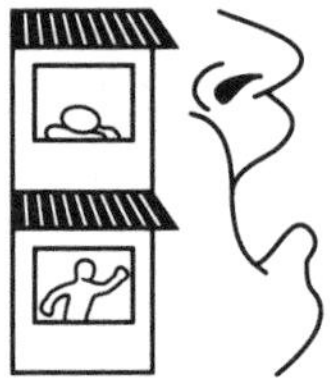

A gaping mouth **sings songs** toward the second-story window.

◧ singing n–552 ◨ gaping mouth 553

LACK 553

欠

KETSU
kaku/keru

This gaping mouth **lacks** teeth.

COOK, BOIL 554

炊

SUI
taku

The **cooked** food goes from the fire to a gaping mouth.

◧ fire 83 ◨ gaping mouth 553

NEXT, FOLLOW 555

次

JI, SHI
tsugi, tsugu

One yawn **follows** another.

◧ freeze 94 ◨ gaping mouth 553

BLOW, BREATHE OUT 556

吹

SUI
fuku

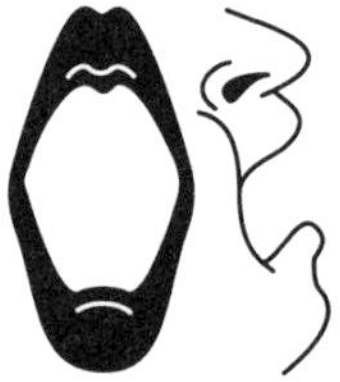

Breathe out through a gaping mouth.

◧ mouth 566 ◨ gaping mouth 553

GOOD LUCK, JOY 557

吉

KICHI, KITSU

A samurai shouts for **joy**.

samurai 753 mouth 566

SHOUT, YELL 558

叫

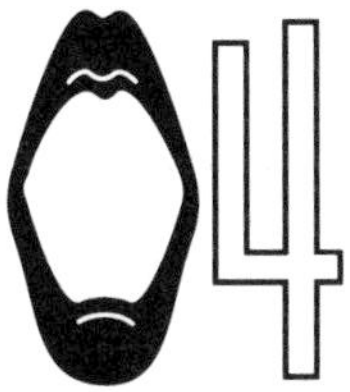

KYŌ
sake<u>bu</u>

A golfer **shouts** "FORE!"

mouth 566 sudden n–558

DISGORGE, VOMIT 559

吐

TO
ha<u>ku</u>

A mouth **vomits** dirt.

mouth 566 soil 101

KNOW 560

知

CHI
shi<u>ru</u>

If you **know**, words fly like arrows.

arrow 818 mouth 566

TO SUCK, INHALE 561

吸

KYŪ
su<u>u</u>

Inhale carbon monoxide, **suck** on a cigarette.

mouth 566 reach 373

CALL, BREATHE 562

呼

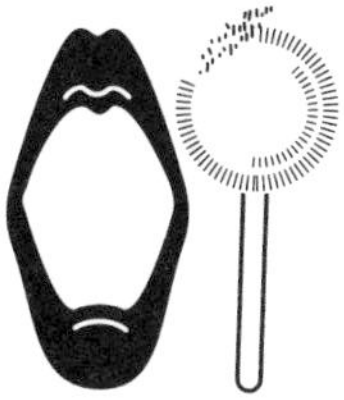

KO
yo<u>bu</u>

In one **breath**, I blew away the milkweed flower.

mouth 566 exhale n–562

INSCRIBE, SIGN 563

銘

MEI

Inscribe your name in metal.

metal 105 name 565

PEACE, SOFT, JAPAN 564

和

WA, O
yawa<u>ragu</u>, nago<u>yaka</u>

Peace is a mouth full of **soft** rice.

rice plant 231 mouth 566

NAME, FAME 565

名

MEI, MYŌ
na

His **name** is on everyone's lips.

moon 14 mouth 566

MOUTH, OPENING 566

口

KŌ, KU
kuchi

The **mouth** is an **opening** in the face.

CARRY IN ONE'S HAND, BRING 567

携

KEI
tazusawaru/eru

To carry a bird in one's hand.

hand 580 | bird 319 | hand n–567

MANAGE, MANIPULATE 570

操

SŌ
misao, ayatsuru

He **manages** to **manipulate** the packages by the Christmas tree.

hand 580 | goods 1038 | tree 126

CHALLENGE, DEFY 573

挑

CHŌ
idomu

Others flee, but I **defy** the omen.

hand 580 | omen 1170

CHOOSE, SELECT 568

択

TAKU
erabu, yoru

I'll hand pick my **selection** after studying all the measurements.

hand 580 | measure 884

CLUMSY, POOR 571

拙

SETSU
tsutanai, mazui

My hands are as **clumsy** as two left feet.

hand 580 | leave 956

PAY, SWEEP AWAY, RID 574

払

FUTSU
harau

Rid yourself of people who don't **pay**.

hand 580 | nose 450

SEARCH 569

捜

SŌ
sagasu

To **search** with a lantern in one's hand.

hand 580 | expound 698 | hand 600

THROW, CAST 572

投

TŌ
nageru

I will **throw** this ax.

hand 580 | hand w/ax 792

INSERT, PINCH, SQUEEZE 575

挟

KYŌ
hasamaru/mu

I need a hand—they put the big **squeeze** on me.

hand 580 | squeeze n–575

Hand

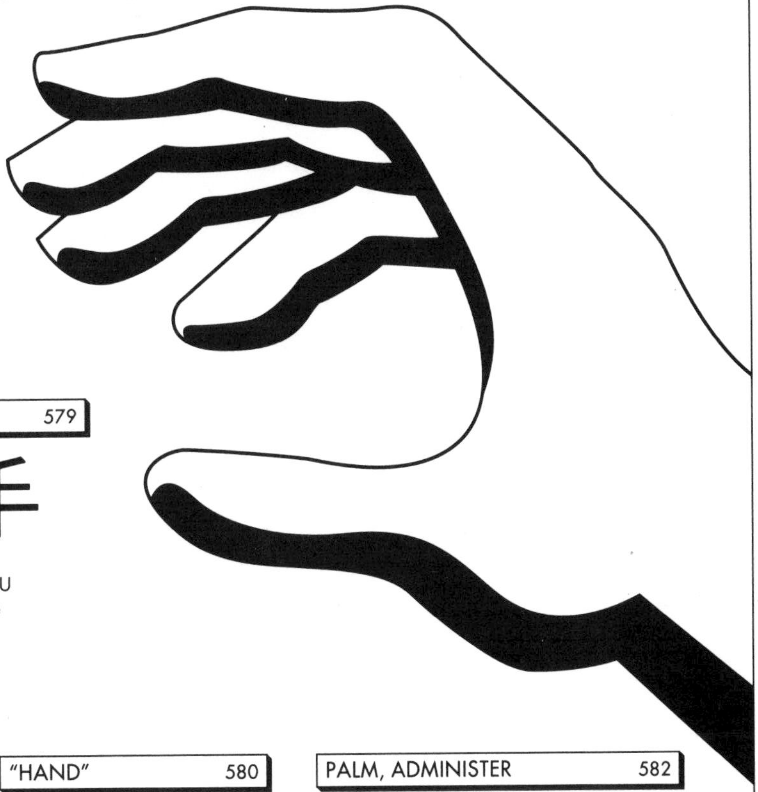

BEAT, TAP, CLAP 576

拍

HAKU, HYŌ

A hand **taps** a white drum.

◧ hand 580 ◨ white 936

LOSE 577

失

SHITSU
ushinau

It slipped out of my hand and was **lost**.

HAND 579

手

SHU
te

A **hand**.

MUTUAL 578

互

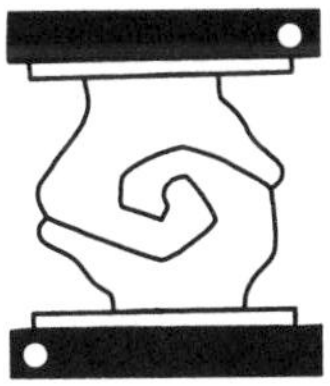

GO
tagai

Mutual dependency.

"HAND" 580

扌

*A common **hand** radical looks like this.*

EMBRACE, HUG 581

抱

HŌ
(i)daku, kakaeru

I was wrapped in an **embrace**.

◧ hand 580 ◨ wrap 944

PALM, ADMINISTER 582

掌

SHŌ,
tsukasadoru,
tanagokoro

I have a shiny coin in the **palm** of my hand.

⬒ shine n–582 ▤ mouth 566 ⬓ hand 579

MEET, JOIN, FIT 583

合

GŌ
au/waseru

The lid **fits** the mouth of the jar.

person 363 | one 897 | mouth 566

ERASE, RUB, PAINT 586

抹

MATSU

Erase the **paint** with the end of my brush.

hand 580 | end 145

CHASE, SEIZE 589

逮

TAI

Chase the animal and **seize** it by the tail.

move 1153 | hand grasping n–589

PICK UP, GATHER, TEN 584

拾

SHŪ, JŪ
hirou

A hand **picks up** the lid.

hand 580 | fit 583

PULL OUT, PLUCK 587

抽

CHŪ
nuku

Pull out in this direction.

hand 580 | cause 76

THING, MATTER, ACT 590

事

JI, ZU
koto

What is that **thing** in your hand?

signboard n–1153 | hand 597

LOAD, BOARD 585

搭

TŌ

Load grass into the container.

hand 580 | grass 124 | fit 583

PUSH 588

押

Ō
osu, osaeru

Push in this direction.

hand 580 | shell 357

LAW, CONTROL 591

律

RITSU, RICHI

The written **law** of the road.

road 1192 | writing n–591

WRITING BRUSH 592

筆

HITSU
fude

A bamboo **brush**.

bamboo 123 | writing n–592

Hold

CONFLICT, VIE 593

争

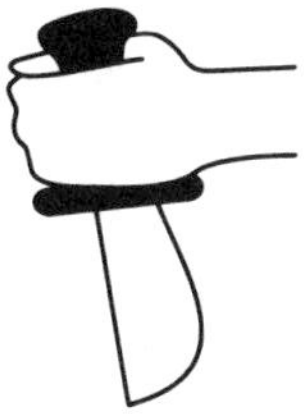

SŌ
arasou

The knife was used in the **conflict** …

PURE, CLEAN 594

浄

JŌ

… and later washed **clean** of blood.

◧ water 66 ◨ conflict 593

APPLY, HIT, MARK, APPROPRIATE 595

当

TŌ
ataru/teru

A few coins **hit the spot**.

⬒ few 924 ⬓ hand 597

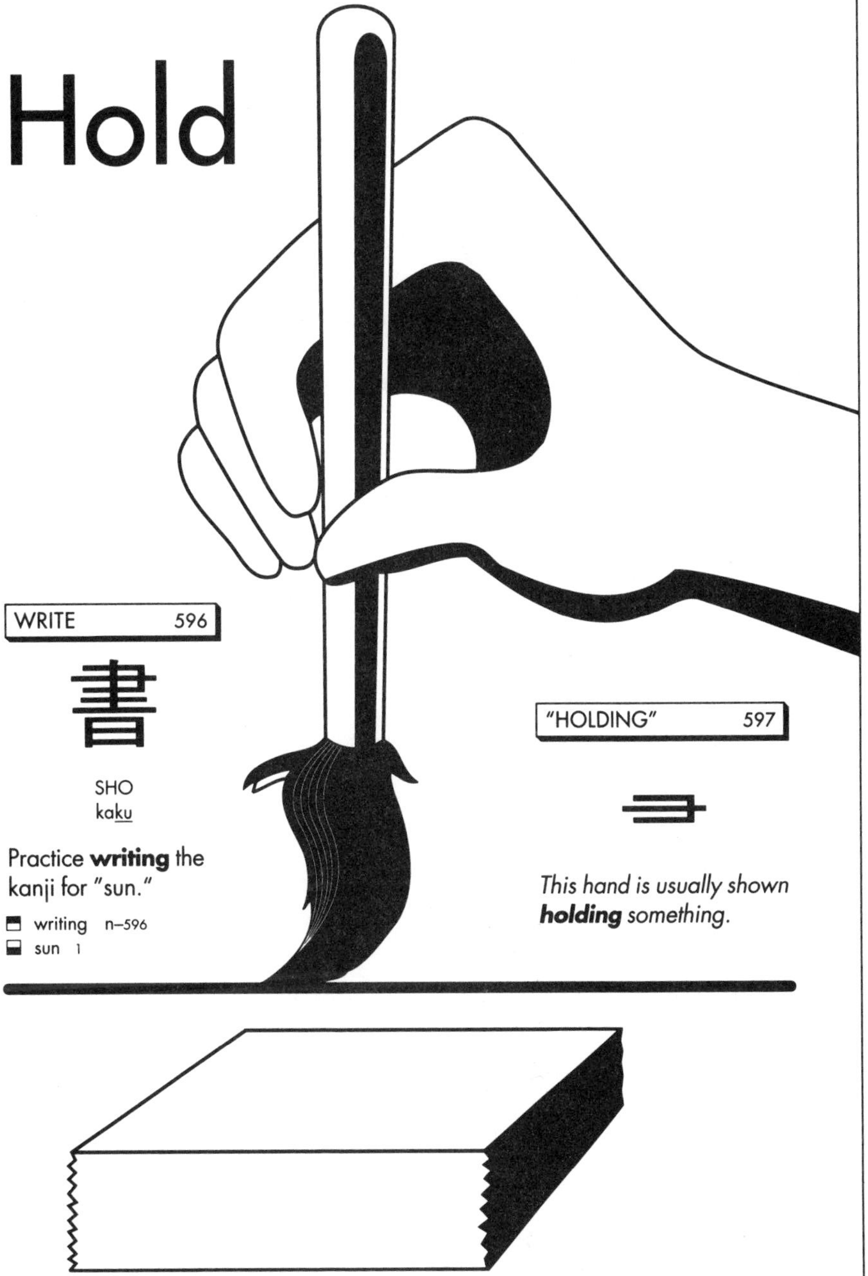

WRITE 596

書

SHO
kaku

Practice **writing** the kanji for "sun."

⬒ writing n–596
⬓ sun 1

"HOLDING" 597

⺕

*This hand is usually shown **holding** something.*

Reach

"HAND" 598

ナ

This is a ***hand****.*

FRIEND 599

友

YŪ
tomo

A hand reaches out in **friendship**.

◧ hand 598 ◨ hand 600

"HAND" 600

又

This is a ***hand****, too.*

LEFT 601

左

SA
hidari

Work with your **left** hand ...

◧ hand 598 ◨ construction 1054

RIGHT 602

右

U, YŪ
migi

... eat with your **right**.

◧ hand 598 ◨ mouth 566

LOOSE, EASY, SLACK 603

緩

KAN
yurui/yaka/mu/meru

Give me some **slack** and make the rope **loose**.

◧ thread 964 ◨ hands w/rope n–603

HELP 604

援

EN

An extra hand **helps** pull up the rope.

◧ hand 580 ◨ hands w/rope n–603

WARM 605

暖

DAN
atatakai/maru/meru

Our hands get **warm** from pulling on the rope all day.

◧ day 1 ◨ hands w/rope n–603

PLUCK, EXTRACT, MISS 606

抜

BATSU
nuku/karu/keru/kasu

A hand **plucks** a friend from danger.

◧ hand 580 ◨ friend 599

Give

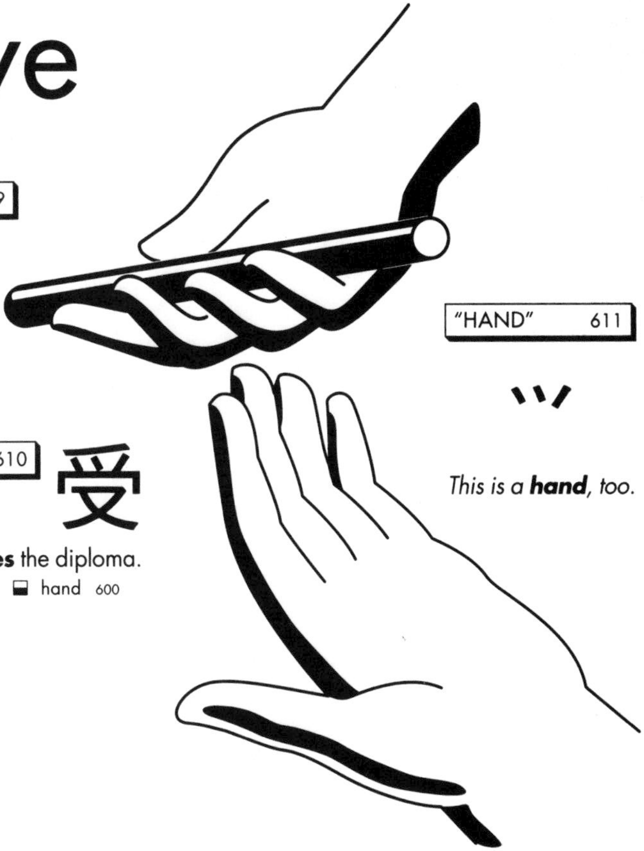

"HAND" 609

⺤

*This is a **hand**.*

"HAND" 611

⺍

*This is a **hand**, too.*

SHAKE, SWING, ROCK 607

揺

YŌ
yuru/reru/ragu/suru,
yusuburu

A basket **swings** from one hand to the other.

◧ hand 580 ◨ hand 609 ◨ basket n–607

RECEIVE 610

受

JU
ukeru

A hand **receives** the diploma.

⬒ hand 609 ⬓ hand 600

GIVE, GRANT, BESTOW 608

授

JU
sazukeru

A **grant** is **given**.

◧ hand 580 ◨ receive 610

OFFER, RAISE, ACT, PERFORM 612

挙

KYO
ageru, kozotte

A **raised** hand is **offered** a diploma in the **performing** arts.

⬒ hand 611 ⬓ hand 579

HONOR, FAME, PRAISE 613

誉

YO
homare

A baccalaureate address filled with **praise** and **honor**.

⬒ hand 611 ⬓ speak 840

Leg

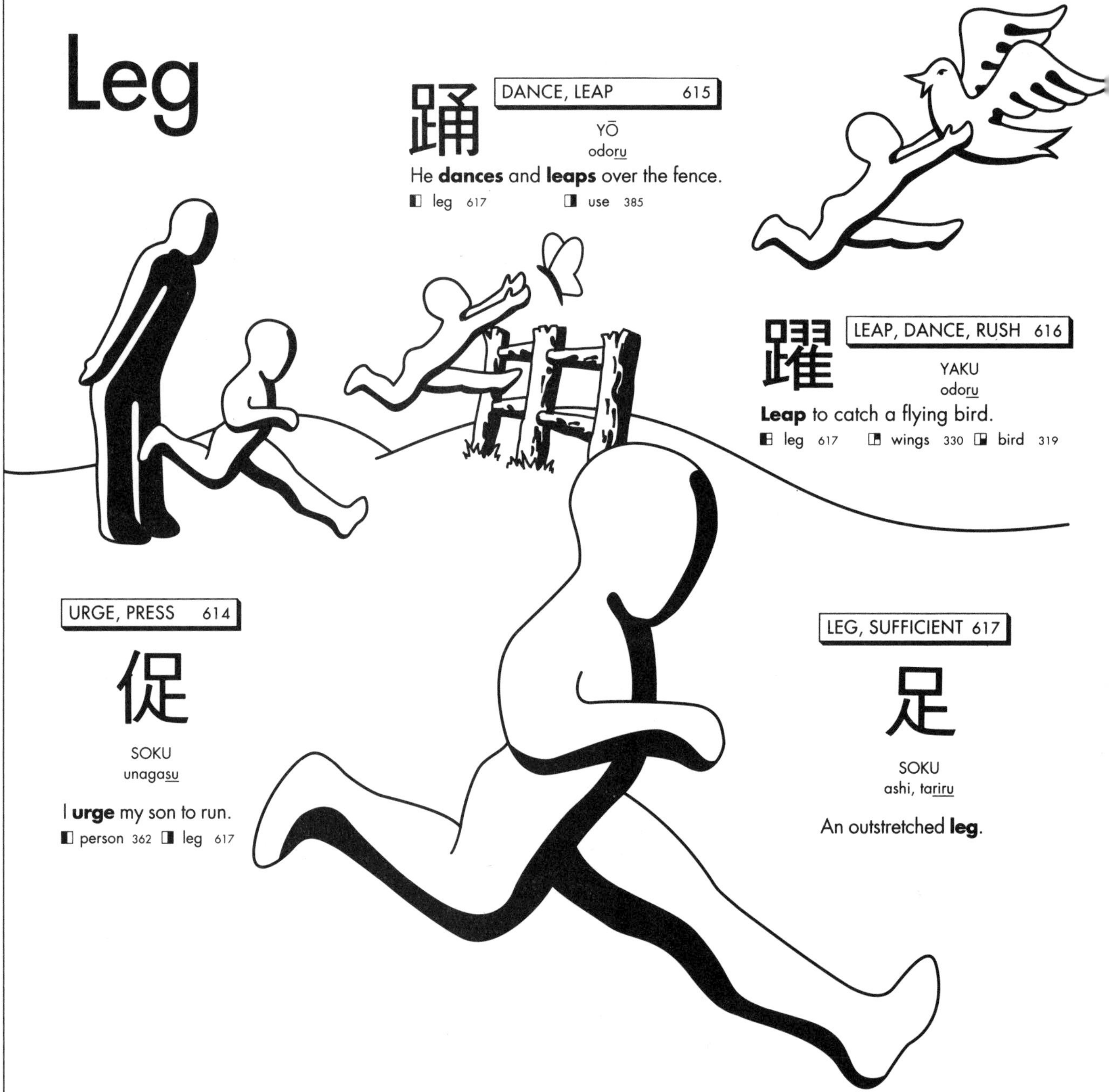

踊 DANCE, LEAP 615

YŌ
odoru

He **dances** and **leaps** over the fence.

◧ leg 617 ◨ use 385

躍 LEAP, DANCE, RUSH 616

YAKU
odoru

Leap to catch a flying bird.

◧ leg 617 ◳ wings 330 ◲ bird 319

URGE, PRESS 614

促

SOKU
unagasu

I **urge** my son to run.

◧ person 362 ◨ leg 617

LEG, SUFFICIENT 617

足

SOKU
ashi, tariru

An outstretched **leg**.

TRACE, REMAINS 618

跡

SEKI
ato

A bird left **traces** of **footprints** in the sand.

leg 617 · red n–65

SPRING, JUMP, LEAP 619

跳

CHŌ
haneru, tobu

Leap a trillion feet

leg 617 · trillion 1170

ARISE, WAKE, CAUSE 620

起

KI
okiru/koru/kosu

I **arise**, stretch, and run out of the house in the morning.

run 625 · self 445

FOLLOW, COMPLY 621

従

JŪ
shitagau

I run from the path of the **complacent followers** ...

path 1192 · follow n–621 · leg 617

CROSS, EXCEED, EXCEL 622

越

ETSU
koeru/su

... and run to **cross** beyond the lance-wielding sentry.

run 625 · halberd 801

HOLD, CARRY, OFFER 623

提

TEI, CHŌ
sageru

My legs and hands **carry** the day.

hand 580 · sun 1 · leg 617

FOLLOWER, FUTILITY 624

徒

TO
ada, itazura

It's **futile** to **follow** such a fast runner.

path 1192 · run 625

RUN 625

走

SŌ
hashiru

Run on the ground.

ground 101 · leg 617

PROCEED, GO 626

赴

FU
omomuku

Proceed when the signal permits.

run 625 · announce n–626

Stand

立 **STAND, RISE, LEAVE 627**

RITSU, RYŪ
tatsu/teru

A **standing** person.

COMPETE, BID 628

競

KYŌ, KEI
kisou

A standing-room-only crowd watches two brothers **compete**.

- stand (x2) 627
- brother (x2) 438

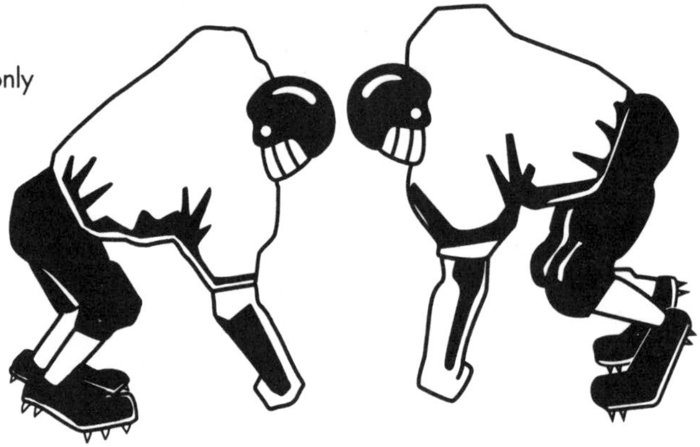

DOUBLE, FOLD 631

倍

BAI

The person's height is **double** that of the standing man.

- person 362
- stand 627
- mouth 566

ATTEND, ACCOMPANY 632

陪

BAI

The **attendant** stood on a box on a hill.

- hill 1094
- stand 627
- mouth 566

WEEP, CRY 629

泣

KYŪ
naku

Stand **weeping** in a puddle of tears.

- water 66
- stand 627

TRADE, DEAL, SELL 630

商

SHŌ
akinau

Stand at a booth and make a **deal**.

- stand 627
- prostitution n–630

ROW, LINE, RANK, ORDINARY 633

並

HEI
nami, narabi/bu

Stand in **line**.

FURIGANA

Small hiragana (and sometimes katakana) symbols can be placed above or to the side of a kanji character to indicate its correct pronunciation. These small kana, called *furigana*, are commonly given for younger readers and whenever there is some question as to how a kanji is read. Kanji used in personal names, for example, often have nonstandard readings, while some kanji are only used in particular contexts and may not be familiar even to educated adult readers. The word "spirit" at right, is read *bōrei*.

PRESIDENT

SHA *shrine 696* 社 しゃ

CHŌ *senior 915* 長 ちょう

HASEGAWA

HA *long 915* 長 は

SE *valley 168* 谷 せ

GAWA *river 55* 川 がわ

*The same kanji, **nagai** 915, is used in Mr. Hasegawa's title, **shachō**, and in his family name. The different readings of the kanji are indicated by* furigana.

亡霊

Spirit

霊 A SOUL, SPIRIT 634

REI, RYŌ
tama

A **spirit** stands in the falling rain.

rain 45 | stand 627

DEATH 635

死

SHI
shi<u>nu</u>

One fallen **dead** in the moonlight …

one 897 | bones 637 | fallen person n–374

BURY 636

葬

SŌ
hōmu<u>ru</u>

… and buried in the grass

grass (x2) 124 | death 635

LEAVE, CRUEL, HARM 637

残

ZAN
noko<u>ru</u>/<u>su</u>

To stab them to the bones is **cruel**.

bones n–637 | halberd 801

SPLIT, RIP, REND 638

裂

RETSU
sa<u>ku</u>/<u>keru</u>

Rip the clothes to shreds.

bones n–637 | knife 1037 | clothes 1021

FIERCE, INTENSE 639

烈

RETSU

A **fierce** line of fire.

bones n–637 | knife 1037 | fire 82

UGLY, INDECENT 640

醜

SHŪ
miniku<u>i</u>

Alcohol is an **ugly** devil in a bottle.

alcohol 251 devil 645

DEMON, WITCH, EVIL SPIRIT 641

魔

MA

A **demon** lives in a building in the forest.

building 1143 forest 142 devil 645

BEWITCH, CHARM 642

魅

MI

The devil easily **charms** the immature.

devil 645 immature 145

SOUL, SPIRIT 643

魂

KON
tama, tamashii

A **spirit** in a cloud.

cloud 54 devil 645

DEVIL, DEMON 645

鬼

KI
oni

A horned **devil** roams the fields.

LOWLY, MEAN, DESPISE 644

卑

HI
iya<u>shii</u>/<u>shimu</u>

The devil is **lowly** and **mean**.

TOMBSTONE, MONUMENT 646

碑

HI

The devil hides near the **tombstone**.

stone 190 mean 644

Pain

凶 BAD LUCK, EVIL, DISASTER 647

KYŌ

Bad luck . . .

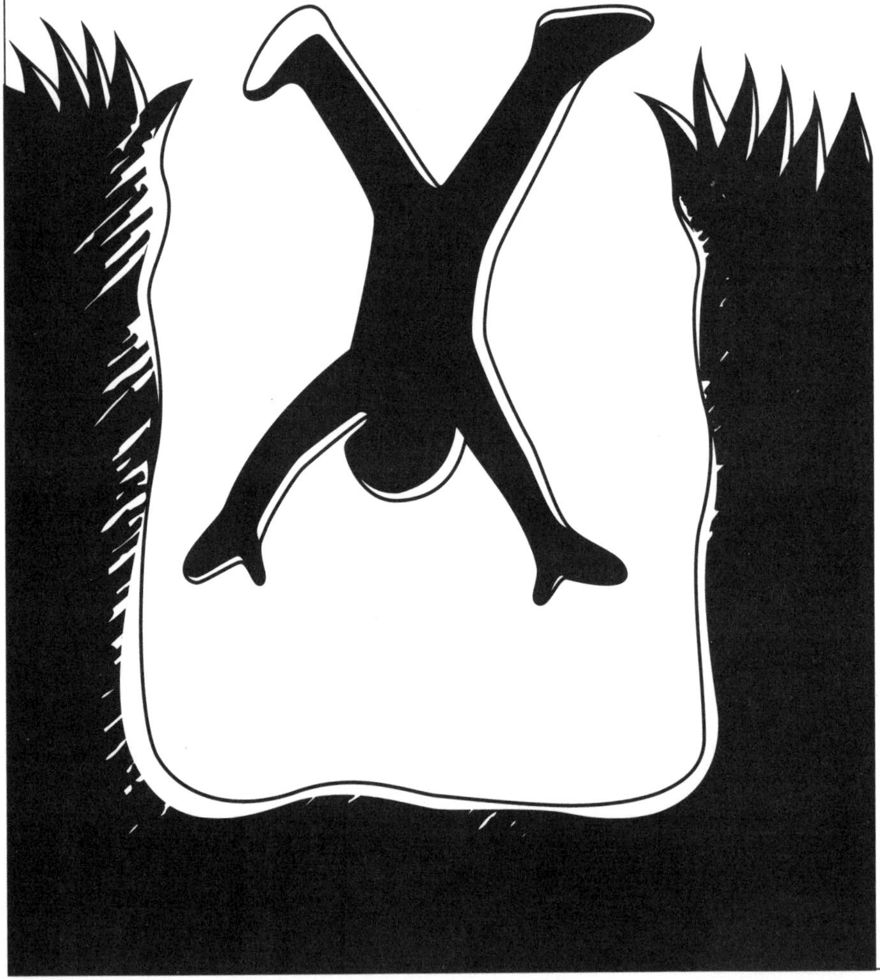

EVIL 648

兇

KYŌ

. . . to be eaten by an **evil** monster.

bad luck 647 legs 647

WORRY, DISTRESS, ANNOY 649

悩

NŌ
naya<u>mashii</u>/<u>mu</u>/<u>masu</u>

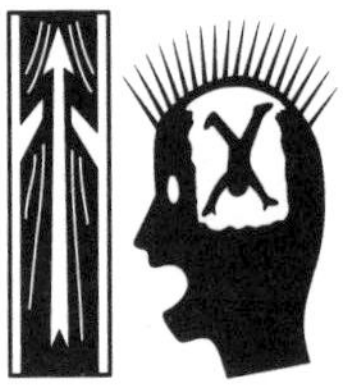

My heart and brain are **worried**.

heart 498 brain n–649

SPIRIT 650

気

KI, KE

My **spirit** rises like steam.

vapors n–650 rice n–650

ILLNESS, SWIFTLY 651

疾

SHITSU

The arrow causing the **illness** is removed **swiftly** …

□ illness 655 ■ arrow 818

HEAL, MEDICAL 652

医

I
iyasu

… and is put in the **medic**'s box when a patient **heals**.

□ enclosed n–652 ■ arrow 818

CAUSE, BASED ON, DEPEND ON 653

因

IN
yoru

A big illness **caused** me to stay in bed.

□ enclosed 778 ■ big 913

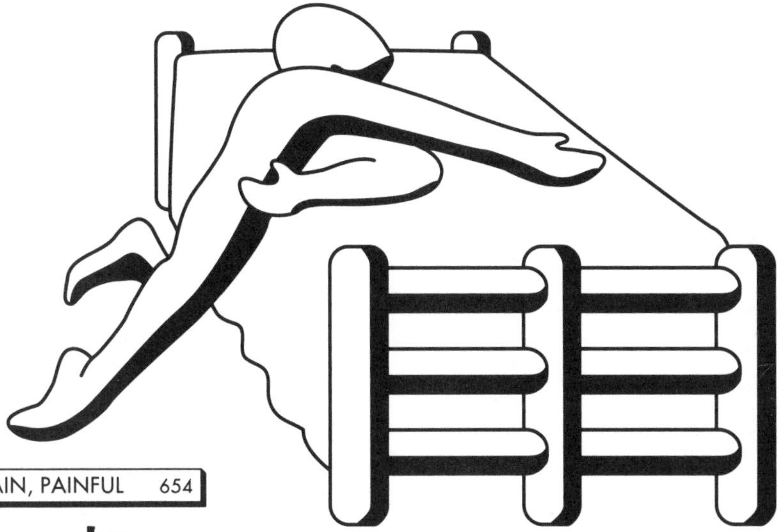

PAIN, PAINFUL 654

痛

TSŪ
itai/mu/meru

He has a **painful** illness.

□ illness 655 ■ use 385

"ILLNESS" 655

疒

*As an element this means **illness**.*

FOOLISH 656

痴

CHI

To **fools**, knowledge is a sickness.

□ illness 655 ■ know 560

FAVOR, KINDNESS 657

恩

ON

He did a **kind**-hearted **favor**.

□ cause 653 ■ heart 499

EPIDEMIC 658

疫

EKI, YAKU

An **epidemic** strikes.

□ illness 655 ■ hand w/ax 792

SYMPTOM, ILLNESS 659

症

SHŌ

Symptoms correctly identify **illness**.

□ illness 655 ■ correct 826

Dead Bodies

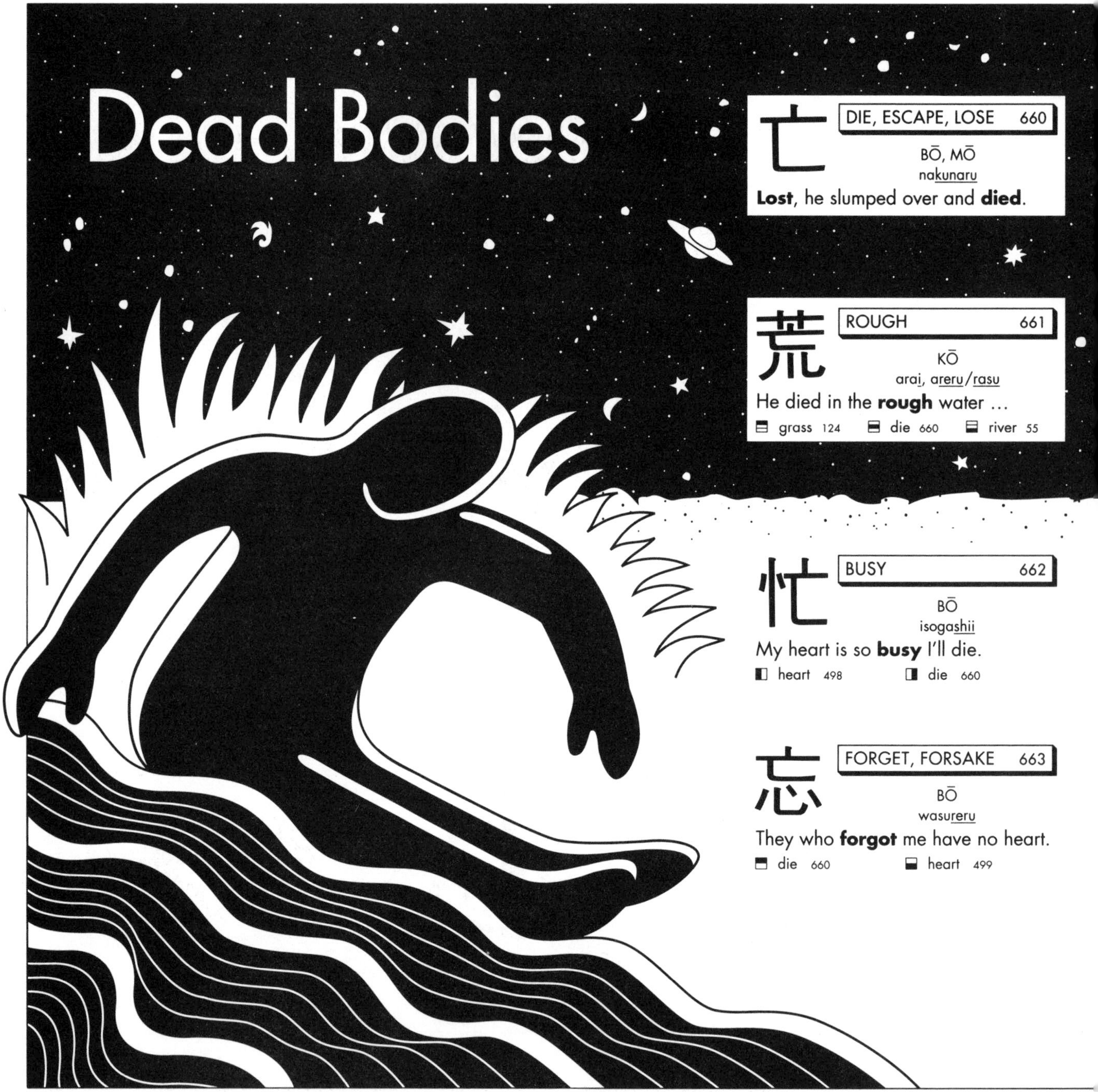

亡 **DIE, ESCAPE, LOSE** 660

BŌ, MŌ
nakunaru

Lost, he slumped over and **died**.

荒 **ROUGH** 661

KŌ
arai, areru/rasu

He died in the **rough** water …

grass 124 — die 660 — river 55

忙 **BUSY** 662

BŌ
isogashii

My heart is so **busy** I'll die.

heart 498 — die 660

忘 **FORGET, FORSAKE** 663

BŌ
wasureru

They who **forgot** me have no heart.

die 660 — heart 499

DANGEROUS 664

危

KI

abu<u>nai</u>, aya<u>ui</u>

Be careful on a **dangerous** cliff …

◧ man on cliff n–664 ◧ slumped body 667

MISFORTUNE, DISASTER 665

厄

YAKU

… or there will be **misfortune**.

◧ cliff n–81 ◧ slumped body 667

CRIME, ASSAULT 666

犯

HAN

oka<u>su</u>

The man was **assaulted** by a dog.

◧ dog 338 ◨ slumped body 667

"SLUMPED BODY" 667

㔾

*This means **slumped body**.*

FLUSTERED, PANIC 668

慌

KŌ

awa<u>teru</u>/<u>tadashii</u>

The rough waters made him **panicky**.

◧ heart 498 ◨ rough 661

IRRATIONAL, RASH 669

妄

MŌ, BŌ

mida<u>ri</u>

To die for a woman is **irrational**.

⬒ die 660 ⬓ woman 411

BLIND 670

盲

MŌ

mekura

Dead, **blind** eyes.

⬒ die 660 ⬓ eye 538

Past

古 OLD (PAST) 671

KO
furui

An **old** tombstone.

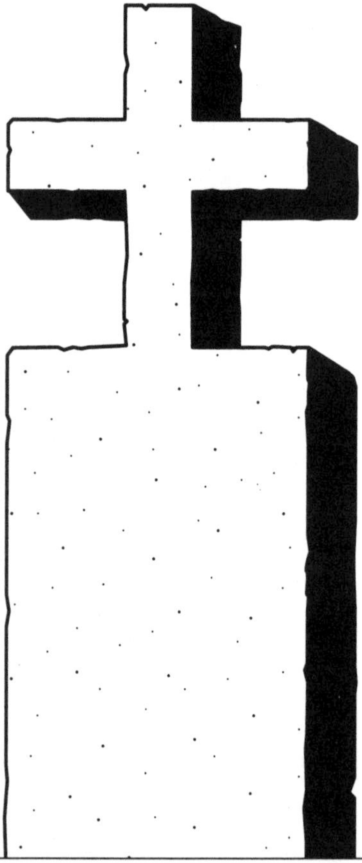

WITHER, DECAY 672

枯

KO
kareru/rasu

An old tree **withers**.

tree 126 | old 671

PAST, REASON 673

故

KO
yue

A violent **past** gives way to reason.

old 671 | strike 802

PAINFUL, BITTER 674

苦

KU
kurushii/shimu, nigai

The old grass tastes **bitter**.

grass 124 | old 671

CONQUER, OVERCOME 675

克

KOKU

Brothers, we shall **overcome**.

old 671 | legs n–675

BURY 676

埋

MAI
umaru/meru,
uzumoreru

He is **buried** outside the village.

soil 101 | village 1088

SUITABLE, FIT, GO 677

適

TEKI

It's **suitable** to visit the grave.

move 1153 | appropriate n–677

MATCH, ENEMY 678

敵

TEKI
kataki

He struck his **enemy** and killed him.

◧ appropriate n–678 ◨ strike 802

DROP, DRIP 679

滴

TEKI
shizuku, shitataru

His tear**drops drip** …

◧ water 66 ◨ appropriate n–679

LEGITIMATE HEIR 680

嫡

CHAKU

… because she, not he, is the **legitimate heir**.

◧ woman 411 ◨ appropriate n–680

GRAVE 681

墓

BO
haka

A sunny **grave**, dug in the grassy soil.

⬒ grass 124
⬒ sun 1
⬒ soil 101

MOURN 682

弔

CHŌ
tomurau

A look of **mourning**.

MOURN, ABHOR, ODIOUS 683

忌

KI
imu/mawashii

I **hate** how my heart still **mourns**.

⬒ self 445 ⬓ heart 499

Temple

BUDDHA, FRANCE 684

仏

BUTSU, FUTSU
hotoke

Buddhist meditation is popular in **France**.

person 362 self 450

HEAVEN 688

天

TEN
ama

Heaven is one big place.

one 897 big 913

GREEDY 689

罪

ZAI
tsumi

The **greedy** miser revels in his net worth.

net 987 oppose 957

TEMPLE 685

寺

JI
tera

He guards every inch of the **temple**.

soil 101 inch 759

WAIT 686

待

TAI
matsu

Wait in the road by the temple.

road 1192 temple 685

SPECIAL 687

特

TOKU

Cows were **special** and worshiped.

cow 276 temple 685

HOLD, HAVE 690

持

JI
motsu

Holding hands in the temple.

hand 580 temple 685

TIME, HOUR 691

時

JI
toki

The temple sun dial tells the **time**.

sun 1 temple 685

Shrine

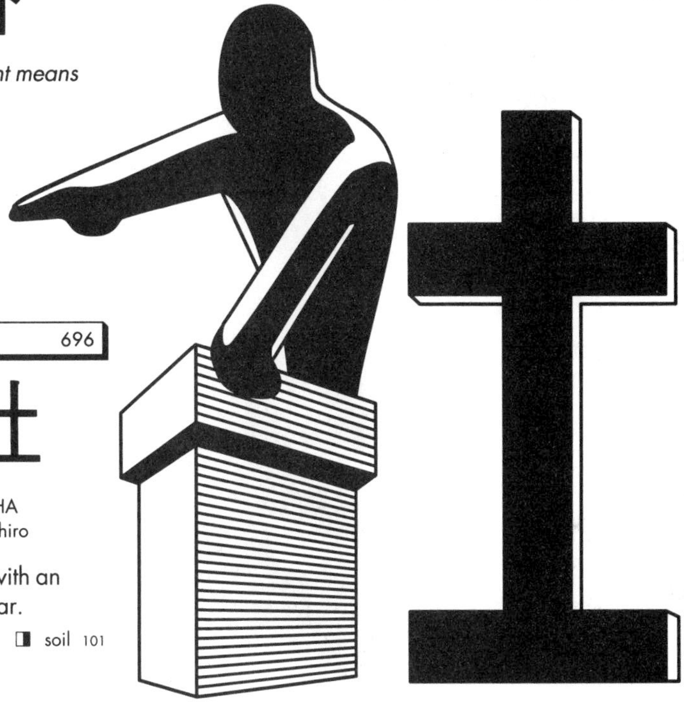

PROPRIETY, BOW 692

礼

REI

Bow at the altar.

◧ altar 696 ◨ kneeling figure n–692

"RELIGION" 695

ネ

*This element means **religion**.*

CALAMITY 693

禍

KA
wazawai

The **calamity** was remembered at the altar.

◧ altar 696 ◨ bones 474

SHRINE 696

社

SHA
yashiro

A **shrine** with an earthen altar.

◧ altar 695 ◨ soil 101

PASS, EXCEED, ERROR 694

過

KA
sugiru/gosu, ayamachi

Quickly **pass** the pile of bones.

◲ move 1153 ◳ bones 474

GOD, SPIRIT 697

神

SHIN, JIN
kami

The preacher expounds the word of **God**.

◧ altar 696 ◨ expound 698

SAY, EXPOUND 698

申

SHIN
mōsu

Ten words he **spoke** out of his mouth.

▢ mouth 566 ▣ ten 906

HAPPINESS 699

祉

SHI

Stop at the altar for **happiness**.

◧ altar 696 ◨ stop 1205

Religion

FESTIVAL, WORSHIP 700

祭

SAI
matsuru, matsuri

Offering meat at the **festival**.

meat 267 hand 600
show 701

SHOW 701

示

JI, SHI
shimesu

Show devotion at the altar.

RELIGION, MAIN 704

宗

SHŪ, SŌ

Practice religion at the main **altar**.

roof 1144 show 701

LOFTY, NOBLE, REVERE 705

崇

SŪ
agameru

In the **lofty** mountains is a **noble** religion.

mountain 167 religion 704

PRIEST, BOY, TOWN 702

坊

BŌ

The **boy** becomes the **town priest**.

soil 101 person 362

OFFER, RESPECTFUL 703

奉

HŌ, BU
tatematsuru

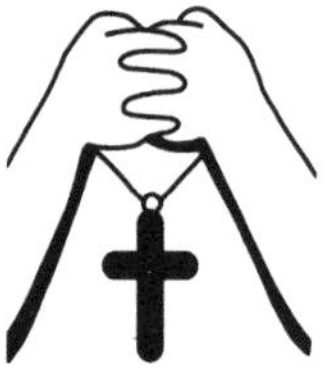

I **respectfully offer** my prayer.

OCCASION, EDGE, CONTACT 706

際

SAI
kiwa

On this **occasion** we worship on the **edge** of the hill.

hill 1094 festival 700

7 POWER

ORIGINAL FORMS

The development of kanji characters began in China in about 2,000 B.C. when people scratched designs into clay pots and tortoise shells to represent the world around them. Lacking a written language, the Japanese borrowed the writing system (and many pronunciations) of Chinese and Korean migrants in the 3rd or 4th century A.D. Simplified, stylized, and miscopied over the centuries by both the Chinese and the Japanese, many kanji today look very different from their pictographic ancestors.

2

3

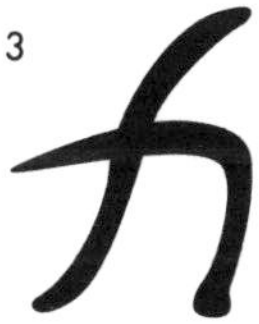

4

Chikara *745, POWER, shown at right, may come from a drawing of an arm with bulging biceps. Others see it as a stooping man working with a spade or pitchfork or as a hand forcefully pressing down.*

力

Money

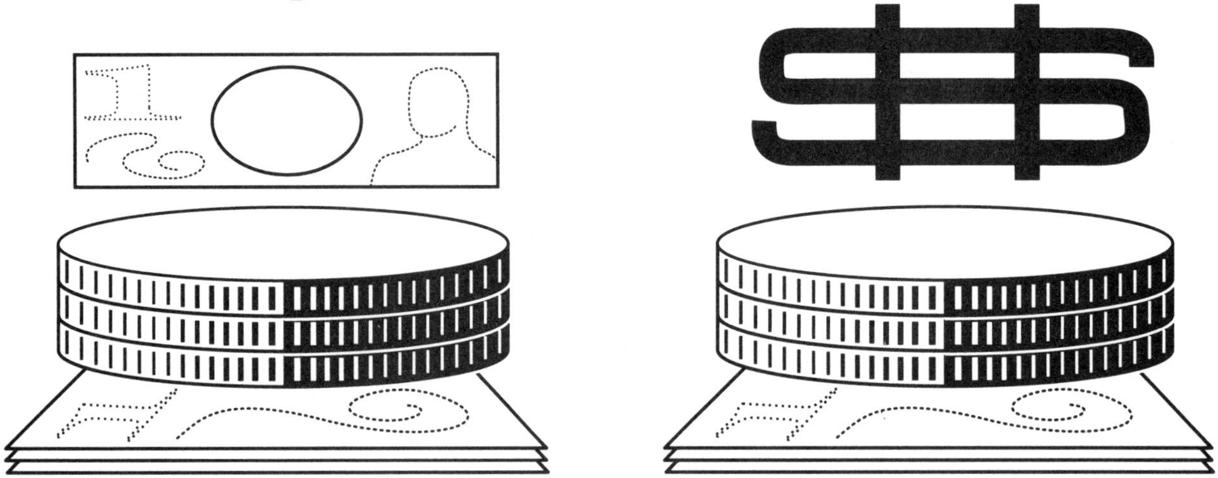

買 BUY 707

BAI
kau

I **buy** a lot with my net income.

net 987 money 708

貝 SHELL 708

KAI

Shells were once used as money.

費 SPEND 709

HI
tsuiyasu

Spend money.

gush 78 money 708

POOR, MEAGER 710

貧

HIN, BIN,
mazushii

Cutting my **meager** income made me **poor**.

divide 1025 money 708

RULE, MODEL, STANDARD 711

則

SOKU
nori, nottoru

Money and weapons are **standard** measures.

money 708 knife 1037

ROUND, YEN 712

円

EN
marui

Yen from a banker's window.

RECOMPENSE, REDEEM 713

償

SHŌ
tsugunau

A person **redeems** …

person 362 prize 714

PRIZE, PRAISE 714

賞

SHŌ

… a monetary **prize**.

shine n–714 mouth 566 money 708

BESTOW 715

賜

SHI
tamawaru

Money was **bestowed** on the field hand.

money 708 easy 23

DEFEAT, BEAR, LOSE 716

負

FU
makeru/kasu,
ou

The one **defeated bears** the financial burden.

bent figure n–716 money 708

LOSS, SPOIL, MISS 717

損

SON
sokonau

The official's money is **lost**. There's zero left!

hand 580 official n–717

PIERCE 718

貫

KAN
tsuranuku

Old coins were **pierced** for threading.

pierce n–708 money 708

DEBT, LOAN 719

債

SAI

A farmer goes into **debt**.

person 362 grow 214 money 708

DUTY, ENTRUST 720

任

NIN
makaseru

My master **entrusts** me with my **duties**.

person 362 burden n–720

WAGES, FEE 721

賃

CHIN

My duties are high, my **wages** are low.

duty 720 money 720

CHASTITY, VIRTUE 722

貞

TEI

Virtue is being above taking money.

above 942 money 720

Wealth

WEALTH, GOODS, MONEY 723

貨

KA

Wealthy money changers.

change 374 money 708

LEND, LOAN 724

貸

TAI
kas<u>u</u>

Replace the money they **lend** you.

replace 376 money 708

TRADE, EXCHANGE 725

貿

BŌ

I'll **trade** money for that knife.

exchange n–725 money 708

SELL, TRADE 726

販

HAN

When you **sell**, money changes hands.

money 708 oppose 957

STORE, SAVE 727

貯

CHO
takuwaeru

Store your **savings** under our roof.

money 708 | roof 1144 | exact 1089

HAPPINESS, LUCK 731

幸

KŌ
saiwai, shiawase, sachi

What **luck** to find yen on the ground.

soil 101 | person n–731

BRIBE, PROVIDE, BOARD 732

賄

WAI
makanau

Bribed with money and steaks.

money 708 | hand 100 | meat 267

PRECIOUS, REVERED 728

貴

KI
tattoi/bu, tōtoi

My **precious** things …

basket 990 | person 100

LEAVE, BEQUEATH 729

遺

I, YUI

… I **leave** behind.

move 1153 | precious 728

MEMBER, OFFICIAL 730

員

IN

An **official** makes money with his mouth.

mouth 566 | money 708

PRESENT, GIVE 733

贈

ZŌ, SŌ
okuru

These **presents** cost a pile of money.

money 708 | give n–733

Master

MASTER, OWNER, MAIN 734

主

SHU
nushi, omo

A lamp indicates the home of the **master**.

RESIDE, LIVE 735

住

JŪ
sumu

The master's **residence**.
◧ person 362 ◨ master 734

POUR, NOTE 736

注

CHŪ
sosogu

Be careful **pouring** water on the lamp.
◧ water 66 ◨ master 734

KOTO (JAPANESE HARP) 737

琴

KIN
koto

Play the **koto** for the two kings. Now!

king 743 king 743 now 31

呈 PRESENT, OFFER 738

TEI

Present the king …
⬒ mouth 566 ⬓ king 743

程 EXTENT, ORDER 739

TEI
hodo

… with the rice he **ordered**.
◧ rice plant 231 ◨ present 738

EMPEROR 740

皇

KŌ, Ō

A pure white **emperor**.

white 936 · king 743

SQUAD, GROUP, ALLOT 741

班

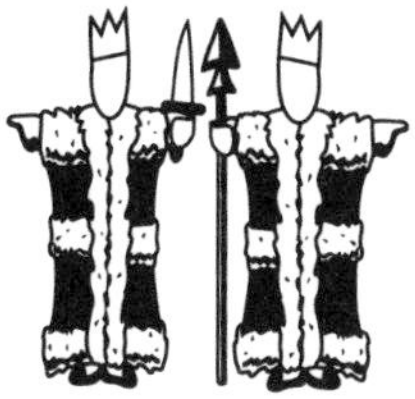

HAN

A **group** of kings.

king 743 · knife 1037 · king 743

IMPERIAL SEAL 742

璽

JI

A jeweled **imperial seal**.

press n–742 · jewel 785

King

KING, RULER 743

王

Ō

Oh! It's the **king**!

LUNATIC, MAD, FANATIC 744

狂

KYŌ

kuruu

The ruler is a **mad** dog.

dog 338 · king 743

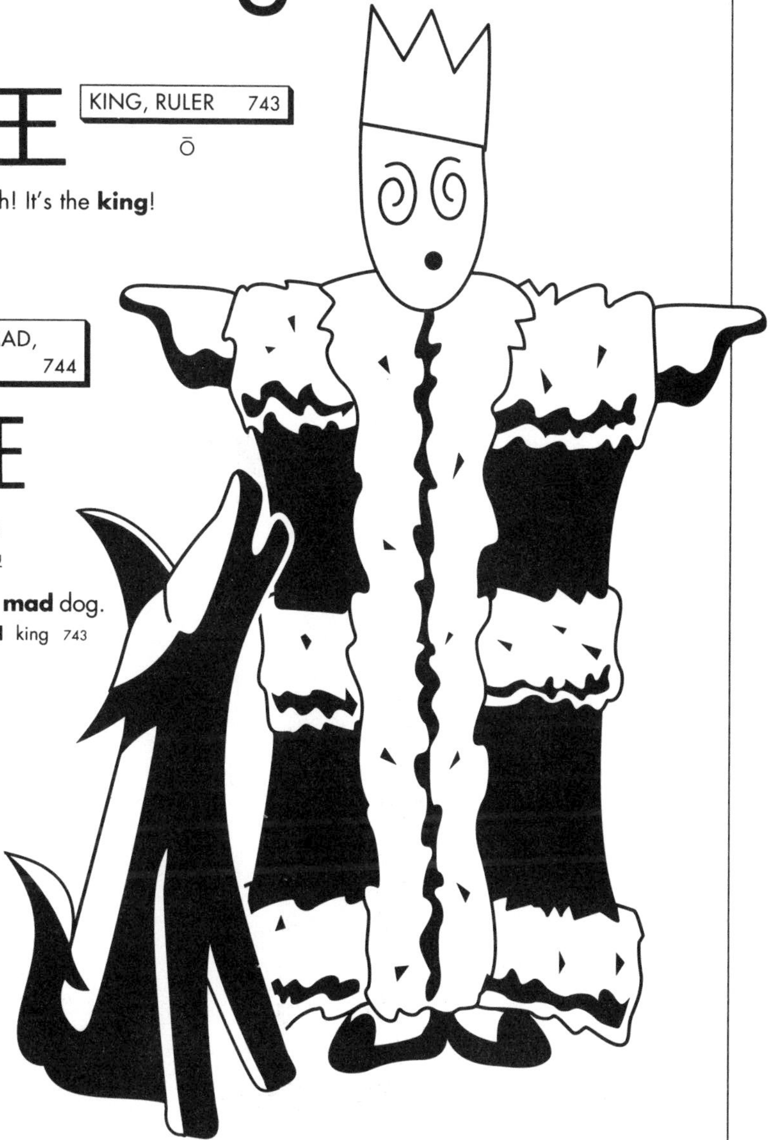

Power

POWER, STRENGTH, EFFORT 745

力

RYOKU, RIKI
chikara

Powerful biceps.

BRAVE, SPIRITED 746

勇

YŪ
isamashii

A **brave** man.

emerge n–746 man 46

THREATEN, COERCE 747

脅

KYŌ
odo(ka)su,
obiyakasu

They **threatened** to beat his flesh to a pulp.

power (X3) 745 meat 267

COOPERATE 748

協

KYŌ

Cooperation increases power tenfold.

ten 906 power (X3) 745

LABOR, TOIL 749

労

RŌ

Labor and **toil** at the break of dawn.

shine n–749 power 745

Soldier

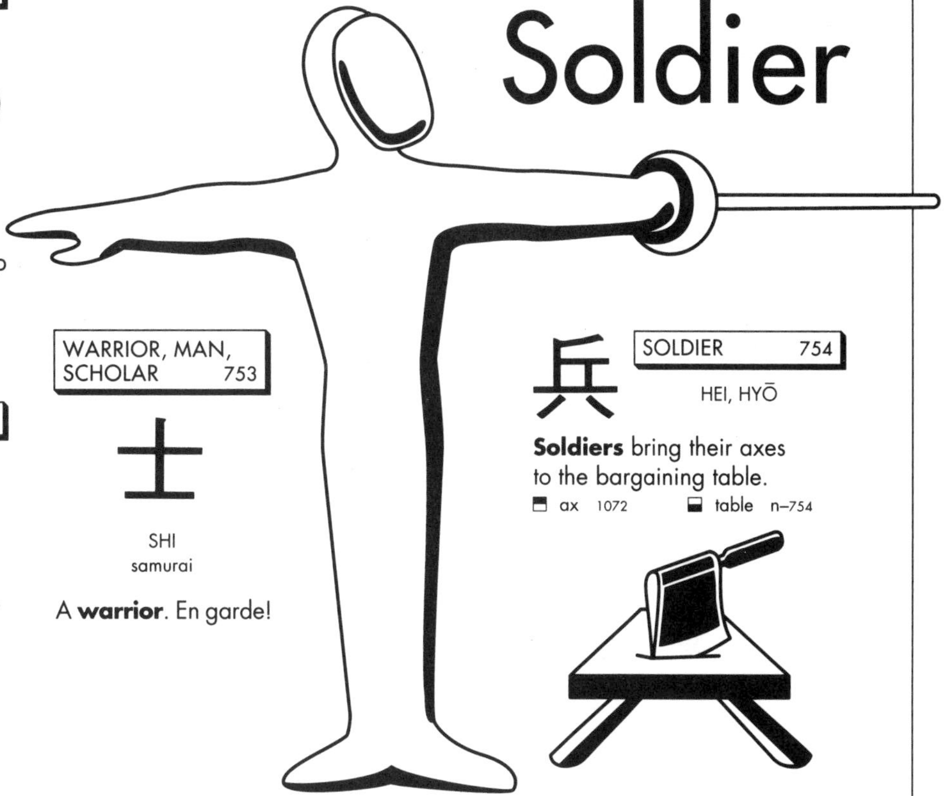

STRIVE, ENCOURAGE 750

励

REI
hagemu/masu

A farmer **strives** to improve his crop a thousandfold.

strive n–750 power 745

SOLDIER 751

卒

SOTSU

A **soldier** reaches for his weapon.

WARRIOR, MAN, SCHOLAR 753

士

SHI
samurai

A **warrior**. En garde!

SOLDIER 754

兵

HEI, HYŌ

Soldiers bring their axes to the bargaining table.

ax 1072 table n–754

ARMY, MILITARY 752

軍

GUN

An armored **military** vehicle.

roof 1144 vehicle 1187

SPARKLE, SHINE 755

輝

KI
kagayaku/kashii

The military vehicles **shine**.

shine 869 military 869

BE INFERIOR 756

劣

RETSU
otoru

An **inferior** weakling.

little 926 strength 745

TRANSPORT, LUCK 757

運

UN
hakobu

Army vehicles on the **move**.

move 1153 army 752

WIELD, COMMAND 758

揮

KI

A hand **commands** the vehicle.

hand 580 army 752

(Never Budge an) Inch

寸

MEASURE, INCH 759

SUN

Never budge an **inch**.

*Although this means **inch**, it is often found in characters that have violent connotations; the illustrations here reflect this.*

CLOSE OFF 760

封

FŪ, HŌ

All boarded up and **closed off**.

soil 101 soil 101 inch 759

FIGHT 761

闘

TŌ

tataka<u>u</u>

If you **fight** outside the gate I'll knock your bean off.

gate 1101 bean + inch n–761

OPPOSE, AGAINST, PAIR 762

対

TAI, TSUI

He **opposes** any violent texts.

text 837 inch 759

ATTACK, (TO) DEFEAT 763

討

TŌ

ut<u>su</u>

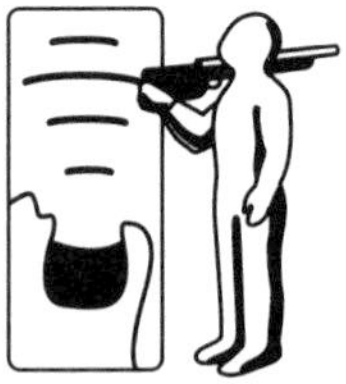

He verbally **attacked** me.

word 840 inch 759

SHOOT 764

射

SHA

i<u>ru</u>

He will **shoot** anybody.

body 459 inch 759

謝

APOLOGIZE, THANKS 765

SHA

ayama<u>ru</u>

Apologize for shooting me.

word 840 shoot 765

奨

URGE, ENCOURAGE 766

SHŌ

The big commander **urges** violence.

command 768 big 913

VALUE, ESTEEM, YOUR 767

尊

SON
tattoi/bu, tōtoi

A hired hand guards the **valuable** wine jar.

wine 249 inch 759

INSULT, HUMILIATE 770

辱

JOKU
hazukashimeru

He trembles in **humiliation** at being held captive.

tremble n-50 inch 759

SEIZE, CAPTURE 774

捕

HO
toraeru, toru

Captured by hand.

hand 580 hold n–774

COMMAND, ABOUT TO 768

将

SHŌ
masa

I'm **about to** hand the **commander** plans.

offer n–768 hand 611 inch 759

ATTACH, APPLY 771

付

FU
tsuku/keru

He **attaches** a medal to a person …

person 362 inch 759

EXCLUSIVE, SOLE 775

専

SEN
moppara

I am the **sole** captive.

hold n–775 inch 759

ENDURE, BEAR 769

耐

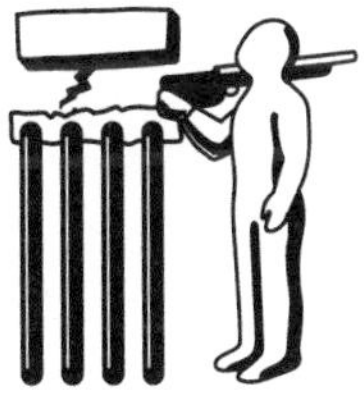

TAI
taeru

Endure being behind bars.

wet n–769 inch 759

ATTACH 772

附

FU

… **attached** to the hill regiment.

hill 759 attach 771

BLESSING, KINDNESS 773

恵

KEI, E
megumu

He is **kind** to the captured people.

hold n–773 heart 499

BIND 776

縛

BAKU
shibaru

The prisoner's hands are **bound** with thread.

thread 775 sole 775

Enclosed

COUNTRY, REGION 779

国

KOKU
kuni

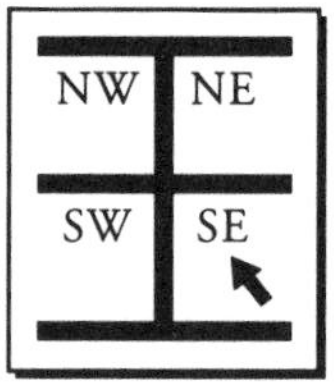

In a certain **region** of the **country** …

◘ enclosed 778 ▣ jewel 785

WARD, SECTION 780

区

KU

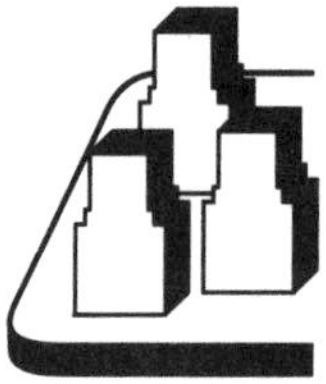

… in a **section** of town …

◘ enclosed 778 ▣ enclosures n–780

GARDEN, PARK 781

園

EN
sono

… is a **garden** …

◘ enclosed 778 ▣ spacious n–100

MAP, CHART, PLAN 777

図

ZU, TO
haka<u>ru</u>

I have a **map**.

◘ enclosed 778 ▣ field n–100

"ENCLOSED" 778

囗

*This box often means **enclosed**.*

DEEP, INSIDE 782

奥

Ō
oku

… with a big hole that leads **deep inside** …

JEWEL, BALL 785

玉

GYOKU
tama

… of **jewels**.

king 743 dot n–785

BE IN DIFFICULTY 786

困

KON
komaru

But I have **difficulty** getting it …

enclosed 778 tree 126

SURROUND 783

囲

I
kakomu/u

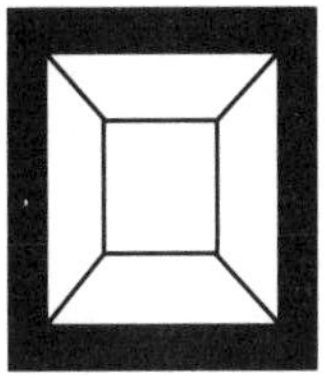

… the walls that **surround** …

enclosed 778 surround n–783

TREASURE 784

宝

HŌ
takara

… the king's **treasure** …

roof 1144 jewel 785

PRISONER 787

囚

SHŪ

… for I am a **prisoner**.

enclosed 778
person 363

STRIKE, ATTACK, FIRE 788

撃

GEKI
utsu

Attack from chariots.

cart 1187 · hand w/ax 100 · hand 579

DESTROY 789

滅

METSU
horobiru/bosu

Destruction by fire and water.

water 66 · fire 83 · halberd 801

COMMAND, ADMONISH 793

戒

KAI
imashimeru

A **commander admonishes** ten men.

halberd 801 · ten 906

HISTORY 790

史

SHI

History is filled with wars.

I, SELF, MY 794

我

GA
ware, waga

My weapon is an extension of **myself**.

me n–794 · halberd 801

没 **SINK, DISAPPEAR, DIE** 791

BOTSU

He **died** of a hatchet wound.

water 66 · hand w/ax 792

義 **RIGHTEOUSNESS** 795

GI

He is so self-**righteous**.

fine 290 · self 794

殳 **"HAND"** 792

An element showing a ***hand holding an ax.***

殴 **HIT, BEAT, ASSAULT** 796

Ō
naguru

Assault people throughout the ward.

ward 780 · hand w/ax 792

Attack

REBEL, PLUNDER, INJURE 797

賊

ZOKU

The commander **plunders** for money.

◧ money 708 ◨ command 793

MILITARY, WARRIOR 798

武

BU, MU

Stop the military **warriors** …

◩ stop 1205 ◨ halberd 801

LEVY, TRIBUTE, ODE 799

賦

FU

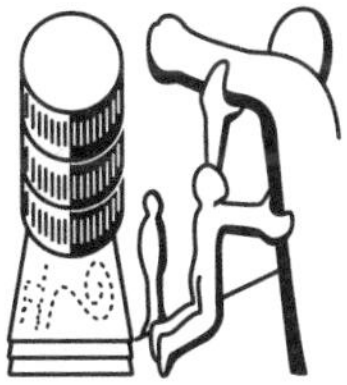

… who make us pay **tribute**.

◧ money 708 ◨ military 798

ATTACK, CUT DOWN 800

伐

BATSU, HATSU

People are **cut down** with halberds.

◧ person 362 ◨ halberd 801

"HALBERD" 801

戈

This element means ***lance*** *or* ***halberd****.*

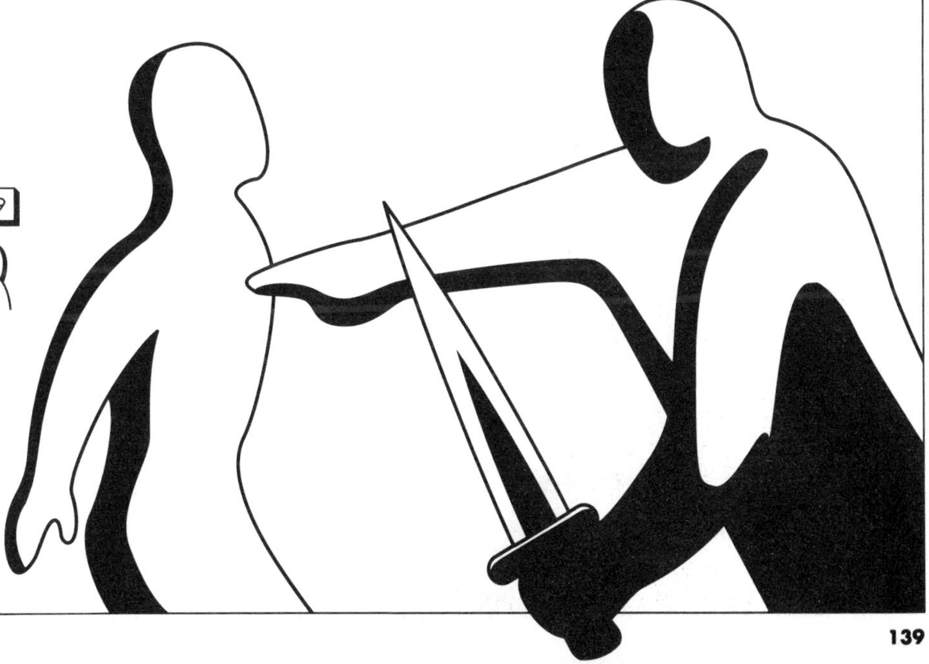

Strike with a Stick

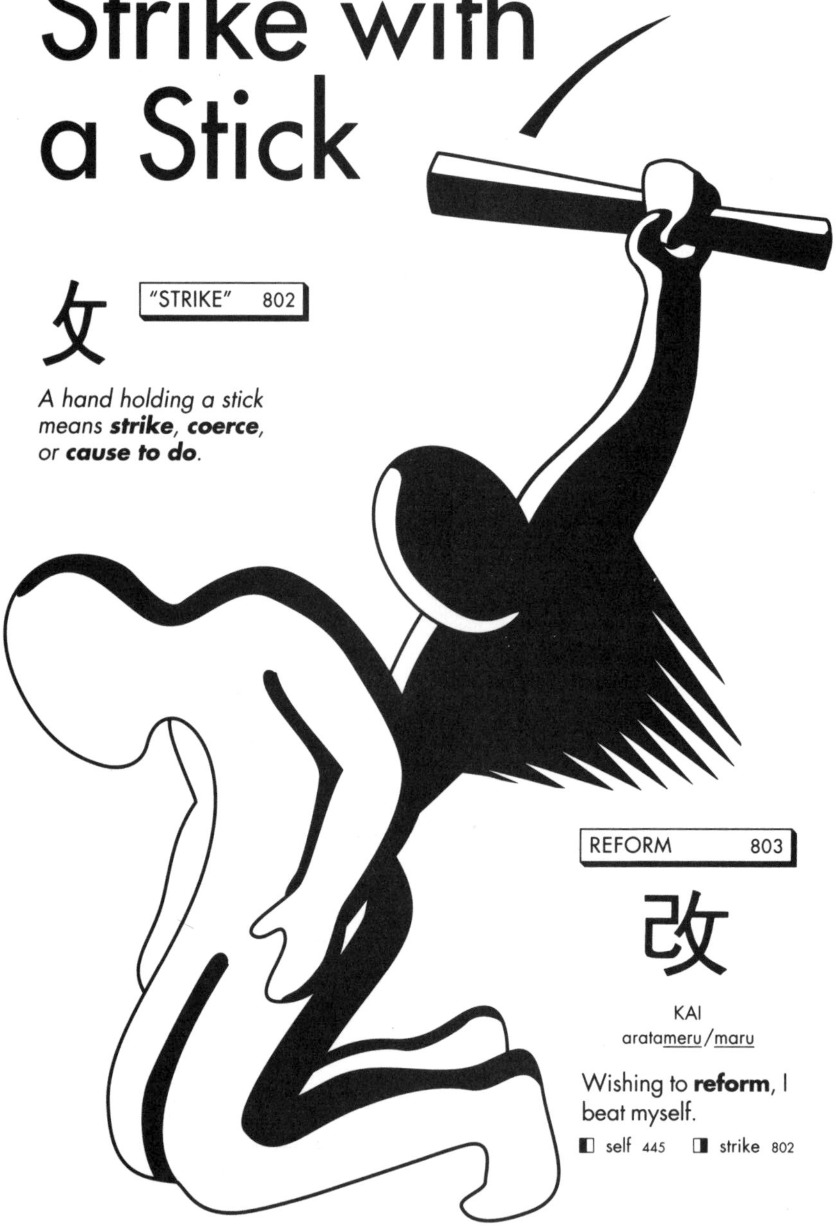

攵 "STRIKE" 802

*A hand holding a stick means **strike**, **coerce**, or **cause to do**.*

REFORM 803

改

KAI
aratameru/maru

Wishing to **reform**, I beat myself.

◧ self 445 ◨ strike 802

BOTH, PAIR, TO RIVAL 804

双

SŌ

Rivals strike at each other.

◧ strike 802 ◨ strike 802

(PERFORM) DUTY 805

務

MU
tsutomeru

A spear carrier, I'm struck until I perform my **duties**.

◧ spear 806 ◨ strike 802 ◨ power 745

SPEAR, LANCE, HALBERD 806

矛

MU, BŌ
hoko

A decorated **lance**.

GO THROUGH, CLEAR, REMOVE 807

徹

TETSU

Clear the path.

path 1192 educate 830 strike 802

REMOVE, WITHDRAW 808

撤

TETSU

People are forcefully **removed** by hand.

hand 580 educate 830 strike 802

SCATTER, DISPERSE 809

散

SAN
chiru/rakaru/rasu

Crowds are **dispersed** by force.

hemp n–809 strike 802

TINY, FAINT, SECRETIVE 810

微

BI

From a **secret** path come **faint** cries of a **tiny** man being beaten.

path 1192 mountain 830 strike 802

DEPEND, PROTECT 811

護

GO

Speak in **defense** of bird **protection**.

speak 840 bird 319 hand 600

DEFEAT 812

敗

HAI
yabureru

Money was lost with the **defeat**.

money 708 strike 802

ATTACK 813

攻

KŌ
semeru

I was **attacked** by a striking construction worker.

construction 1054 strike 802

PRACTICE, MASTER 814

修

SHŪ, SHU
osameru/maru

I'll **master** my stroke with **practice**.

person 362 strike 802 delicate 536

政 GOVERNMENT 815

SEI, SHŌ
matsurigoto

The **government** corrects problems.

correct 826 strike 802

馭 DRIVE (A HERD) 816

GYO

Drive a herd of horses with a stick.

horse 291 strike 802

Bow & Arrow

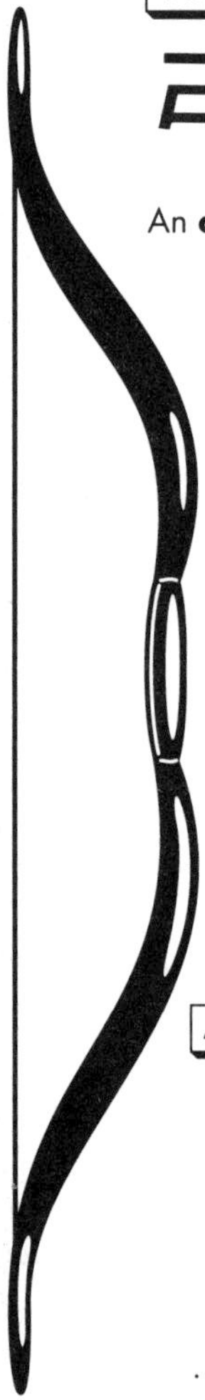

BOW, ARCHERY 817

弓 KYŪ yumi

An **archery bow** …

ARROW 818

矢 SHI ya

… and **arrow**.

WEAK 819

弱 JAKU yowai

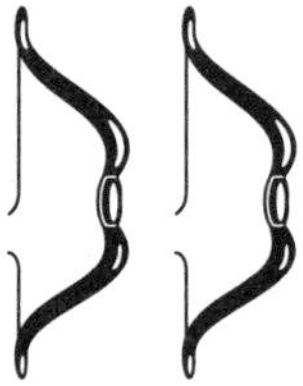

Two **weak** bows.

◧ bow 817 ◨ bow 817

ARC, ARCH, BOW 820

弧 KO

Arc-shaped bows.

◧ bow 817 ◨ rounded n–820

(BOW) STRING 821

弦 GEN tsuru

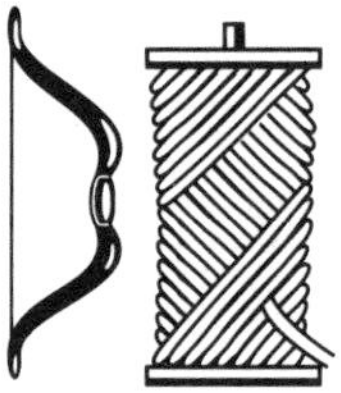

A bow is **strung** with thread.

◧ bow 817 ◨ thread 964

DOUBT, SUSPECT 822

疑 GI utagau

I doubt we'll catch the **suspects**.

⊞ 2 persons n–822 ◰ arrow 818 ◲ leg 617

FIGHT, WAR 823

戦 SEN tatakau, ikusa

Each warrior **fights** with a simple weapon.

◧ simple 824 ◨ halberd 801

単 SIMPLE, SINGLE, UNIT 824

TAN

An arrow is a **simple** weapon.

弾 BULLET, SPRING, PLAY 825

DAN hiku, hazumu, tama

Bullets beat simple bows and arrows.

◧ bow 824 ◨ simple 824

OKURIGANA

The tense and voice of Japanese verbs are indicated by "trailing kana," or *okurigana*, which are added to the kanji that represents the verb root. For example, the verb *narau*, "to learn," shown at right, uses the kanji **SHŪ** 326 for the root *nara-* and the kana *u* to create the plain, present-tense form. Other forms—past, negative, passive, etc.—are similarly indicated by kana following the root.

LEARNED

習った

nara (t) ta

IS LEARNED

習われる

nara wa re ru

MAKES LEARN

習わせる

nara wa se ru

習う

Learn

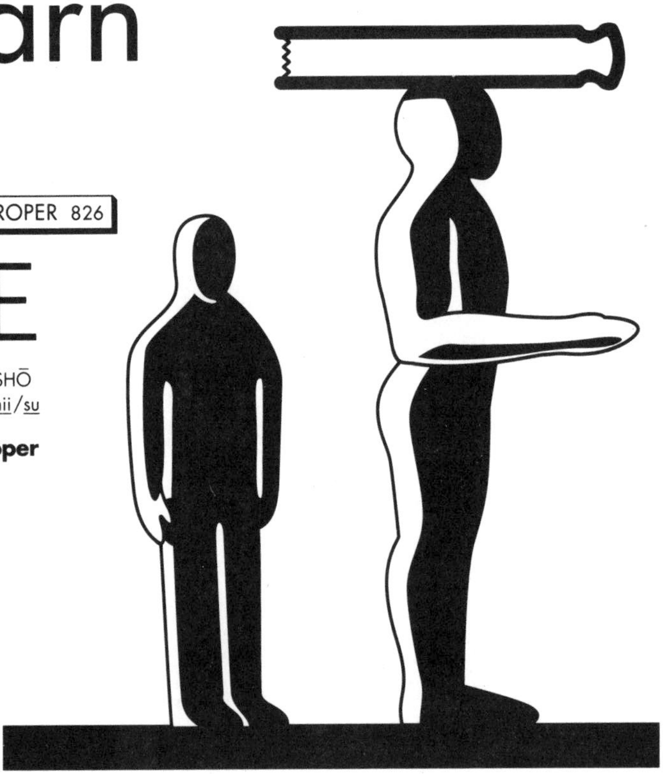

CORRECT, PROPER 826

正

SEI, SHŌ
tadashii/su

Correct, **proper** posture.

RAISE, EDUCATE 830

育

IKU
sodatsu/teru

A woman **raises** and **educates** her child.

person n–58 flesh 267

MIX, EXCHANGE 831

交

KŌ
majiru, kawasu

Mix them up.

CEREMONY, FORM 827

式

SHIKI

Hal is sworn in at the official **ceremony**.

halberd 801 construction 1054

試 TRIAL, TEST 828

SHI
kokoromiru, tamesu

He speaks out at the **trial**.

speak 840 ceremony 827

証 PROOF 829

SHŌ
akashi

Here is **proof** that my words are correct.

words 840 correct 826

校 SCHOOL, CHECK 832

KŌ

In **schools** ideas are exchanged by trees.

tree 126 exchange 831

較 COMPARISON 833

KAKU, KŌ

Compare the cartloads of goods.

vehicle 1187 exchange 831

GIVE 834

呉

GO
kureru

The woman opens her mouth to **give** advice.

mouth 566 man n–834

WRITING, TEXT 837

文

BUN, MON
fumi

He's **writing** an "X" in the sand.

CREST, PATTERN 838

紋

MON

The **pattern** is "written" in thread.

thread 964 writing 837

GIVE, CONVEY, IMPART 835

与

YO
ataeru

This man **gives** generously.

LEARNING 839

学

GAKU
manabu

The child is **learning**.

shine n–127 child 447

FINISH, COMPLETE, UNDERSTAND 836

了

RYŌ

I don't **understand**. This doesn't look **finished**.

Speak

言 **WORD, SAY, SPEAK 840**

GEN, GON
koto, iu

He **spoke** four **words**.

feelings n–840 · mouth 566

KNOWLEDGE 841

識

SHIKI

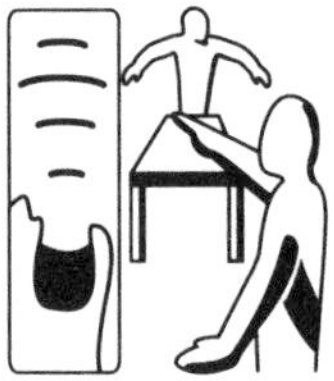

Every day I must stand and say something **knowledgeable**.

word 840 · stand 627 · halberd 801

SUE, APPEAL 842

訴

SO
uttaeru

The lawyer's words repelled the **suit** and led to an **appeal**.

word 840 · repel 1076

PRISON, LITIGATION 843

獄

GOKU

A good argument at **litigation** can hound a man into **prison**.

dog 338 · word 840 · dog 335

TRUST, BELIEVE 844

信

SHIN

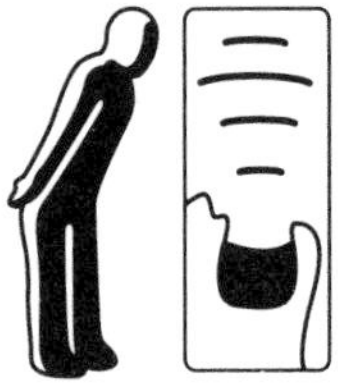

If you **trust** me, **believe** what I say.

person 362 · word 840

INVITE, TEMPT, LEAD 845

誘

YŪ
sasou

I was **tempted**, **led on**, with an **invitation** to have ...

word 840 · rice plant 231 · reach n–567

EXCEL, EXCELLENT 846

秀

SHŪ
hiideru

... **excellent** rice.

rice plant 231 · hand n–567

LANGUAGE, SPEAK 847

語

GO
kataru

Fifty words of **language** …

word 840 five 901 mouth 566

PERCEIVE, DISCERN 848

悟

GO
satoru

… filled fifty hearts with new **perception**.

heart 498 five 901 mouth 566

MISTAKE, MIS- 849

誤

GO
ayamaru

What she said was filled with **mistakes**.

word 840 give 834

CONVERSATION, TALK 850

談

DAN

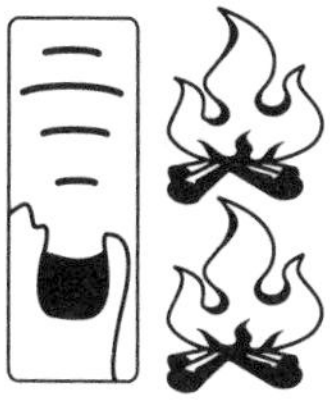

He **talks** like his tongue is aflame.

word 840 flame 86

LESSON, TEACH, READ 851

訓

KUN

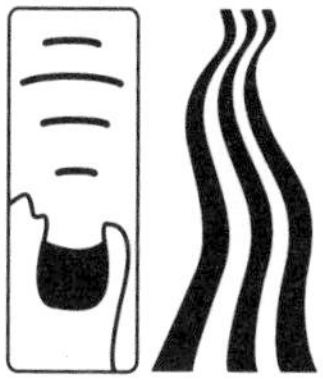

His **lessons** flow like a river.

word 840 river 55

ACKNOWLEDGE, RECOGNIZE 852

認

NIN
mitomeru

Endure his words and you will **recognize** how true they are.

word 840 endure 510

WORD, PART OF SPEECH 853

詞

SHI
kotoba

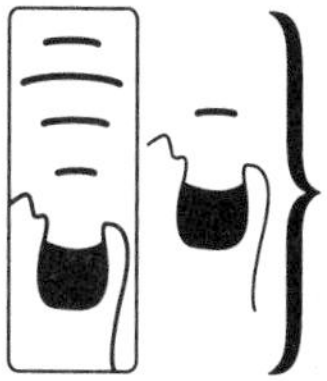

Identify the part of **speech** of each of the four words spoken.

word 840 administer n–853

CORRECT, REVISE 854

訂

TEI

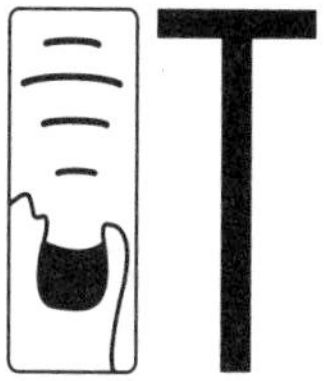

He **corrected** my pronunciation of the letter "t."

word 840 exact 1089

NOH CHANT, SONG 855

謡

YŌ
utai, utau

Sing a **song** while swinging the basket.

speak 840 hand 609 basket n–607

Read

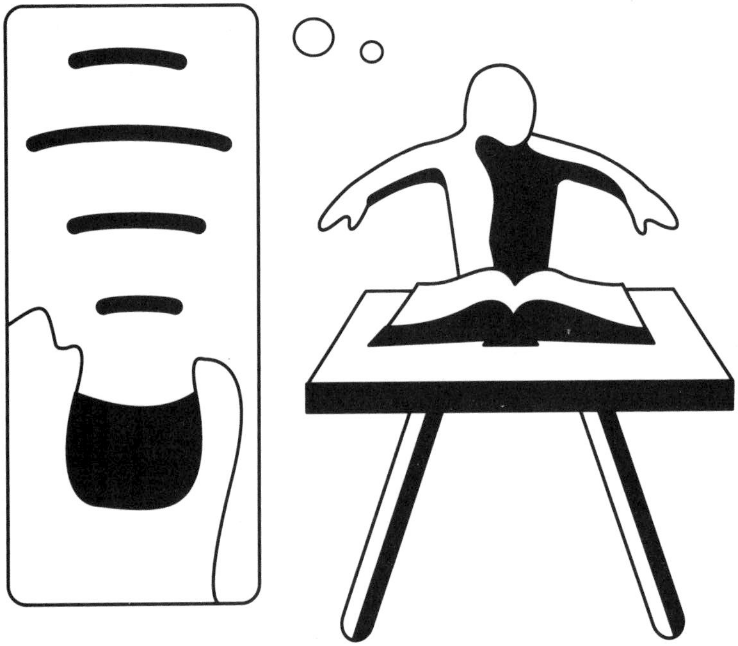

読 READ 856

DOKU, TOKU
yomu

He **reads** the words from the book.

word 840 · soil 101 · call n–856

PHRASE, CLAUSE 857

句

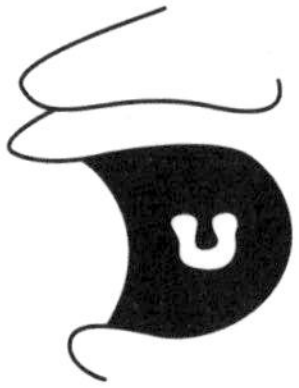

KU

He wraps his tongue around a **phrase**.

wrap 944 · mouth 566

SEIZE, ADHERE TO 858

拘

KŌ
kakawaru

A hand **adheres** to his mouth.

hand 580 · phrase 857

RECITE, PREACH 859

唱

SHŌ
tonaeru

They **recite** with clear voices.

mouth 566 · clear 2

PREACH, EXPLAIN 860

説

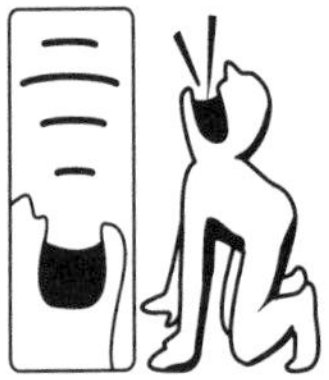

SETSU
toku

His words **preach** brotherly love.

word 840 · split 456 · brother 438

ANSWER 861

答

TŌ
kotaeru

He **answered** a question about bamboo.

bamboo 123 · join 583

SEAL, SIGN, SYMBOL 862

印

IN
shirushi

A "top secret" **seal**.

ROLL, REEL, VOLUME 863

巻

KAN
maki, maku

This **rolled** up document speaks **volumes** about my personal life.

hands n–863 personal 445

ARGUMENT, OPINION 864

論

RON

When we got into an **argument** over the book's **opinions**, he walked out.

speak 840 person 362 book 868

ONE OF A PAIR, ONE SIDE, PIECE 865

片

HEN
kata

The man in the chair is holding **one of a pair** of aces.

PRINT, BOARD 866

版

HAN

Paper is pressed against a **board** to make **prints**.

piece 865 against 957

TRANSLATION 867

訳

YAKU
wake

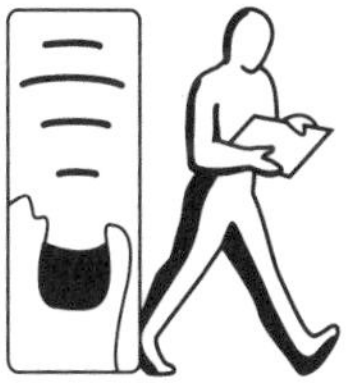

Translation means carrying words from one language to another.

word 840 measure 884

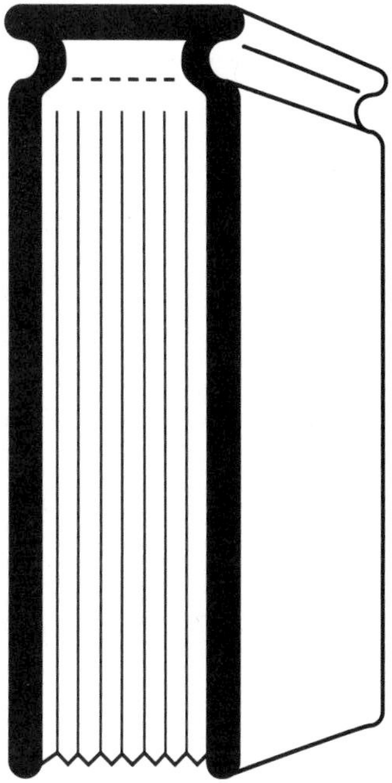

冊 BOOK, VOLUME 868

SATSU

A bound **book**.

The Arts

LIGHT, SHINE, BRILLIANCE 869

光

KŌ
hikari, hikaru

The candle **light** shines **brilliantly**.

CODE, RULE, PRECEDENT 870

典

TEN
nori

A book of legal **codes** and **precedents**.

TALENT, YEAR OF AGE 871

才

SAI

He shows great theatrical **talent** for someone his **age**.

EXIST, KNOW, THINK 872

存

SON, ZON

I teach my child all that I **know** of **existence**.

dam n–872 child 447

DWELL, COUNTRYSIDE, BE 873

在

ZAI
aru

A farmer **dwells** in the **countryside**.

dam n–872 soil 101

INFER, PUSH AHEAD 874

推

SUI
osu

I **infer** that the hand is pushing the bird forward, not backward.

hand 580 bird 319

PRESSURE 875

圧

ATSU

My friend Cliff is under a lot of **pressure**.

cliff n–81 soil 101

MATCH, ANIMAL COUNTER 876

匹

HITSU
hiki

Two wrestlers in loincloths have a sumo **match**.

BEND, MELODY 877

曲

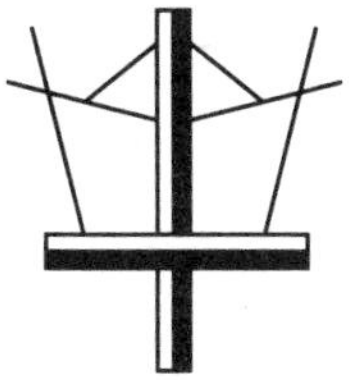

KYOKU
magaru/geru

The music stand holds my **melody**.

PICTURE, STROKE 880

画

GA, KAKU

The **picture** has simple **strokes**.

ILLUSION, MAGIC 881

幻

GEN
maboroshi

The **illusion** is done with invisible threads.

thread n–881 illusion n–881

CARVE, SCULPTURE 878

彫

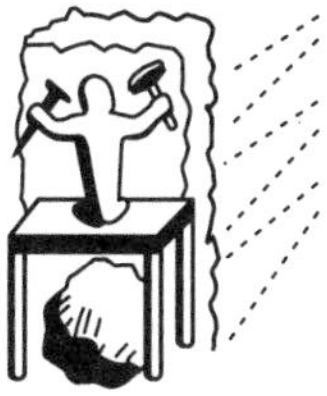

CHŌ
horu

The artist **carves** delicate features in his **sculpture**.

circumference n–878 delicate 536

PLEASURE, MUSIC 882

楽

RAKU, GAKU
tanoshii/shimu

The **music** brings **pleasure** to my ears.

drum n–882 tree 126

SOUND 883

音

ON, IN
oto, ne

I can't stand *The **Sound** of Music.*

stand 627 sun 1

MEDICINE, DRUG 879

薬

YAKU
kusuri

Some grasses are "pleasure **drugs**."

grass 124 pleasure 882

音楽 *These two kanji together form the word for **music**.*

ON GAKU

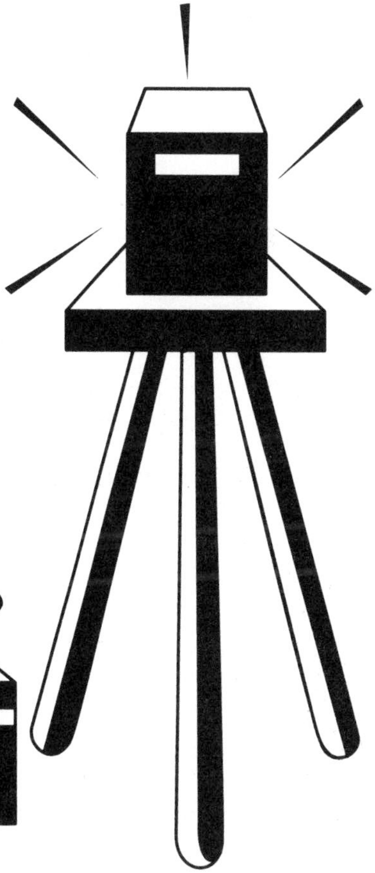

尺

MEASURE, FOOT 884

SHAKU, SEKI

I pace off the **measure** with my feet.

MEASURE 885

計

KEI
hakaru

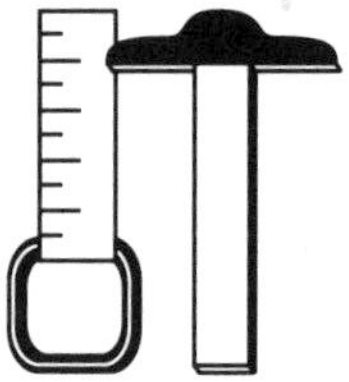

Metric **measures** are based on ten.

◧ word 840 ◨ ten 906

DIPPER, MEASURE 886

斗

TO

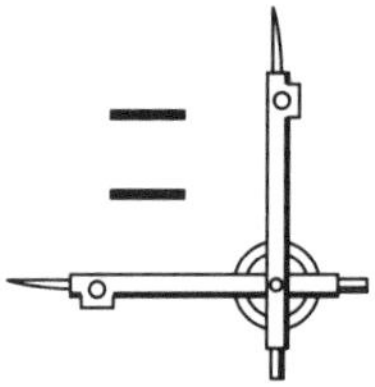

I **measure** with calipers.

STARTING POINT, MEANS, USE 887

以

I
motte

This line is the **starting point**.

EQUAL, LEVEL 888

均

KIN
hitoshii

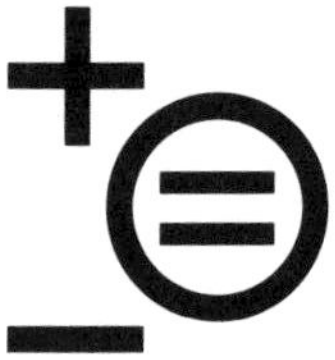

Positive and negative **equals** zero.

◧ soil 101 ◨ flat n–888

SAME 889

同

DŌ
onaji

The diameter of a circle is the **same** in all directions.

MANY 890

多

TA
ōi

Many moons ago—99 months to be exact.

⬒ moon 14 ⬓ moon 14

Measure

BOTH, PAIR, COIN 891

両

RYŌ

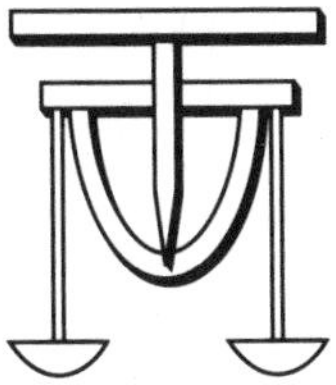

A **pair** of coins are on **both** sides of the scale.

FULL, FILL 892

満

MAN
michiru/tasu

Both halves of the melon are **full** of water.

water 66 grass 124 both 891

LENGTH, MEASURE, STATURE 894

丈

JŌ
take

I'll measure the **length** with this rule.

INCLUDE, CONTAIN 893

含

GAN
fukumu/meru

Now the box **contains** a puppet.

now 31 opening 566

OBTAIN, STORE, SUPPLY 895

収

SHŪ
osameru/maru

Keep a **supply** of sticks on hand in the **storage** box.

seek out n–895 hand 600

WHAT, HOW MANY 896

何

KA
nan, nani

What's in the box?

person 362 opening 566

Numbers

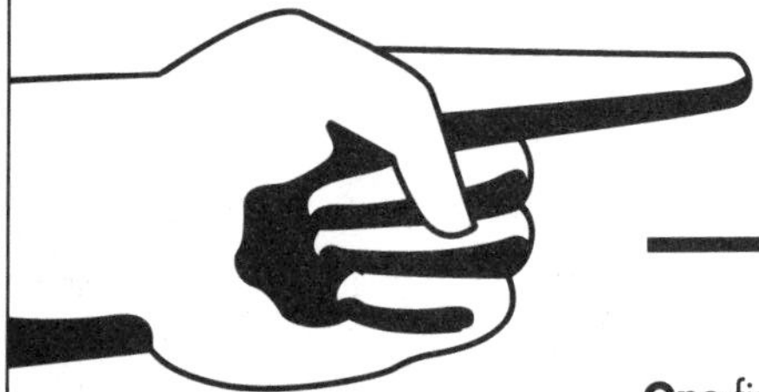

一

ONE 897

ICHI, ITSU
hito-

One finger.

二

TWO 898

NI
futa-

Two fingers.

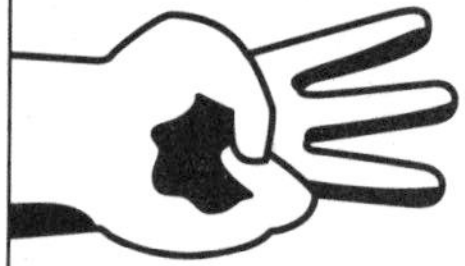

三

THREE 899

SAN
mi-

Three fingers.

四

FOUR 900

SHI
yon, yo-

A square has **four** corners.

五

FIVE 901

GO
itsu-

Find the number **five**.

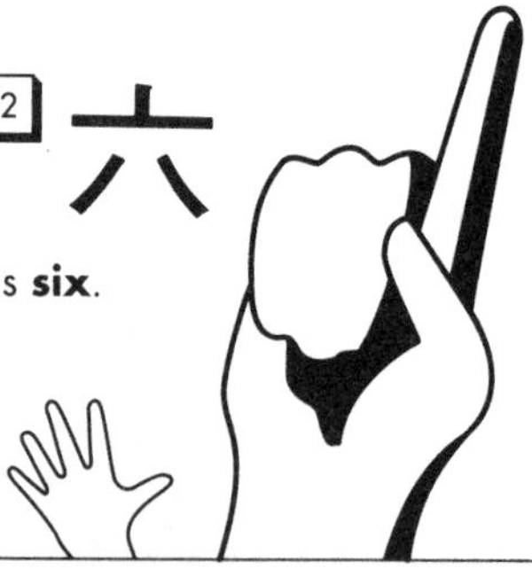

六

SIX 902

ROKU
mu-

Five plus one is **six**.

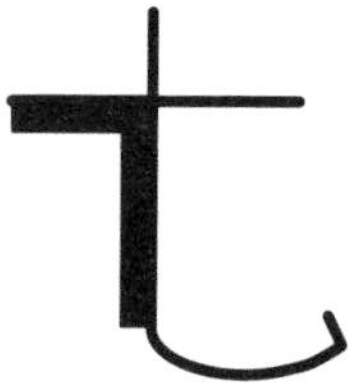

七

SEVEN 903

SHICHI
nana-

Find the number **seven**.

八

EIGHT 904

HACHI
ya-

Eight is easily divided in half.

九

NINE 905

KYŪ, KU
kokono-

A broken number **nine**.

十 **TEN 906**

JŪ
tō

A slant Roman numeral **ten**.

半 **HALF, MIDDLE 907**

HAN
naka<u>ba</u>

I broke it in **half**—right down the **middle**.

号 **NUMBER 908**

GŌ

Fractions are **numbers**.

千 **THOUSAND 909**

SEN
chi

Here's the "t" in **thousand**.

百 **HUNDRED 910**

HYAKU

The price tag says a **hundred** cents.

乙 **ODD, B, 2ND, STYLISH 911**

OTSU, ITSU

An **odd**, upside-down two.

弐 **TWO (LEGAL STYLE) 912**

NI

Two strokes of the banker's pen.

Sizes

大

BIG 913

TAI, DAI
ōkii

"It was this **big**!"

FAT 914

太

TAI, TA
futoi/ru

See the **fat** man with the big belly button.

big 100 two n–914

LONG, SENIOR 915

長

CHŌ
nagai

Long hair is a sign of old age.

STRETCH 916

張

CHŌ
haru

Pulled back, his hair **stretches** a long way.

pull 817 long 915

HOLLOW, CONCAVE, DENT 917

凹

Ō
kubo, boko
hekomu

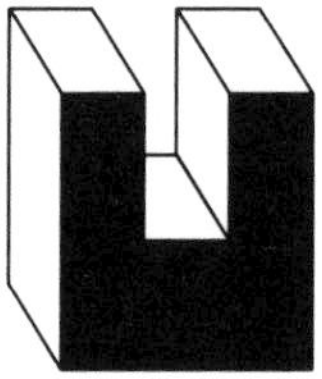

A **concave** figure.

CONVEX, PROTRUSION 918

凸

TOTSU
deko

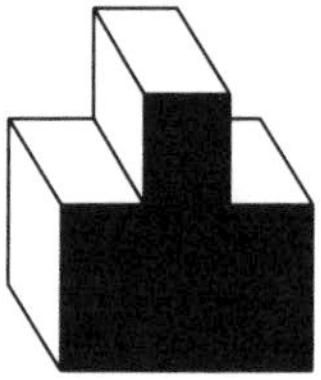

A **convex** figure.

ROUND, CIRCLE, BALL, SHIP 919

丸

GAN
maru, marui

Curl up in a **ball**.

SHAPE, PATTERN 920

形

KEI, GYŌ
kata, katachi

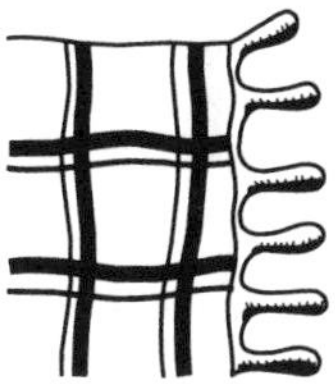

The blanket has a plaid **pattern** and a delicate fringe.

◧ lattice window n–920 ◨ delicate 536

EXTRACT, EXCERPT 924

抄

SHŌ

A hand **extracts** …

◧ hand 580 ◨ a little 925

FLAT, EVEN, CALM 921

平

HEI, BYŌ
taira, hiratai

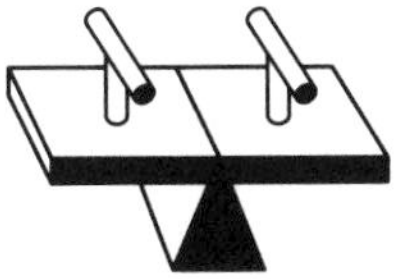

This seesaw is **flat** and **calm**.

FEW, A LITTLE 925

少

SHŌ
sukoshi, sukunai

… a **little** strand of thread …

⬒ small 926 ⬓ little dot n–925

評 CRITICISM, COMMENT 922

HYŌ

The **criticism** was even and fair.

◧ words 840 ◨ even 921

坪 SQUARE, MEASURE 923

HEI
tsubo

The **square** was built on level ground.

◧ ground 101 ◨ flat 921

小 SMALL 926

SHŌ
ko-, o-, chiisai

… from a **small** needle.

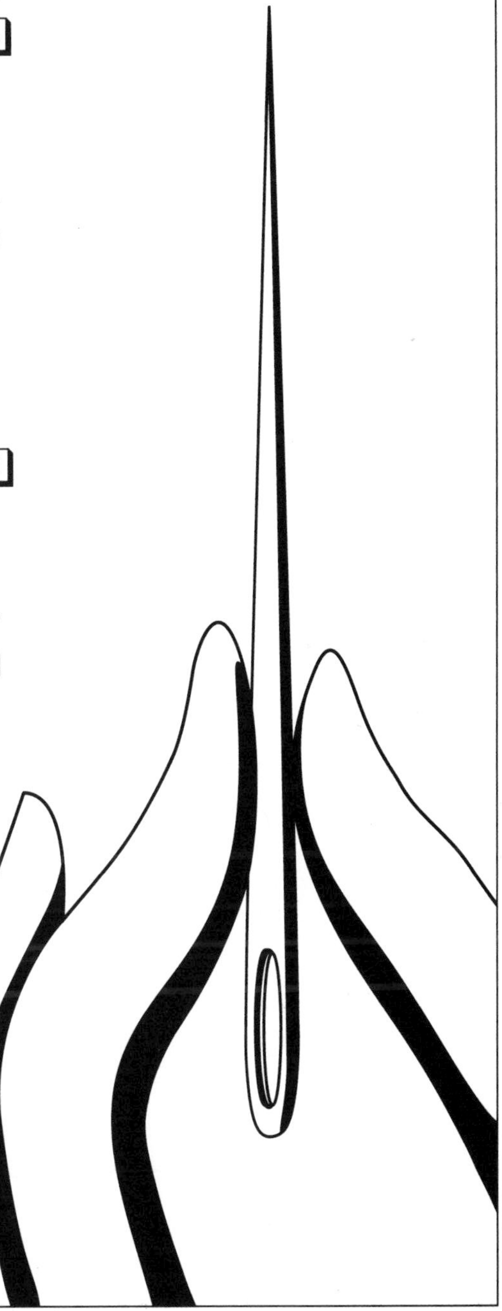

Colors

COLORS, SENSUALITY 927

色

SHOKU, SHIKI
iro

A variety of **sensual colors** are squeezed from the tubes.

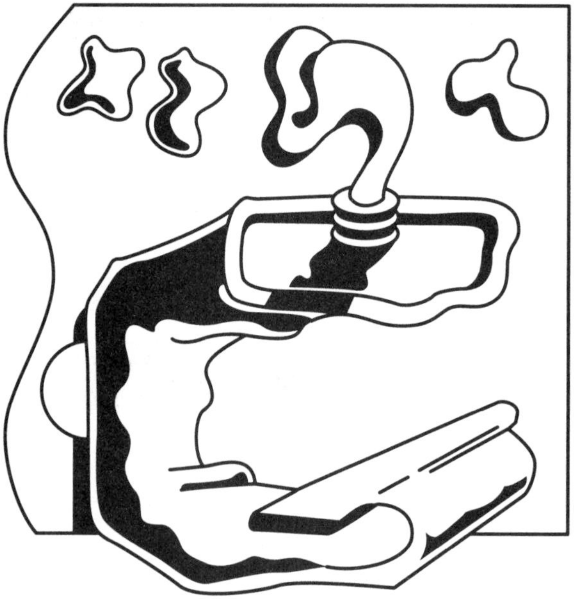

RED, CRIMSON, ROUGE 930

紅

KŌ, KU
kurenai, beni

A **red** construction sign.

thread 964 constructrion 1054

BLACK 931

黒

KOKU
kuroi

Black soot is on the BBQ grill.

village 1087 fire 82

COLOR 928

彩

SAI
irodoru

Rays of light shine on the **colorful** hand-picked tree blossoms.

hand 609 tree 126 delicate 536

RED 929

赤

SEKI, SHAKU
akai

A **red** cross is on the first aid kit.

soil 101 fire 82

墨 INK, INKSTICK 932

BOKU
sumi

An **inkstick** is made of black soot.

black 931 soil 101

赦 FORGIVENESS 933

SHA

I'll **forgive** you after you're beaten red.

red 929 strike 802

DARK BLUE, DYE 934

紺

KON

The **blue** thread is dyed in sweet blueberries.

◧ thread 964 ◨ sweet 272

GREEN 935

緑

RYOKU, ROKU
midori

Pour the **green** liquid over the thread.

◧ thread 964 ◨ liquid n–935

WHITE 936

白

HAKU
shiroi

A **white** ray of sunshine.

⬒ ray n–936 ⬓ sun 1

BLUE, YOUNG 937

青

SEI, SHŌ
aoi

A **green** plant grows on the moon.

⬒ plant 214 ⬓ moon 14

CLEAR, BRIGHT 938

晴

SEI
hareru

Bright and sunny with **clear** blue skies.

◧ sun 1 ◨ blue 937

SPIRIT, VITALITY 939

精

SEI, SHŌ

Eat blue/green rice for **vitality**.

◧ rice 217 ◨ blue 937

FEELING, PITY 940

情

JŌ, SEI
nasake

Pity me, my heart **feels** blue.

◧ heart 498 ◨ blue 937

PURE, CLEAN 941

清

SEI, SHŌ
kiyoi/meru

The water is a **pure**, clear blue.

◧ water 66 ◨ blue 937

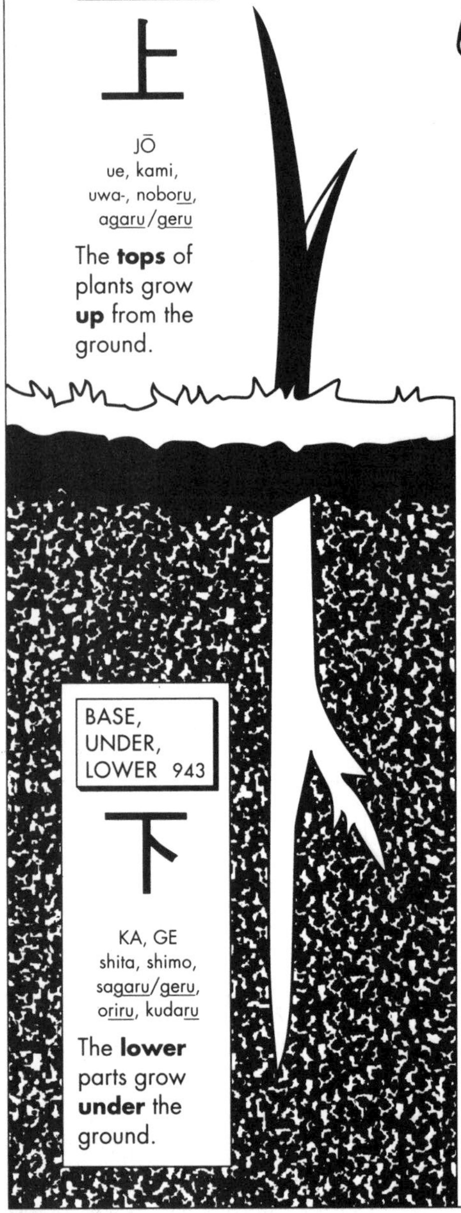

UP, TOP, OVER, GO UP 942

上

JŌ
ue, kami, uwa-, noboru, agaru/geru

The **tops** of plants grow **up** from the ground.

BASE, UNDER, LOWER 943

下

KA, GE
shita, shimo, sagaru/geru, oriru, kudaru

The **lower** parts grow **under** the ground.

WRAP, ENVELOP 944

包

HŌ
tsutsumu

Wrap myself in a warm blanket.

◧ encircle 949 ◧ self 445

GUN, CANNON 945

砲

HŌ

The **cannon** fires stones wrapped in **gun** powder.

◧ stone 190 ◧ wrap 944

THIRST, PARCHED 946

渇

KATSU
kawaku

The sun wrapped me in heat and made me **thirsty**.

◧ water 66 ◧ sun 1 ◧ dry up n-946

TIRE, SATIATE 947

飽

HŌ
aku/kiru/kasu

I'm **tired** of eating; let's wrap things up.

◧ eat 232 ◧ wrap 944

泡 FROTH, BUBBLE, FOAM 948

HŌ
awa

A **bubble** is air wrapped in water.

◧ water 66 ◧ wrap 944

勹 "COVER, ENCIRCLE" 949

*This element means **cover**, **encircle**, and **protect**.*

Positions

MIDDLE, INSIDE, CHINA 950

中

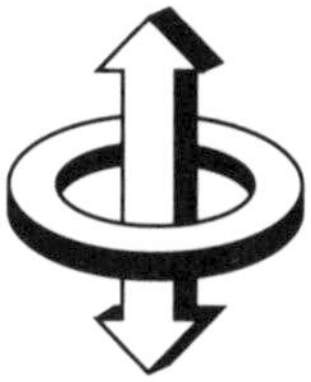

CHŪ
naka

A line through the **middle** of the opening.

CENTER 951

央

Ō

Lines radiate from the **center** of the opening.

INSIDE, WITHIN 952

内

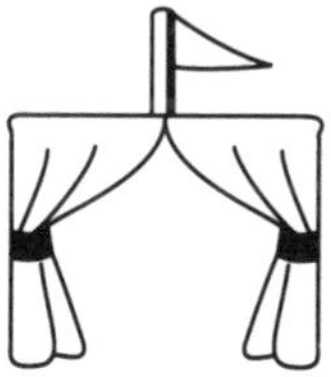

NAI, DAI
uchi

We kept things **inside** the tent.

PUT IN, CROWDED 953

込

komu/meru

He didn't enter the **crowded** tent.

◻ move 1153 ◼ enter 950

ENTER, PUT IN 954

入

NYŪ
hairu, ireru/ru

Enter the tent.

EMERGE, PUT OUT 955

出

SHUTSU
deru, dasu

He **emerged** from the tent feeling **put out**.

OBTAIN, STORE, SUPPLY 956

納

NŌ, NA,
NATSU, TŌ
osameru

Our **supply** of thread is **stored** inside the tent.

◧ thread 964 ◨ inside 952

Oppose

OPPOSE, ANTI-, REVERSE, BEND, CLOTH 957

反

HAN, TAN
soru/rasu

He **opposed** the movie with a thumb's down.

turn over n–957
hand 600

NOT, UN-, FAULT 960

非

HI

The signs are **not** pointing in one direction.

REJECT, EXPEL, PUSH, ANTI- 961

排

HAI

He **rejected** the handout by covering his mouth.

hand 580 not 960

NOT, NONE, CEASE TO BE 958

無

MU, BU
nai/shi

Burn the books til there are **none**.

book 868 fire 82

NOT, UN-, DIS- 959

不

FU, BU

He **dis**likes something.

俳 **ACTOR 962**

HAI

It was not really him; he was **acting**.

person 362 not 960

否 **NO, DECLINE, DENY 963**

HI
ina, inamu

He always says **no**.

not 958 mouth 566

STROKE ORDER

Kanji are written according to rules of stroke order established long ago by calligraphers and teachers. Generally: (1) strokes are written from top to bottom and from left to right; (2) horizontal crossing strokes precede vertical crossing strokes; (3) enclosures are drawn first, but a closing line at bottom is drawn last; (4) strokes that slant from right to left are written before strokes that slant left to right; (5) piercing vertical lines are written last. There are many exceptions, however. In the kanji **DŌ** 534 of *dōgu,* meaning "tool," shown at right, the element MOVEMENT 1153 that stretches from upper left to lower right is actually written last. In the examples here, stroke order numbers have been placed at the beginning point of each stroke.

DŌ
way 534

GU
equipment 1039

道
具

9 — TOOLS

Thread

糸 THREAD 964

SHI
ito

A spool of **thread**.

SILK 965

絹

KEN
kinu

Silk comes from a worm.

thread 964 mouth 566 flesh 267

EDIT, KNIT, BOOK 966

編

HEN
a<u>mu</u>

Editing a book is like **knitting** words.

thread 964 door 1113 book 868

SPIN (YARN) 967

紡

BŌ
tsumu<u>gu</u>

Spin a spool of thread.

thread 964
direction 386

REEL, TURN 968

繰

SŌ
ku<u>ru</u>

The wooden **reel** **turns** thread.

thread 964
goods 1038
tree 126

HOW MANY, HOW MUCH 969

幾

KI
iku-

Hal asks **how much** thread …

thread 964 thread 964 halberd 801

LOOM, DEVICE, OCCASION 970

機

KI
hata

… is **needed** for the wooden loom …

tree 126 how much 969

WEAVE 971

織

SHOKU, SHIKI
oru

… to **weave** a scarf for his son.

thread 964 sound 883 halberd 801

FINE, SLENDER 972

纖

SEN

Fine threads.

thread 964 leek n–972

ENTWINE, EXAMINE 973

糾

KYŪ

The thread is **entwined** on the loom.

thread 964 seek out n–895

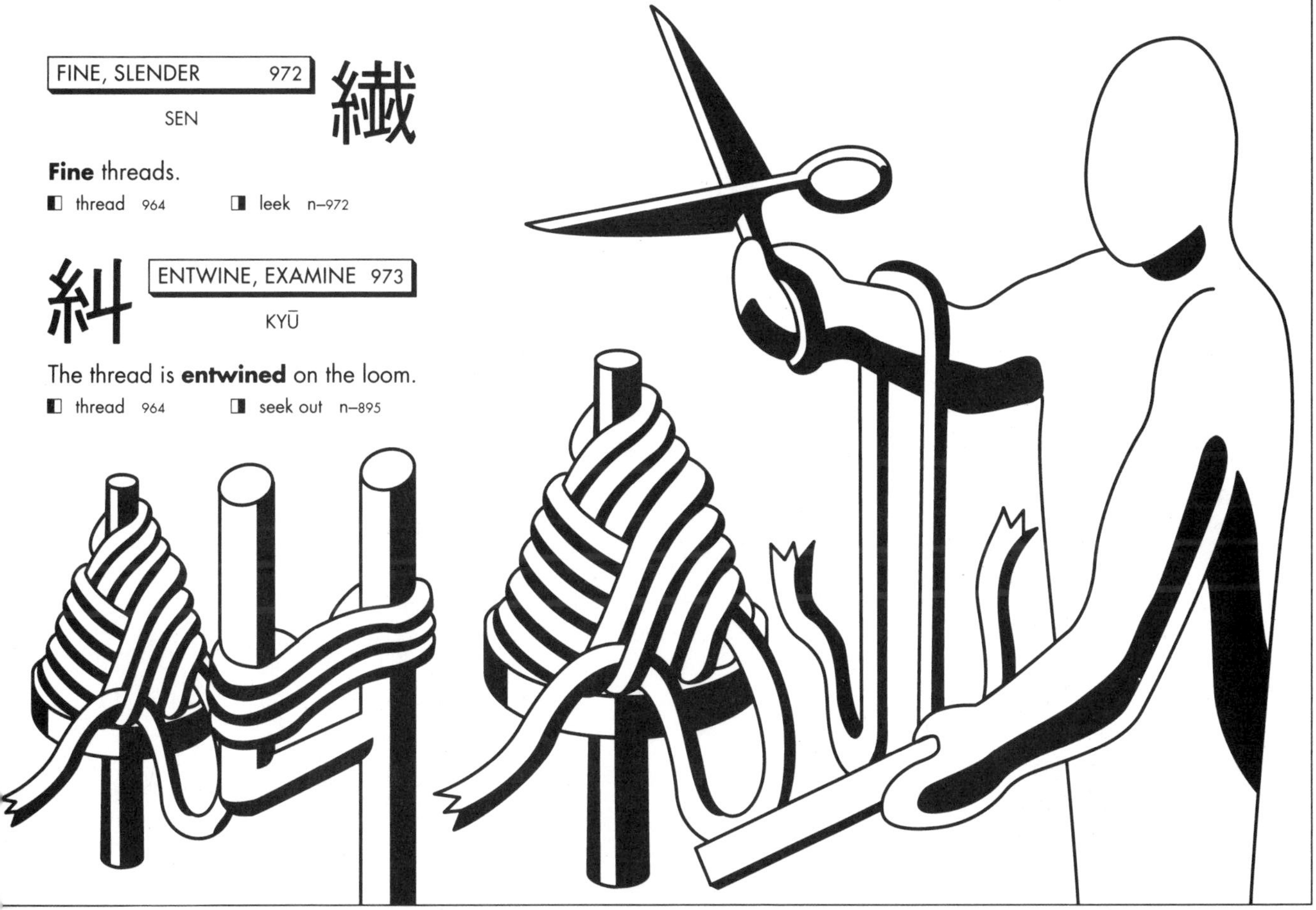

PAPER	974

紙

SHI
kami

This **paper** is made of stringy fibers.

◧ thread 964 ◨ family 396

LINE	975

線

SEN

Thread, water, and rays of sunshine travel in a **line**.

◧ thread 964 ◨ white 936 ◨ water 57

INVOLVEMENT	976

係

KEI
kakari

This person is **involved** in finding …

◧ person 362 ◨ lineage 977

LINEAGE, CONNECTION	977

系

KEI

… where one string **connects** to another.

⬒ hand n–977
⬓ thread 964

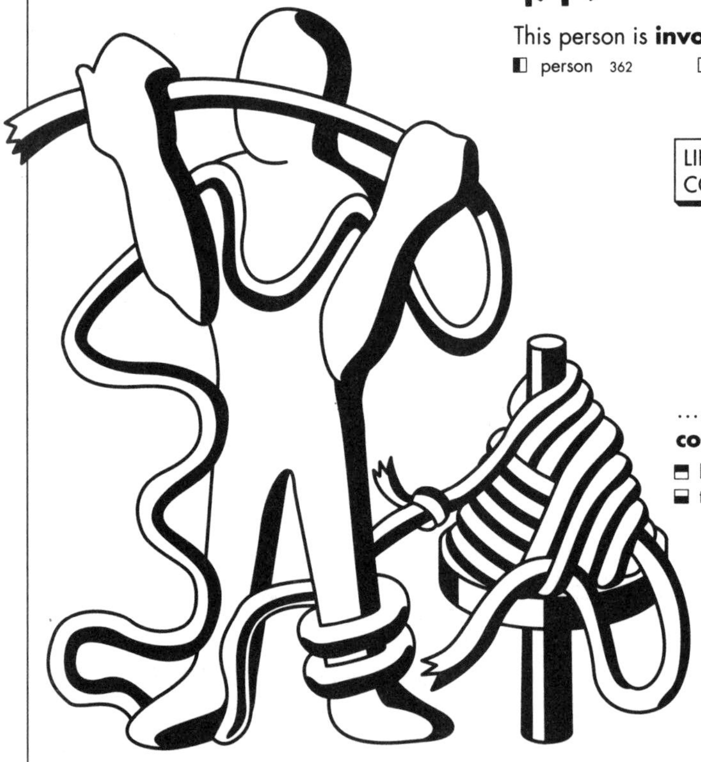

ACCUMULATE, INVOLVE	978

累

RUI

Thread has **accumulated** in the field.

⬒ field 201 ⬓ thread 964

STRAW, CORD	979

縄

JŌ
nawa

Two knots are tied in the **straw** cord.

◧ thread 964 ◨ twist n–979

FINISH	980

終

SHŪ
owaru/eru

The ends of the string are **finished** with a knot.

◧ thread 964 ◨ winter 42

STRANGLE, WRING 981

絞

KŌ
shiboru, shimeru

This mixed-up person **strangles** people with string.

thread 964 mix 831

BIND, TIGHTEN, CLOSE 982

締

TEI
shimaru/meru

Bind the broom straws with thread.

thread 964 stand 627 broom n–982

STOP, FASTEN 983

留

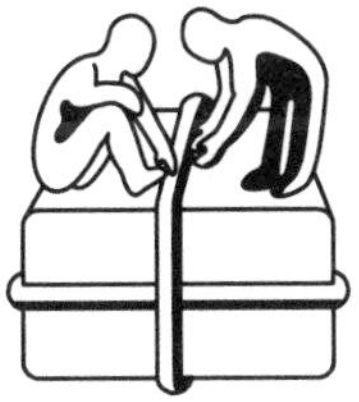

RYŪ, RU
tomaru/meru

Stop and help me **fasten** this package.

family n–983 knife 1023 field 201

NET, NETWORK 984

網

MŌ
ami

The dead body is entwined in a **net**.

thread 964 net n–984 die 660

ELEMENT, BASE, BARE 985

素

SO, SU
moto

A plant is made of threadlike **elements**.

plant 214 thread 964

FINE, NARROW 986

細

SAI
hosoi, komakai

The field is as **narrow** as thread.

thread 964 field 201

"NET" 987

罒

*This element means **net**, but also looks like an eye on its side.*

GAUZE, NET, INCLUDE 988

羅

RA

A **gauze net** and a rope …

net 987 thread 964 bird 319

FASTEN, ROPE, SUPPORT 989

維

I

… **fastened** to its leg hold the bird.

thread 964 bird 319

Baskets

"BASKET" 990 覀

*This element means **basket**.*

PRICE, VALUE, WORTH 996

価

KA
atai

A person rings up the **price** of a basket.

person 362 basket 990

NECESSARY 991

要

YŌ
iru

The woman finds it **necessary** to carry the basket on her head …

basket 990 woman 411

HIP, LOWER BACK, BEARING 992

腰

YŌ
koshi

… to prevent **lower back** pain.

flesh 267 basket 990 woman 411

VOTE, SLIP OF PAPER 993

票

HYŌ

Votes are collected in the basket.

basket 990 altar 701

SIGN(POST), MARK 994

標

HYŌ
shirushi

A **sign** is **marked** with a slip of paper.

tree 126 vote 993

"BASKETS" 995

冓

*This element means **baskets**.*

LECTURE 997

講

KŌ

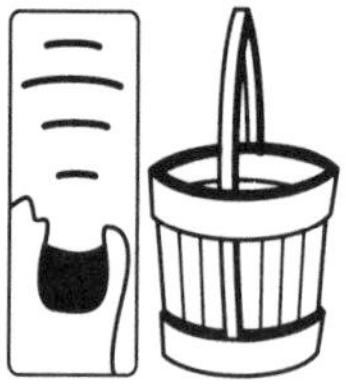

A wordy **lecture** on baskets.

speak 840 baskets 995

BUY 998

購

KŌ

With inflation, you need baskets of money to **buy** anything.

money 708 baskets 995

DITCH, CHANNEL 999

溝

KŌ
mizo, dobu

Baskets were used to fill the **ditch** with water.

water 66 | baskets 995

BUILD, MIND 1000

構

KŌ
kamau/eru

Baskets are **built** from trees.

tree 126 | baskets 995

NEW 1001

新

SHIN
atarashii, arata

A **new** ax is needle-sharp.

needle 1006 | ax 1072

AVOID 1002

避

HI
sakeru

Move quickly to **avoid** getting a needle in your rear.

move 1153 | needle + buttocks n–1002

HABIT, KINK 1003

癖

HEKI
kuse

Any bad **habit** can be cured by a needle in your rear.

illness 655 | needle + buttocks n–1002

ADMINISTER 1004

宰

SAI

Needles are **administered** in this building.

roof 1144 | needle 1005

Needles

SHARP, BITTER 1005

辛

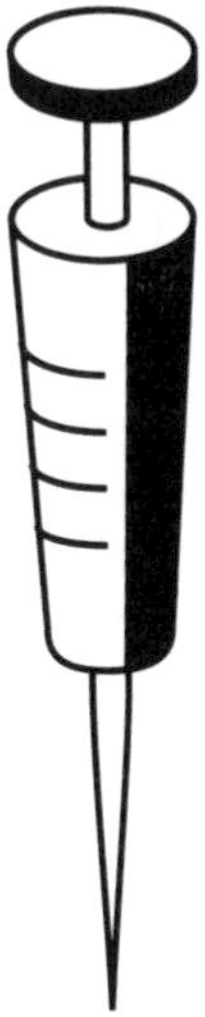

SHIN
karai, tsurai

A **sharp** needle.

"NEEDLE" 1006

亲

This element means ***needle****.*

Cloth

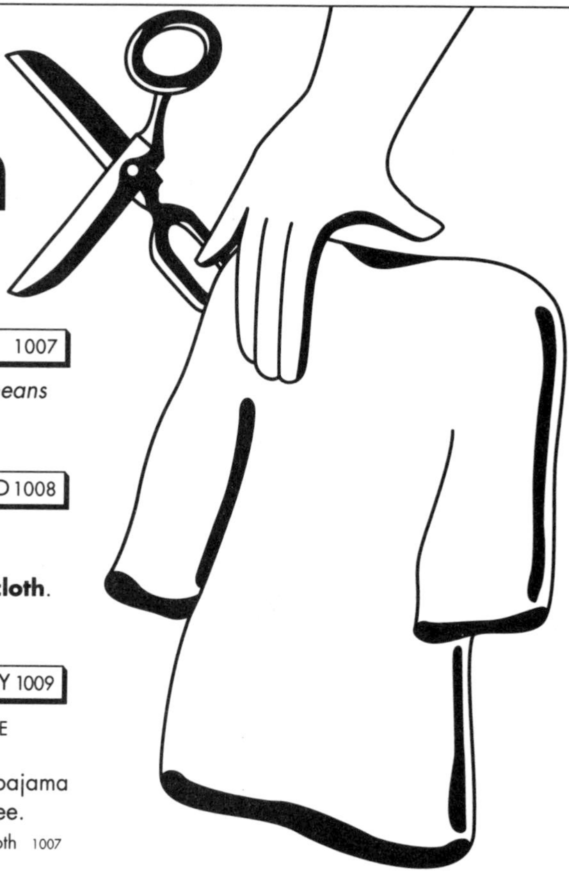

巾

"CLOTH" 1007

This element means ***cloth****.*

布

CLOTH, SPREAD 1008

FU
nuno

A hand spreads out the **cloth**.

hand 598 cloth 1007

希

DESIRE, SCANTY 1009

KI, KE

I **desire** to cut this cloth pajama top into a **scanty** negligee.

weave n–1009 cloth 1007

EMPEROR 1010

帝

TEI

What is an **emperor** but a man standing in fine clothes?

stand 627 cloth 1007

REGISTER, DRAPE 1011

帳

CHŌ

Cloth and long hair **drape** down her back.

cloth 1007 long 915

SAIL 1012

帆

HAN
ho

A cloth **sail**.

cloth 1007 wind n–1012

CURTAIN, TENT, ACT 1013

幕

MAKU, BAKU

A cloth **tent** protects you from the sun and itchy grass.

grass 124 sun 1 cloth 1007

綿

COTTON 1014

MEN
wata

Cloth is made of white **cotton** thread.

thread 964 white 936 cloth 1007

旅

JOURNEY 1015

RYO
tabi

Clothing fit for a **journey**.

flag n–387 clothing 1021

WEAR, CLOTHING, GEAR 1016

装

SŌ, SHŌ
yosōu

I **wear** manly **gear**.

manly 420 clothing 1021

CLOTHES, YIELD, SERVE 1019

服

FUKU

I keep my **clothes** on the shelf.

flesh 267 hand w/tool n–1019

REPORT, REWARD 1020

報

HŌ
mukuiru

Reportedly, the **reward** was yen plus clothes.

happiness 731 seize n–1020

REVERSE SIDE, INSIDE, LINING 1017

裏

RI
ura

The label is on the **inside lining** of the clothes.

shelter 1147 village 1086 clothing 1021

NAKED, BARE 1018

裸

RA
hadaka

He hung his clothes on the fruit tree while running **naked**.

clothing n–1015 field 201 tree 126

JUDGE, CUT, DECIDE 1022

裁

SAI
sabaku, tatsu

Hal **decides** to **cut** the sleeves from his clothes.

halberd 801 clothing 1021

CLOTHING 1021

衣

I
koromo

A piece of **clothing**.

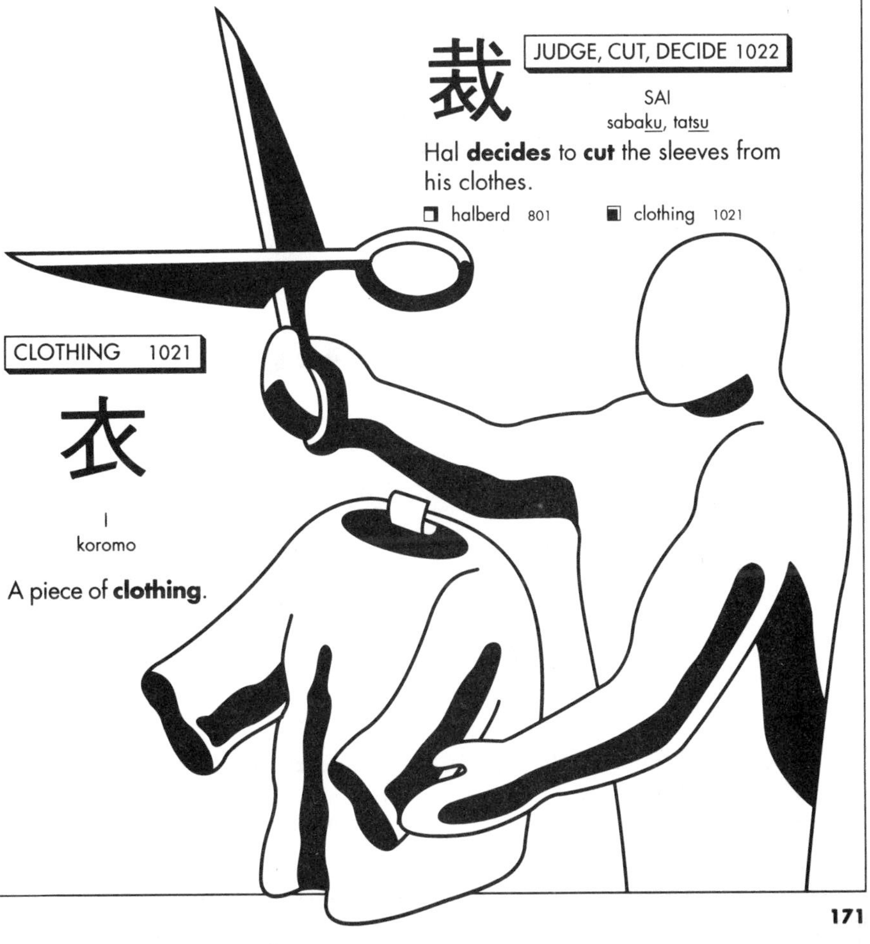

Knife

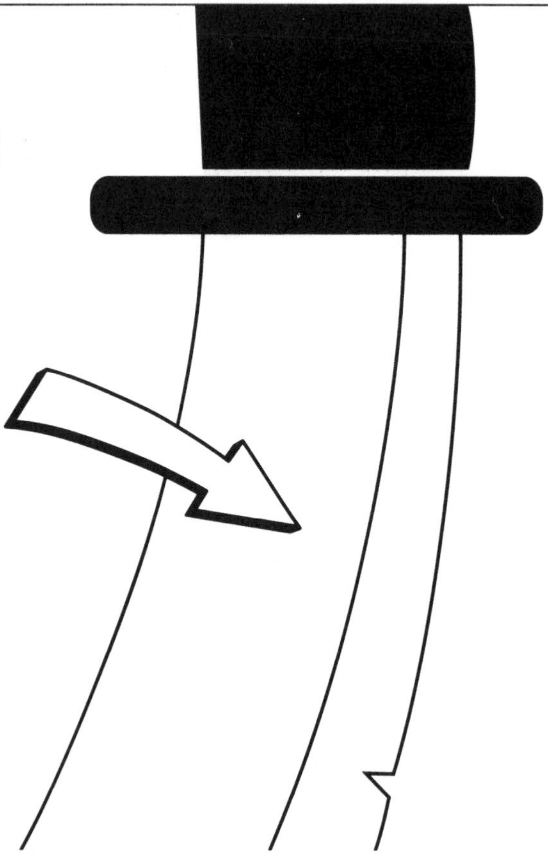

SWORD 1023

刀

TŌ
katana

A mighty **sword** …

BLADE, SWORD 1024

刃

JIN
ha, yaiba

… has a sharp **blade**.

PIERCE, STAB, THORN 1027

刺

SHI
sasu/saru, toge

The **thorn pierces** like a knife.

thorn n–1027 knife 1037

CHOP, MINCE, ENGRAVE 1028

刻

KOKU
kizamu

The **chopped** wood becomes an **engraved** bedpost.

pig n–1028 knife 1037

DIVIDE, MINUTE, UNDERSTAND 1025

紛

BUN, FUN, BU
wakaru/keru

I fell into confusion when my lifeline **divided** in two.

split 456 sword 1023

PUNISH 1026

刑

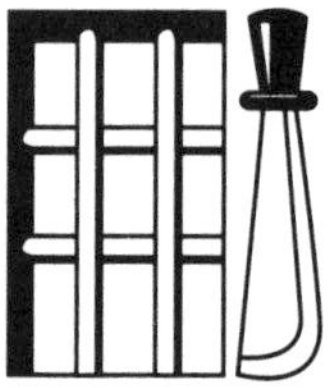

KEI

Stabbing is **punished** by imprisonment.

grill n–920 knife 1037

CORE, NUCLEUS 1029

核

KAKU

A bedpost was made of a tree's **core**.

tree 126 pig n–1028

PUNISHMENT 1030

罰

BATSU, BACHI

Speaking gets the knife/net **punishment**.

net 987 speak 840 knife 1037

PUBLISH, ENGRAVE 1031

刊

KAN

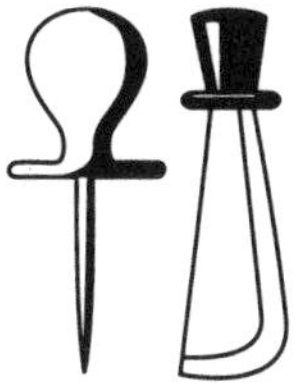

Engraving tools.

◧ dry 73 ◨ knife 1037

DIVERGE, SPLIT, DIFFER 1032

別

BETSU
waka<u>reru</u>

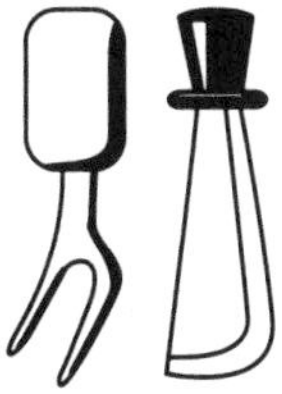

The fork **splits** into two prongs.

◧ bone n–1032 ◨ knife 1037

TYPE, MODEL, MOLD 1033

型

KEI
kata

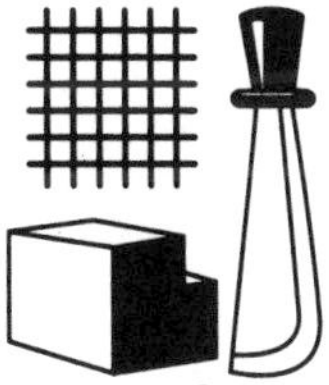

Clay **modeling** tools.

◰ grill n–920 ◳ knife 1037 ⬓ soil 101

CUT 1034

切

SETSU, SAI
ki<u>ru</u>

I **cut** it into seven pieces.

◧ seven 903 ◨ sword 1023

REAP, CUT, SHEAR 1036

刈

ka<u>ru</u>

Cut and **shear** with scissors and a knife.

◧ shears n–1036 ◨ knife 1037

"KNIFE" 1037

刂

*This element means **knife**.*

JUDGE, SEAL, SIZE 1035

判

HAN, BAN

The **judge** cut the **seal** in two with a knife.

◧ half 907 ◨ knife 1037

Equipment

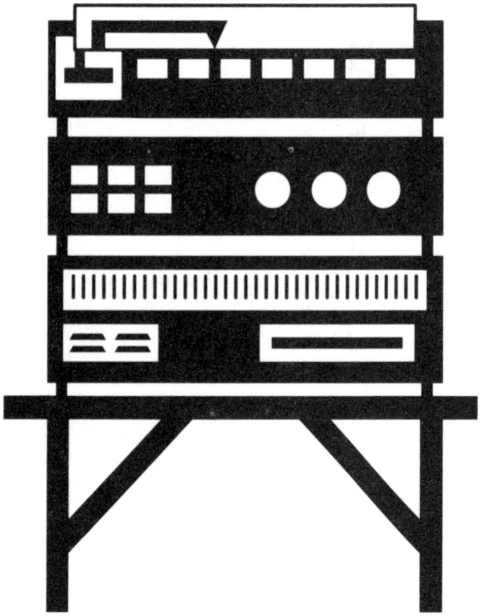

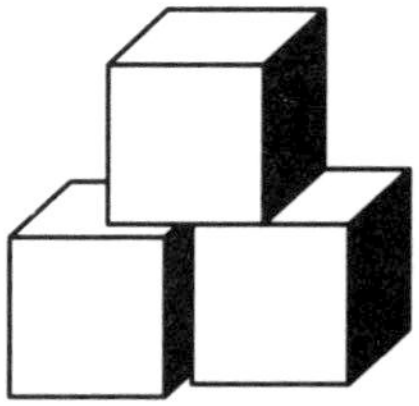

GOODS, QUALITY, KIND 1038

品

HIN
shina

Three opened boxes of **goods**.

opening 566
opening 566 opening 566

EQUIPMENT, MEANS 1039

具

GU
sonaeru

Stereo and video **equipment**.

eye 538 utensil n–1039

TURN, ROTATE 1042

回

KAI
mawaru/su

Nuts **rotate** around bolts.

enclose 778 opening 566

UMBRELLA, PARASOL 1043

傘

SAN
kasa

This **umbrella** can comfortably shade four people.

enter 950 person (x4) 363

VESSEL, UTENSIL, SKILL 1040

器

KI
utsuwa

A big kitchen **utensil**.

opening (x4) 566 big 913

SPEECH, KNOW, VALVE, PETAL 1041

弁

BEN

I wish I could put a shut-off **valve** on his **speech**.

HIT, STRIKE 1044

打

DA
utsu

Hold a nail and **strike** it exactly on its head.

hand 580 exact 1089

Brooms

HONEST, CHEAP, ANGLE 1045

廉

REN

Every house can buy two brooms at one **honest**, **cheap** price.

building 1143 combine 1051

DISLIKE 1046

嫌

KEN, GEN
kirau/i,
iya

The woman **dislikes** housework.

woman 411 combine 1051

ORDINARY, WORK 1047

庸

YŌ

This building is used for **ordinary work**.

building 1143 hand 597 use 385

SWEEP 1048

掃

SŌ
haku

A hand **sweeps** the broom.

hand 580 hand w/broom 1052

RETURN 1049

帰

KI
kaeru

I'm **returning** your broom.

follow n–1049 hand w/broom 1052

SOAK, IMMERSE 1050

浸

SHIN
hitasu/ru

A mop **soaked** up the water.

water 66 hand 597 hand 600

COMBINE, UNABLE 1051

兼

KEN
kaneru

Two brooms are **combined** into one.

"BROOM" 1052

*This element shows a hand holding a **broom**.*

帚

Build

MERIT, SERVICE 1053

功

KŌ, KU

He offers his construction **services**.

- construction 1054
- power 745

CONSTRUCTION, WORK 1054

工

KŌ, KU

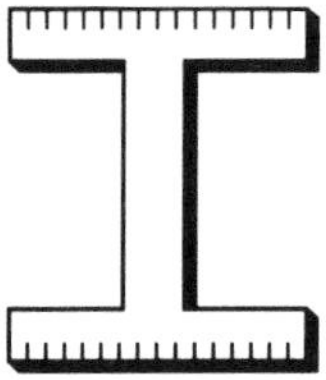

A carpenter's square is used in **construction**.

BUILD 1055

築

CHIKU
kizu<u>ku</u>

The Japanese commonly **build** their homes of bamboo and wood.

bamboo 123 · work 1054 · common 1056

MEDIOCRE, COMMON 1056

凡

BON, HAN
oyo<u>so</u>

This **common** person tries to hide his **mediocrity**.

TRIBUTE 1057

貢

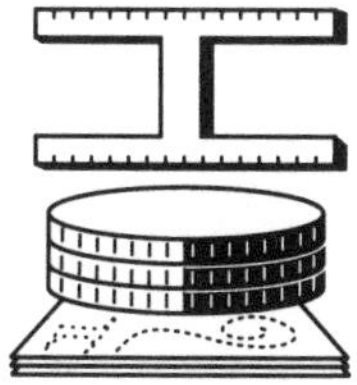

KŌ, KU
mitsugu

The **tribute** was paid with money and construction labor.

construction 1054 money 708

MAKE 1058

作

SAKU, SA
tsukuru

What shall I **make** with my saw?

person 362 adze n–1058

VINEGAR, SOUR 1059

酢

SAKU
su, suppai

Vinegar is made from alcohol.

alcohol 249 adze n–1058

LIE, DECEIVE 1060

詐

SA

Lies are fabricated words.

words 840 adze n–1058

LARGE BEAM, FLAG POLE 1061

杠

KŌ
chigi

A wooden **beam** is used in construction.

tree 126 construction 1054

SUSPEND, HANG DOWN 1062

垂

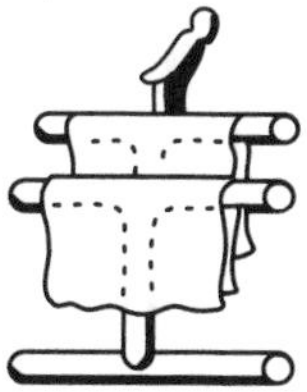

SUI
tareru/rasu

The blankets **hang** on the drying racks.

SPINDLE, SINKER 1063

錘

SUI
tsumu, omori

The metal **sinker** hangs in the water.

metal 105 hang down 1062

SLEEP 1064

睡

SUI
nemuru

When I'm **sleepy** my eyelids hang down.

eye 538 hang down 1062

BECOME, MAKE, CONSIST 1065

成

SEI, JŌ
naru/su

Hal **becomes** a **maker** of things with his ax.

halberd 100 exact n–1065

CASTLE 1066

城

JŌ
shiro

In Hal's hands, earth is piled up and becomes a **castle**.

earth 101 become 1065

PROSPER, HEAP, SERVE 1067

盛

SEI, JŌ
moru, sakaru/n

Hal's dish is **heaping** with rice.

become 1065 dish 261

SINCERITY 1068

誠

SEI
makoto

Hal's **sincere**. His words become true.

word 840 become 1065

Ax

CUT, DECLINE, WARN, JUDGE 1069

断

DAN
kotowaru, tatsu

Cut up the rice.

rice 217 ax 1072

QUALITY, PAWN 1070

質

SHITSU,
SHICHI, CHI

Pawn two **quality** axes for some money.

ax (x2) 1072 money 708

BEND, BREAK, OCCASION 1071

折

SETSU
ori, oru/reru

Grab the **bent** and **broken** ax.

hand 580 ax 1072

AX, WEIGHT 1072

斤

KIN

A **weighty ax**.

CRAFTSMAN 1073

匠

SHŌ

A **craftsman** keeps his tools in a box.

enclosed 778 ax 1072

PLEDGE, VOW, OATH 1074

誓

SEI
chikau

I **pledge** never to break my word.

break 1071 word 840

DIE, PASS ON, DEATH 1075

逝

SEI
yuku

Death breaks life's motion.

movement 1153 break 1071

REPEL, REJECT 1076

斥

SEKI
shirizokeru

I **repelled** it with an ax.

RADICALS

Thousands of kanji are built from a few hundred basic elements. Of these basic elements, roughly eighty of the most frequently used elements are known as radicals. Radicals often indicate the "topic" of a character. Kanji with the radical SOIL 101 often have meanings associated with soil or ground, such as **BA** 28, PLACE, in *basho*, "location," shown at right. Below are a handful of frequently used radicals.

WATER 66	FIRE 82	SOIL 101
氵	灬	土
GRASS 124	HEART 498	HAND 580
艹	忄	扌
WORD 840	KNIFE 1037	MOVE 1153
言	刂	辶

場所

Places

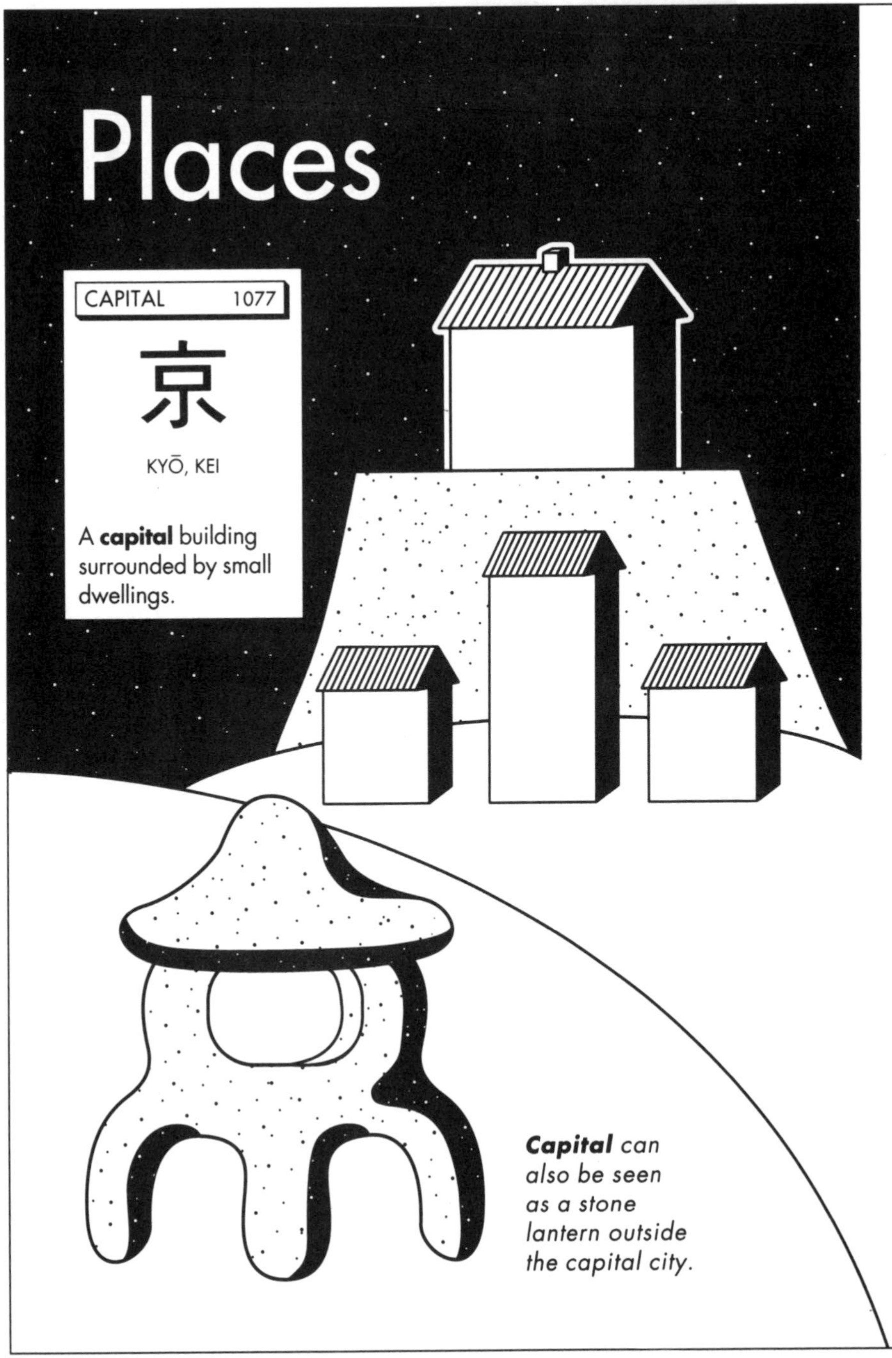

CAPITAL 1077

京

KYŌ, KEI

A **capital** building surrounded by small dwellings.

Capital *can also be seen as a stone lantern outside the capital city.*

COOL 1078

涼

RYŌ
suzumu/shii

Cool raindrops fall.

water 66 capital 1077

SCENE, VIEW, BRIGHT 1079

景

KEI, KE

A **bright** and sunny **view** of the capital.

sun 1 capital 1077

SHADOW, LIGHT, IMAGE 1080

影

EI
kage

The sun's rays cast **light** and dark **shadows**.

sun 1 capital 1077 delicate 536

WORLD, GENERATION 1081

世

SEI, SE
yo

Longitude and latitude lines on a **world** map.

NEXT, SUB-, ASIA 1082

亜

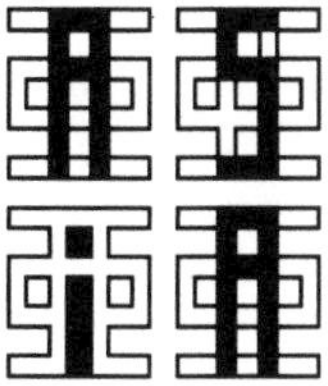

A

Lattice and design motifs from **Asia**.

(T'ANG) CHINA 1083

唐

TŌ
kara

In a building in **China**, a hand practices k'ung fu chops.

building 1143 hand 597 opening 566

CITY, MARKET 1084

市

SHI
ichi

I buy clothes in the **city market**.

RISE, RAISE, INTEREST 1085

興

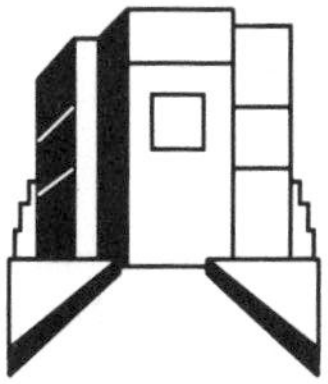

KYŌ, KŌ
oko<u>su</u>/<u>ru</u>

High-**rise** apartments all look the same—of no **interest**.

VILLAGE 1086

村

SON
mura

A sentry protects every inch of our **village**.

tree 126 inch 759

VILLAGE 1087

里

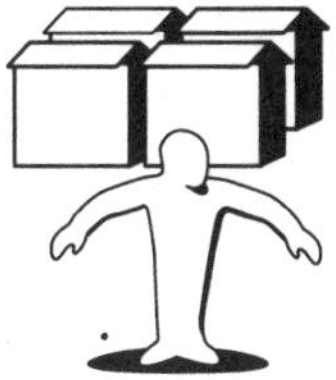

RI
sato

A samurai stands in a field before the **village**.

field 201 soil 101

TOWN, BLOCK 1088

町

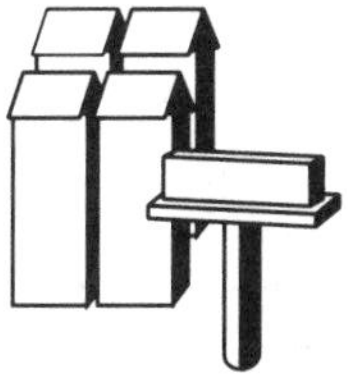

CHŌ
machi

This sign shows what **town** you're in …

field 201 soil 101

BLOCK, EXACT 1089

丁

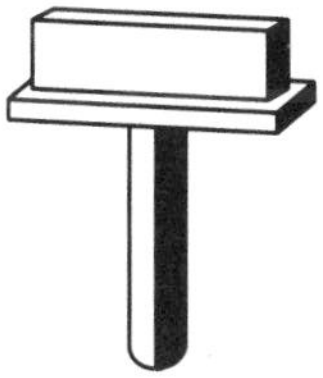

CHŌ, TEI

… but this sign tells you **exactly** what **block** you're in.

Village

都 CAPITAL, METROPOLIS 1090

TO, TSU
miyako

People flock to the **metropolis** to sell their wares.

◧ person 408 ◨ village 1094

SUBURBS 1091

郊

KŌ

The **suburbs** are beyond the village.

◧ mix 831
◨ village 1094

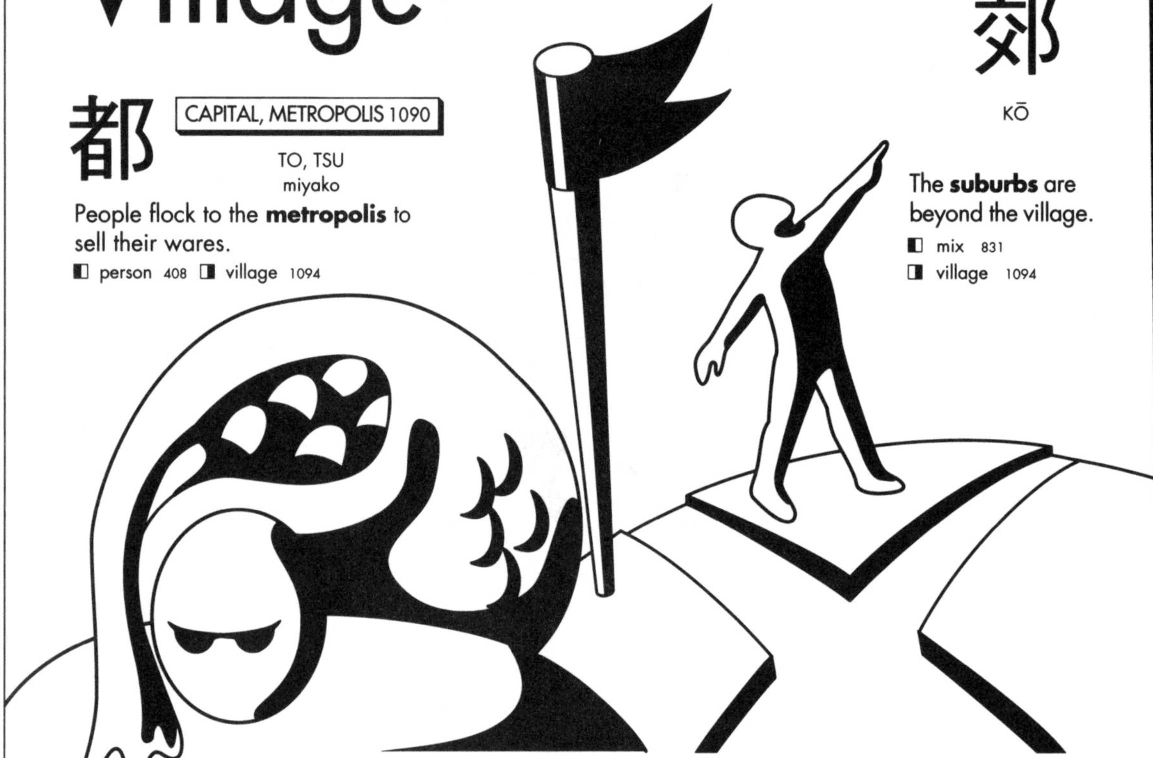

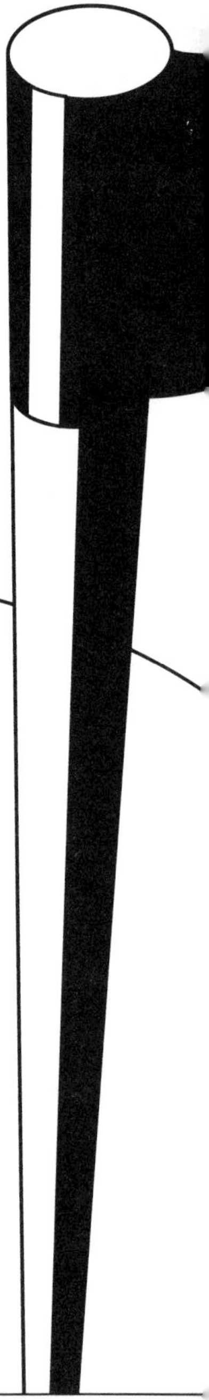

COUNTY, DISTRICT 1092

郡

GUN
kōri

Lord of the **county**.

◧ lord 417 ◨ village 1094

MAIL, RELAY STATION 1093

郵

YŪ

A **mail** bag waits at the **relay station**.

◧ hand down 1062 ◨ village 1094

"VILLAGE/HILL" 1094

阝

*This element means **village** when on the right side of a character and **hill** when on the left. Picture a flag placed on a hill to mark a village.*

Hill

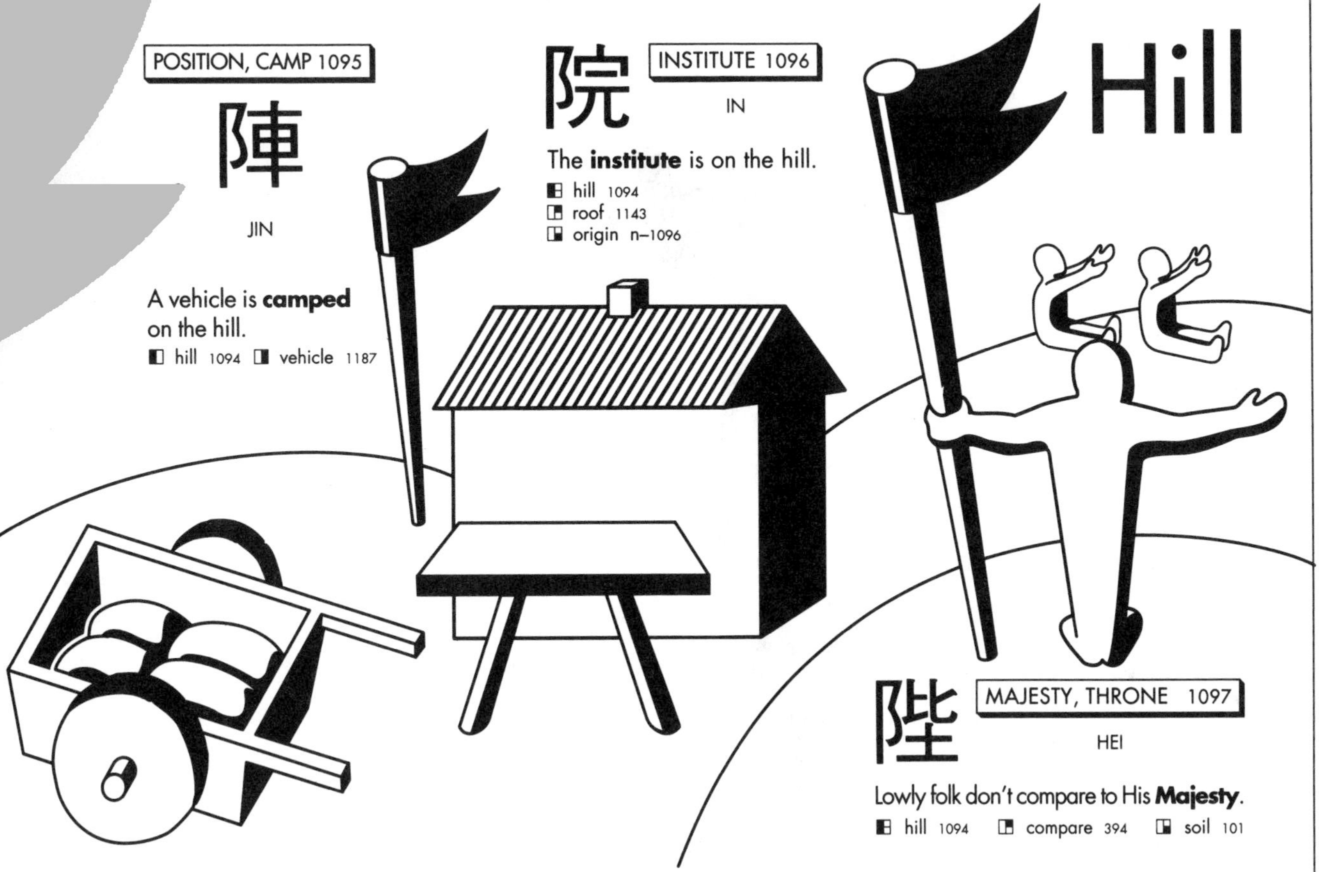

POSITION, CAMP 1095

陣

JIN

A vehicle is **camped** on the hill.

◧ hill 1094 ◨ vehicle 1187

院 INSTITUTE 1096

IN

The **institute** is on the hill.

hill 1094
roof 1143
origin n–1096

陛 MAJESTY, THRONE 1097

HEI

Lowly folk don't compare to His **Majesty**.

hill 1094 compare 394 soil 101

PREVENT, DEFEND 1098

防

BŌ
fusegu

A person **defends** his position on the hill.

◧ hill 1094 ◨ person 386

LAND 1099

陸

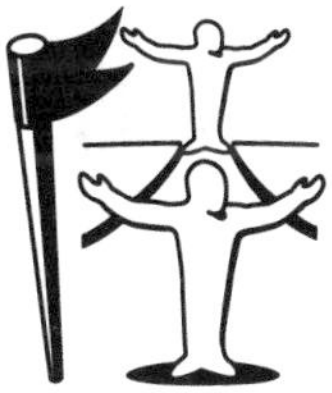

RIKU

We plant a flag on our **land**.

hill 1094 mound n–1099 soil 101

HIGH, PEAK, PROSPEROUS 1100

隆

RYŪ

It's slow progress reaching the **peak** of the hill.

hill 1094 slow progress 1218 plant 214

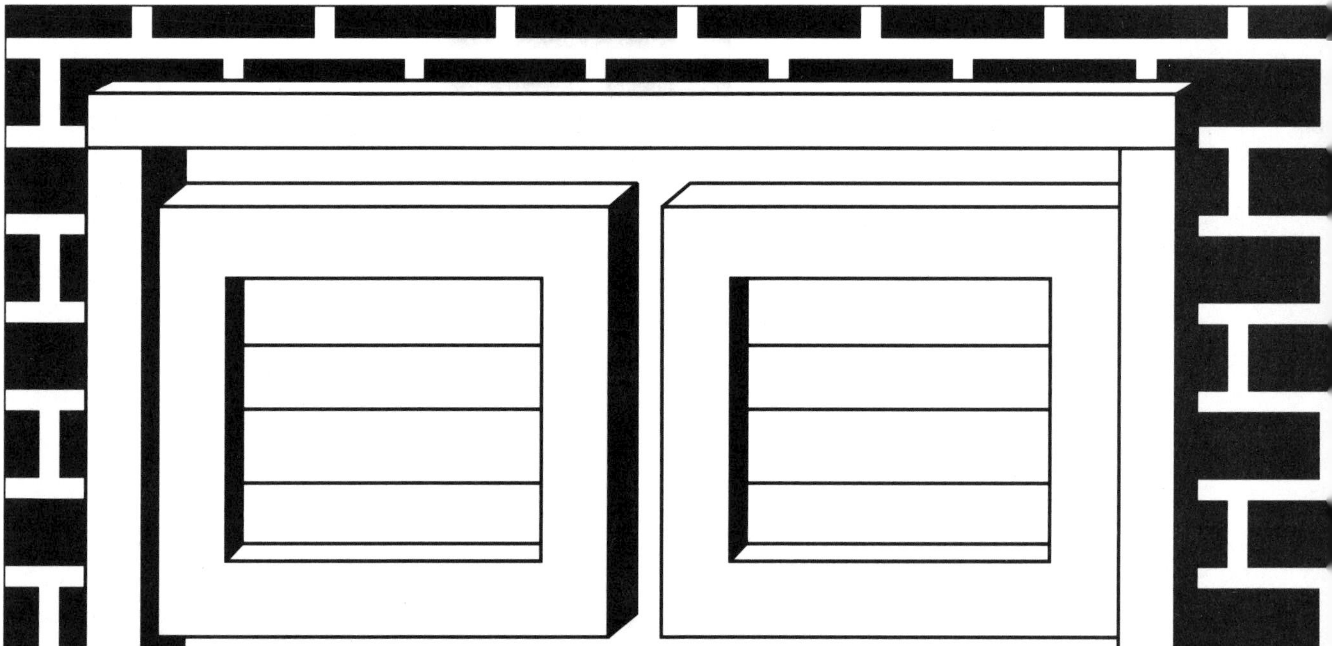

Gate

門 GATE, DOOR 1101

MON
kado

Two **doors** form a **gate**.

閑 LEISURE, QUIET 1102

KAN

There's a **quiet**, peaceful scene of trees outside my gate.

gate 1101 tree 126

CLOSE, SHUT 1103

閉

HEI
tojiru,
shimaru/meru

A post holds the gate **shut**.

gate 1101 talent 871

OPEN 1104

開

KAI
hiraku, akeru

Two hands **open** the gate.

gate 1101 hands n–1104

SPACE, GAP 1105

間

KAN, KEN
aida, ma

Sunshine pours through the **gap** in the gate.

gate 1101 sun 1

FACTION, CLAN LINEAGE 1106

閥

BATSU

One **faction** attacks outside the gate.

gate 1101 attack 800

DARKNESS, GLOOM 1107

闇

AN
yami

Gloom stood at the gate, shrouded in **darkness**, making no sound

gate 1101 sound 883

BE OBSTRUCTED 1108

閊

tsukaeru

The gate **obstructs** my view of the mountain.

gate 1101 mountain 167

SUDDEN ENTRY, INQUIRE 1109

闖

CHIN

Suddenly, a horse **entered** the gate.

gate 1101 horse 291

BARRIER, CONNECTION 1110

関

KAN
seki

A **barrier** prevents me from leaving the gate.

gate 1101 bar n–1110

ASK 1111

問

MON
tou

Ask by putting your mouth to the gate.

gate 1101 ear 551

HEAR, ASK, LISTEN 1112

聞

BUN, MON
kiku/koeru

Hear more with your ear to the gate.

gate 1101 mouth 566

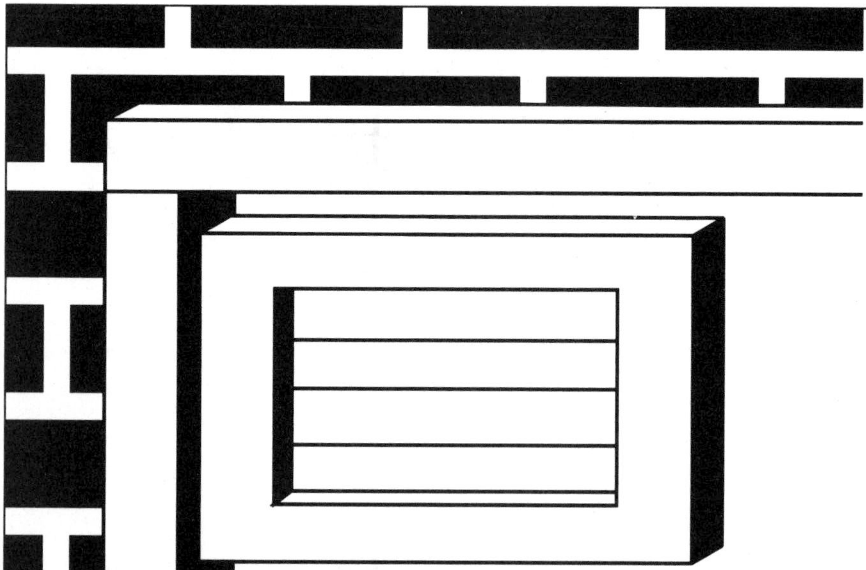

Door

戸 **DOOR 1113**

KO
to

Half of a saloon **door**.

尸 **"DOOR" 1114**

*This **door** is really the element* BODY *460.*

TEAR 1115

涙

RUI
namida

Big John shed **tears** when his wife walked out the door.

water 66 · door 1113 · big 913

PLACE, SITUATION 1116

所

SHO
tokoro

The **place** to chop wood is by the door .

door 1113 · ax 1072

FURNACE 1117

炉

RO

A **furnace** has fire behind its door.

fire 83 · door 1113

ROOM, WIFE, TUFT 1118

房

BŌ
fusa

My **wife** is in the **room** on the other side of the door.

door 1113 · person 1113

FAN 1119

扇

SEN
ōgi, aogu

A **fan** is like a flapping door.

door 1113 · wings 330

STORE, BUILDING 1120

屋

OKU
ya

Go through a door to reach the **store**.

door 1113 · reach 1135

DOOR, FRONT PAGE 1121

扉

HI
tobira

Automatic **doors** slide open in opposite directions.

door 1113 | opposite 960

PALACE, LORD, MR. 1122

殿

DEN, TEN
tono, -dono

The **lord** of the **palace** shakes an ax at all who come to his door.

door 1113 | together 383 | hand/ax 1113

WEAR, WALK, FOOTWEAR 1123

履

RI
haku

Wear shoes when **walking** outdoors.

door 1114 | walk n–1123

DELIVER, REPORT 1124

届

todoku/keru

Deliver the pizza to my door.

door 1114 | cause 76

SUBMIT, CROUCH 1125

屈

KUTSU

You must **crouch** to leave through this strange door.

door 1114 | leave 956

LEAK 1126

漏

RŌ
moru/reru/rasu

Drops of rain **leak** through the door.

water 66 | door 1114 | rain 45

MOAT, DITCH CANAL 1127

堀

hori

A drawbridge door covers the **moat**, but people still have trouble leaving.

soil 101 | submit 1125

FENCE, WALL 1128

塀

HEI

We built this **fence** to keep people out.

soil 101 | fence n–1128

DIG 1129

掘

KUTSU
horu

I often have to **dig** them out by hand.

hand 580 | submit 1125

HALL, TEMPLE 1130

堂

DŌ

A chalice is used in **temples** and **halls**.

roof 1144 · opening 566 · soil 101

PALACE, SHRINE, PRINCE 1131

宮

KYŪ, GŪ, KU
miya

The prince lives in a two-storied **palace**.

roof 1144 · joined blocks n–1131

LODGE, SHELTER, HOUSE 1132

宿

SHUKU
yado, yadoru

The **lodge** holds a hundred people.

roof 1144 · person 362 · hundred 909

HOUSE, HOME 1133

宅

TAKU

Home is a roof over your head.

roof 1144 · open up n–1133

ROOM, HOUSE 1134

室

SHITSU
muro

Reach for some flowers to decorate the **house**.

roof 1144 · reach 1135

REACH, GO, PEAK 1135

至

SHI
itari/ru

Reach for the plant in the soil.

arrow n–1135 · soil 101

SPREAD 1136

拡

KAKU

Spread your hand wide.

hand 580 · wide 1139

GOV'T OFFICE, PREFECTURE 1137

府

FU

Government office workers give themselves medals.

building 1143 · attach 771

GOV'T OFFICE, AGENCY 1138

庁

CHŌ

The sign marks the **government agency**.

building 1143 · exact 1089

WIDE, SPACIOUS 1139

広

KŌ
hiroi/geru

I have a wide and **spacious** building for myself.

building 1143 · private 450

Building & Roof

STOREHOUSE 1140

庫

KO

Store the cart in the garage.

◧ building 100 ◨ vehicle 100

广 "BUILDING" 1143

*This element means **building**.*

宀 "ROOF" 1144

*This element means **roof**.*

SEAT, PLACE 1141

席

SEKI

This **place seats** one person.

◧ building 1143 ◨ cloth 1007

STORE, PREMISES 1145

店

TEN
mise, tana

The **store** is ...

◧ building 1143
◨ occupy 1146

BED, FLOOR, ALCOVE 1142

床

SHŌ
toko, yuka

In the **alcove** is a bonsai tree.

◧ building 1143 ◨ tree 126

DIVINE, OCCUPY 1146

占

SEN
uranau, shimeru

... **occupied** by a green grocer.

Shelter

亠 "SHELTER" 1147

*This element means **to shelter**.*

停 STOP 1148

TEI

A person **stops** ...

person 362 inn 1149

亭 INN, PAVILION 1149

TEI

... at the **inn**.

TALL, HIGH, SUM 1150

高

KŌ
taka, takai

An expensive **high**-rise building.

shelter 1147 tower n–1150

QUARTER, ENCLOSURE 1151

郭

KAKU

Children's **quarters** are on the hill.

shelter 1147 child 447 village 1094

PRIVATE SCHOOL 1152

塾

JUKU

A child attends a mediocre **private school**.

castle n–1152 mediocre 1056 soil 101

READINGS

Kanji in dictionaries can be found by three methods: radical search, stroke counting, and pronunciation. Each method is laborious and uncertain. Which element is the defining radical? Which is the correct reading of several possibilities? Even after you identify the reading/meaning of an individual character, you may then have to search in a separate compound dictionary to find the definition of a word like *ryokō*, at right, which means "trip," "travel," or "journey." Kanji dictionaries are usually arranged by radical and stroke count. Word dictionaries are arranged in the order of the syllabaries—*a, i, u, e, o, ka, ki, ku, ke, ko,* etc.

TRIP	1015

旅

radical: 方
stroke count: 10
readings: RYO, tabi
other meanings: TRAVEL, JOURNEY

GO	1192

行

radical: 彳
stroke count: 6
readings: KŌ, AN, GYŌ, iku, okonau, -yuki
other meanings: CONDUCT, COLUMN

旅行

Move

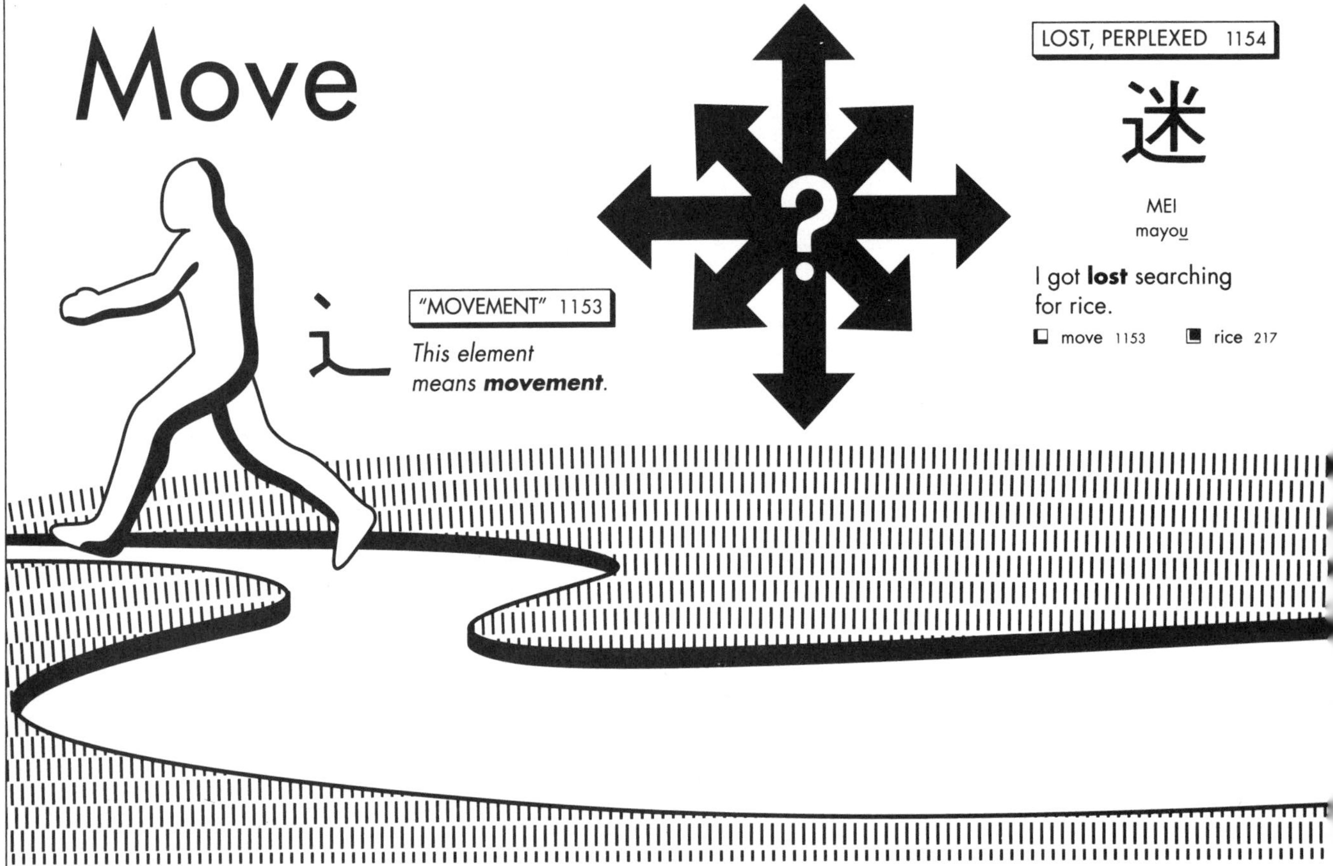

⻌

"MOVEMENT" 1153

*This element means **movement**.*

LOST, PERPLEXED 1154

迷

MEI
mayou

I got **lost** searching for rice.

◻ move 1153 ◼ rice 217

A CROSSING 1155

辻

tsuji

I **cross** ten intersections …

◻ move 1153 ◼ ten 906

PASS, WAY, COMMUTE 1156

通

TSŪ
tōru/su, kayou

… and **pass** many things as I **commute** to work.

◻ move 1153 ◼ use 385

GO AROUND 1157

巡

JUN
meguru

Go around the river.

◻ move 1153 ◼ river 55

FAST, INTENSE 1158

迅

JIN
hayai

Move **fast**!

◻ move 1153 ◼ fast n–1158

EXCESS, AMPLE 1161

余

YO
amari/ru/su

There was an **excess** of material for building the road.

SPEED, FAST 1159

速

SOKU
hayai, sumiyaka

A **speedy** delivery of a bundle of branches.

◻ move 1153 ◼ bundle 153

ROAD, WAY 1162

途

TO

The **road** was built with excess materials.

◻ move 1153 ◼ excess 1161

PRESS, DRAW NEAR 1160

迫

HAKU
semaru

Press on, for dawn is **drawing near**.

◻ move 1153 ◼ white 936

RETURN 1163

返

HEN
kaeru/su

It **returns** in the opposite direction.

◻ move 1153 ◼ oppose 957

FOLLOW, OBEY 1164

遵

JUN

I **follow** out of respect.

◻ move 1153 ◼ respect 767

EXCLUDE, REMOVE 1165

除

JO, JI
nozoku

Remove the excess materials from the road.

◧ hill 1094 ◨ excess 1161

Escape

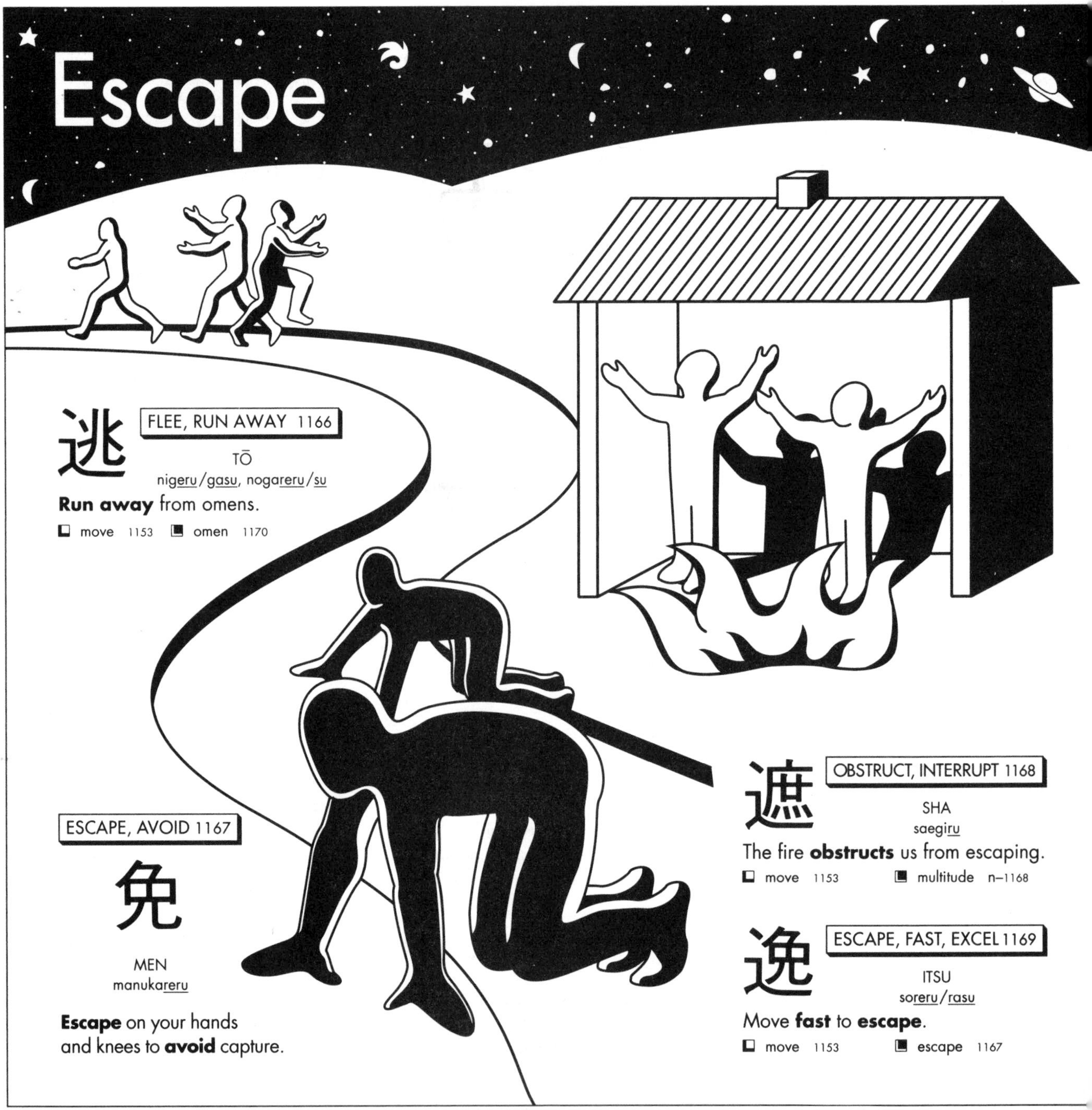

逃 FLEE, RUN AWAY 1166

TŌ
nigeru/gasu, nogareru/su

Run away from omens.

□ move 1153 ■ omen 1170

ESCAPE, AVOID 1167

免

MEN
manukareru

Escape on your hands and knees to **avoid** capture.

遮 OBSTRUCT, INTERRUPT 1168

SHA
saegiru

The fire **obstructs** us from escaping.

□ move 1153 ■ multitude n–1168

逸 ESCAPE, FAST, EXCEL 1169

ITSU
soreru/rasu

Move **fast** to **escape**.

□ move 1153 ■ escape 1167

SIGN, OMEN, TRILLION 1170

兆

CHŌ
kizashi/su

A **trillion** people were frightened by the **omen**.

FLEE, EVADE 1171

逋

HO

Flee from the prison.

move 1153 capture n–773

CHASE, PURSUE 1172

追

TSUI
ou

Move your butt in hot **pursuit**.

move 1153 buttocks 466

VICINITY, BOUNDARY 1173

辺

HEN
atari, be

Men with swords guard the **boundary**.

move 1153 sword 1023

NEAR 1174

近

KIN
chikai

This way "chopped" time off our journey. We are **near**.

move 100 ax 100

CONTRARY, UPSIDE DOWN 1175

逆

GYAKU
sakasa, sakarau

She's walking **upside down** just to be **contrary**.

move 1153 big n–1175

RETREAT, WITHDRAWAL 1176

退

TAI
shirizoku/keru

Retreat from the scary sight.

move 1153 stop/stare 1178

RESENT, REGRET 1177

恨

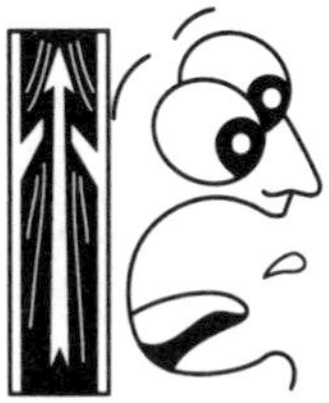

KON
uramu

I **resent** people staring at me.

heart 498 stop/stare 1178

"STOP AND STARE" 1178

艮

*As an element this can mean **stop and stare** with bulging eyes and gaping mouth.*

ALTERNATE, ROTATE 1179

迭

TETSU

I took an **alternate** path and got lost.

move 1153 lose 577

Boat

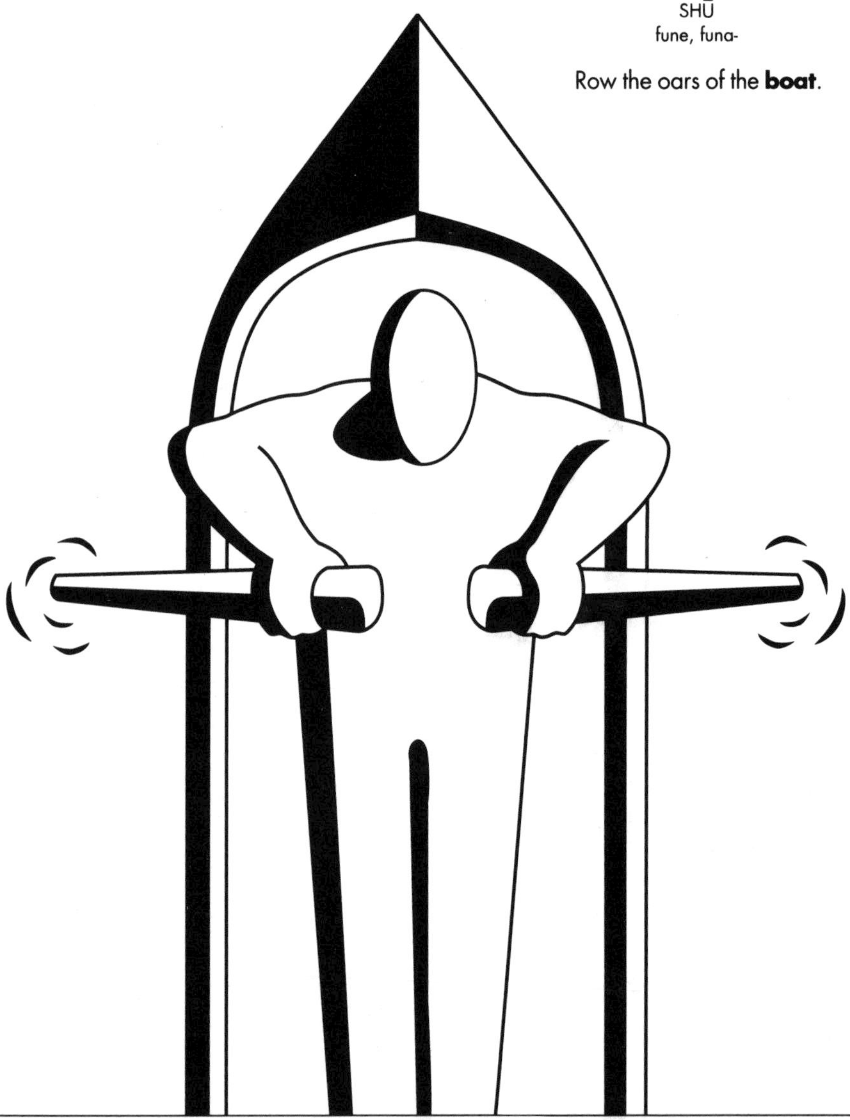

BOAT, SHIP 1180

舟

SHŪ
fune, funa-

Row the oars of the **boat**.

SAIL, VOYAGE 1181

航

KŌ

My **voyage** begins from the shelter of the dock.

boat 1180 shelter 1147 desk n–157

GENERAL, TIME, CARRY 1182

般

HAN

The boat **carries** the ax-wielding **general**.

boat 1180 hand w/ax 792

BOAT, SHIP 1183

船

SEN
fune, funa-

The hull of a **ship** is an opening made of wood.

boat 1180 split 456 opening 566

Cart

LOAD, CARRY 1184

載

SAI
noru/seru

Hal **loads** the cart with soil.

soil 101 · cart 1187 · halberd 801

VEHICLE, CHARIOT, CART 1187

車

SHA
kuruma

This **cart** carries things from the field.

TRACK, RUT, WAY 1188

軌

KI

Nine times the cart got stuck in the **rut**.

cart 1187 · nine 905

RICKSHAW 1185

俥

kuruma

A person pulls the **rickshaw**.

person 362 · cart 1187

ACCOMPANY

連

REN
tsureru, tsuraneru

Ride in the cart and **accompany** me on my trip.

move 1153 · cart 1187

WHEEL, HOOP 1189

輪

RIN
wa

The **wheel** fell off my cart.

cart 1187 · person 363 · book 868

AXLE, SHAFT, SCROLL 1190

軸

JIKU

The **axle** was the cause of my problem.

cart 1187 · cause 76

Road

ROAD, AREA 1191

街

GAI, KAI
machi

I'm new to this **area**.
Which **road** ...

path 1192 soil (x2) 101

GO, CONDUCT, COLUMN 1192

行

KŌ, GYŌ, AN
iku, yuku, okonau

... **goes** into town?

WANDER ABOUT 1195

彷

HŌ

That person **wandered** about in all directions.

path 1192 direction 386

ROLE, SERVICE, DUTY 1196

役

YAKU, EKI

Ax-wielding sentries do their **duty**.

path 1192 hand w/ax 792

PATH, DIRECT 1193

径

KEI

Cut a **direct path** through the jungle.

path 1192 hand 600 soil 101

GO, GONE, PAST 1194

往

Ō

My master has **gone** down this path.

path 1192 master 743

SUBJUGATE, TRAVEL 1197

征

SEI

You must only **travel** the correct path.

path 1192 correct 826

ROAD / CRASH! 1198 – 1204

ROAR, THUNDER, REVERBERATE 1198

轟

GŌ
todoroku

Three **Thunder**birds **roar** down the road.

car 1187 · car 1187 · car 1187

ROTATE, ROLL, TUMBLE 1199

転

TEN
korobu/garu/geru/gasu

The car **rolls** and **tumbles** in a cloud of smoke.

car 1187 · cloud 54

Crash!

COLLIDE, ROAD 1201

衝

SHŌ

A **collision** in the **road** …

path 1192 · heavy 1202

HEAVY, PILE, FOLD 1202

重

JŪ, CHŌ
kasaneru/naru, omoi, e

… left a **heavy pile** of **folded** metal.

MOVE 1200

動

DŌ
ugoku/kasu

A man tries to **move** the heavy car with all his power.

heavy 1202 · power 745

MERIT 1203

勲

KUN

Gain **merit** by trying to move the heavy, burning car.

move 1200 · fire 82

WORK 1204

働

DŌ
hataraku

We **worked** to get the car to move on its own power.

person 362 · move 1200

Stop . . .

STOP 1205

止

SHI
tomaru/meru

Stop.

EACH 1209

各

KAKU
ono-ono

Step in **each** box.

⬒ slow progress 1218 ⬓ opening 566

DEAL WITH, PLACE 1210

処

SHO

I do business **deals** at my desk.

◧ slow progress 1218 ◨ desk n–157

PLAN, UNDERTAKE 1206

企

KI
kuwadateru

We **plan** to stop that person.

⬒ person 363 ⬓ stop 1205

歩 WALK 1207

HO
aruku, ayumu

We **walk** a little then stop a while.

⬒ stop 1205 ⬓ little 924

渉 CROSS OVER, LIAISE 1208

SHŌ

Walk **across** the river.

◧ water 66 ◨ walk 1207

BASE, BASIS 1211

拠

KYO, KO
yoru

The deals are **based** on handshakes.

◧ hand 580 ◨ deal with 1210

ENTWINE, CONNECT 1212

絡

RAKU
karamu/maru

He became **entwined** in the thread.

thread 964 each 1209

CABINET, CHAMBER 1213

閣

KAKU

Each official retreated to his **chamber**.

gate 1101 each 1209

ROAD, ROUTE 1214

路

RO
ji

We leg it down each and every **road**.

leg 617 each 1209

FALL, DROP 1215

落

RAKU
ochiru/tosu

Each person **falls** on the wet grass.

grass 124 water 66 each 1209

GUEST, VISITOR 1216

客

KYAKU, KAKU

Each man is a **guest** at this house.

roof 1144 each 1209

FALL, ALIGHT, DESCEND 1217

降

KŌ
furu, oriru/rosu

It's slow work **descending** these steps.

hill 1094 slow progress 1094

"FOLLOW, SLOW PROGRESS" 1218

夂

This element suggests ***slow progress****,*
or stops and starts.

. . . & Start Again

Come

来 **COME** 1219

RAI
kuru

Come follow me.

ENCOUNTER, MEET 1220

遭

SŌ
au

I will **meet**...

move 1153 companion 1220

OFFICIAL, COMPANION 1221

曹

SŌ, ZŌ

... my **companion** ...

east n–1220 sun 1

TANK, TUB, VAT 1222

槽

SŌ

... for our Hot **Tub** Encounter Group.

wood 100 companion 1221

GREET, WELCOME 1223

迎

GEI
mukaeru

He went to **greet** his friend at the turnstile.

move 1153 bending person n–1223

LOOK UP, STATE, RESPECT 1224

仰

GYŌ, KŌ
aogu, ōse

This person **respectfully looks up** at his friend by the turnstile.

person 362 bending person n–1223

RESTRAIN, PRESS DOWN 1225

抑

YOKU
osaeru

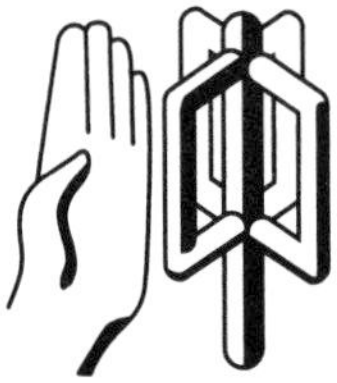

The turnstile **restrains** visitors.

hand 580 bending person n–1223

NOTES

These brief notes give information about elements not covered in the main text. The evolution of phonetic, symbolic, and graphic connotations over centuries makes it difficult to fully describe the meaning of each element. See Kenneth Henshall's *A Guide to Remembering Japanese Characters*, from which much of this information is derived.

n-6 **wet** Part of a phonetic element meaning "wet."

n-9 **rise** The sun rising through the grass. Compare with EARLY 19.

n-13 **crack** Phonetic meaning.

n-18 **winged bird** See WING 330 and BIRD 319.

n-19 **grass** Variant of GRASS 124.

n-20 **clear/high** Entry 20 refers to the element's phonetic meaning of "clear." Entry 85 refers to a Chinese character meaning "high."

n-21 **high** Phonetic meaning.

n-22 **kneeling** From a pictograph of a person kneeling.

n-23 **big-eyed lizard** May refer to the chameleon which can change colors.

n-26 **rays** From a pictograph of rays of sunlight. Distinguish from EASY 23.

n-40 **mask** From a pictograph of a summer festival mask.

n-43 **branches** From a pictograph of branches.

n-49 **lightning** From a pictograph of lightning.

n-50 **tremble** Phonetic meaning.

n-58 **person** From a pictograph of an upside-down child. Compare with CHILD 447.

n-62 **planks** From a pictograph of a tree cut in half.

n-65 **red** Variant of RED 929.

n-68 **previous** As a stand-alone character, this element has the readings *SEN*, *saki*.

n-69 **steam** From a pictograph of swirling vapors.

n-70 **stagnant** From a pictograph of a waterweed.

n-78 **emerge** Refers to a geyser; can also mean "boil."

n-81 **cliff** From a pictograph of a cliff.

n-89 **offer** From a pictograph of two hands holding an offering.

n-93 **plants** Picture a variant of LIFE 214 doubled.

n-94 **crack** Represents a crack in the ice.

n-102 **creature** From a pictograph of a scorpion.

n-106 **scene** Picture it as a standing mirror. Distinguish from LOOK 543.

n-111 **path** May derive from MOVEMENT 1153.

n-117 **speak** As a stand-alone character, this has the readings *UN*, *iu*, and is sometimes used to mean "speak." It can also mean "cloud." See entry 54.

n-118 **flower** From a pictograph of a flower.

n-122 **hands** From a pictograph of two hands. Graphically identical to GRASS 124.

n-125 **roots** Think of the line as representing the roots of a tree. Distinguish from TREE 126.

n-127 **shine** Picture rays of light radiating outward.

n-128 **flow** Looks graphically similar to a bent willow.

n-130 **basket** From a pictograph of a basket.

n-133 **extreme** Phonetic meaning.

n-137 **upright** As a stand-alone character, this has the readings *CHOKU*, *JIKI*, *naoru*, *sugu*.

n-157 **desk** From a pictograph of a table or desk.

n-170 **clothes** This is the radical form for CLOTHING 1021. Distinguish from the radical RELIGION 695.

n-172 **thread (x2)** A variant of THREAD 964.

n-175 **slow progress** Actually a combination of SLOW PROGRESS 1218 and a variant of COW 275.

n-176 **insert** From a pictograph of a person being squeezed by a person on either side.

n–177 **plant** From a pictograph of a plant.

n–187 **uniformity** From a pictograph of uniform gridwork, such as a lattice window or a grill.

n–202 **person** Picture PERSON 362 and its mirror image.

n–212 **well** As a stand-alone character, this has the reading *I*.

n–219 **quantity** As a stand-alone character, this has the readings *RYŌ, hakaru*.

n–220 **stop** A variant of SLOW PROGRESS 1218.

n–256 **pair** Convoluted etymology, acc. to Henshall.

n–256 **vessel** From a pictograph of a vessel.

n–257 **water** A variant of WATER 57.

n–295 **humility** From a pictograph of a bent-over body.

n–297 **all** Convoluted etymology, acc. to Henshall, meaning "all" in the sense of "bringing together," with the extension "examine."

n–336 **protect** Phonetic meaning. See also BASKET 130.

n–341 **leap** Phonetic meaning.

n–344 **group** Phonetic meaning.

n–347 **hand** Variant of HOLDING 597.

n–350 **play** Phonetic meaning.

n–351 **stomach** As a stand-alone character, this has the reading *I*.

n–359 **dragon** Old style of DRAGON 358.

n–366 **tower** A variant of TALL 1150, which comes from a pictograph of a tower.

n–371 **what?** As a stand-alone character, this has the readings *KA, nani, nan*.

n–373 **hand** A variant of HAND 600.

n–374 **fallen person** From a pictograph of a fallen or seated person.

n–375 **order** Phonetic meaning of "put in order."

n–384 **use** Possibly a variant of USE 385. Convoluted etymology acc. to Henshall.

n–387 **flag** From a pictograph of a flag fluttering.

n–387 **device** Obscure. Acc. to Henshall, it is from a picture of a winnowing mechanism for cleaning grain.

n–417 **hand w/stick** A variant of HOLDING 597.

n–418 **elbow** From a pictograph of an elbow.

n–420 **big** Henshall has an interesting discussion about whether the element here means "big" or "bed."

n–422 **depend** From a Chinese meaning of "depend on." Note similarity to BE IN DIFFICULTY 786.

n–449 **breast** This element's shape suggests a woman's breast. See n-692, "kneeling figure."

n–478 **lungs** Symbolizes a lung, with the element at right for "flesh" supporting the meaning.

n–483 **north** As a stand-alone character, this has the readings *HOKU, kita*.

n–494 **order** As a stand-alone character, this has the readings *REI, RYŌ*.

n–497 **necessarily** As a stand-alone character, this has the readings *HITSU, kanarazu*.

n–500 **pull apart** From a pictograph of an archer's hand pulling on a bow.

n–502 **crouch** From a pictograph of a crouching person.

n–514 **pierce** Depicts two objects pierced by a stake.

n–516 **progress** The element SLOW PROGRESS 1218.

n–542 **nose** Entire character comes from a pictograph of a nose.

n–546 **subject** As a stand-alone character, this has the readings *SHIN, JIN*.

n–546 **person** Acc. to Henshall, this represents a person bending over to stare at water in a bowl.

n–552 **singing** Phonetic meaning.

n–558 **sudden** Phonetic meaning.

n–562 **exhale** Symbolic meaning.

n–567 **hand** Think of this as REACH 373.

n–575 **squeeze** Think of this as two men back to back being squeezed from top and bottom.

n–589 **hand grasping** From a pictograph of a hand grasping an animal's tail.

n–596 **writing** From a pictograph of a hand holding a brush.

n–603 **hands w/rope** Comprises HAND REACHING DOWN 609, HAND REACHING UP 600, and a knotted rope.

n–607 **basket** From a pictograph of a basket.

n–621 **follow** From a pictograph of PERSON 363 doubled.

n–626 **announce** Phonetic meaning.

n–630 **prostitution** Graphically similar to a character meaning "sell."

n–649 **brain** From a pictograph of a brain. Imagine the X marking the brain enclosed in a skull topped with hair.

n–650 **vapors** From a pictograph. See STEAM 69.

n–650 **rice** A simplification of RICE 217.

n–652 **enclosed** A simplification of ENCLOSED 778.

n–664 **man on cliff** From a pictograph of a bent figure on a cliff.

n–677 **appropriate** Phonetic meaning.

n–692 **kneeling figure** From a pictograph of a kneeling person.

n–716 **bent figure** From a pictograph of a bent figure.

n–717 **official** As a stand-alone character, this has the reading IN.

n–718 **pierce** From a pictograph of money threaded on a string.

n–720 **burden** Phonetic meaning. It looks like WARRIOR 753 carrying a load.

n–725 **exchange** Acc. to Henshall, this is from a picture of a horse's bit, suggesting "change of direction."

n–731 **person** Of convoluted etymology

n–733 **give** Phonetic meaning.

n–742 **press** Phonetic meaning.

n–749 **shine** From a pictograph of FIRE 83 doubled.

n–750 **strive** Phonetic meaning.

n–754 **hands** From a pictograph of two hands wielding an ax, as a soldier does in battle.

n–761 **bean + inch** Convoluted etymology. Derives from a character meaning "hit."

n–768 **offer** Phonetic meaning.

n–769 **wet** Phonetic meaning. Obscure relation to endure.

n–773 **hold** Acc. to Henshall, from a pictograph of a child holding a toy.

n–780 **enclosures** The enclosed X is a simplification of what was originally three enclosed squares.

n–783 **surround** Phonetic meaning.

n–785 **dot** Acc. to Henshall, the dot was used to distinguish a pictograph of a string of beads from the similarly shaped character KING 743.

n–794 **me** Phonetic meaning.

n–809 **hemp** Acc. to Henshall, a simplification of plants.

n–820 **rounded** Phonetic meaning

n–822 **2 persons** Two persons, one fallen, the other crouched.

n–834 **man** From a pictograph of a man opening his mouth to brag. Evolved into meaning of "give."

n–840 **feelings** Phonetic meaning.

n–853 **administer** As a stand-alone character, this has the readings *SHI, tsukasadoru*.

n–863 **hands** From a pictograph of hands rolling rice. This is the kanji used in *temaki sushi*.

n–872 **dam** From a pictograph of a dam; borrowed meanings lead to "exist."

n–878 **circumference** As a stand-alone character, this has the readings *SHŪ, mawari*.

n–881 **thread** Borrowed meaning from graphically similar character meaning occult.

n–881 **illusion** Unclear origin and meaning.

n–882 **drum** From a pictograph of a tasseled drum.

n–888 **flat** Phonetic meaning.

n–895 **seek out** Phonetic meaning.

n–914 **two** A simplification of TWO 898 to suggest twice as big and fat.

n–925 **little dot** Whole character was once written as four little dots.

n–935 **liquid** A variant of WATER 57.

n–936 **ray** Acc. to Henshall, the entire character derived from a picture of a pointed thumbnail. It is easier to think of this top element as a "ray."

n–946 **dry up** Phonetic meaning.

n–957 **turn over** Phonetic meaning.

n–972 **leek** Convoluted etymology acc. to Henshall.

n–979 **twist** Phonetic meaning.

n–982 **broom** From a pictograph of a broom. Often shown with a hand as in BROOM 1052.

n–1002 **needle + buttocks** A combination of SHARP 1005 and BUTTOCKS 466.

n–1009 **weave** From a pictograph of interwoven sticks.

n–1012 **wind** Actually a stand-alone character (*BON, HAN, oyoso*) meaning "mediocre," but used here as a simplification of WIND 44.

n–1019 **hand w/tool** From a pictograph of a hand with a tool.

n–1020 **seize** Graphically identical to entry n-1019, but this element comes from a pictograph of a hand seizing a bent-over figure.

n–1027 **thorn** This combines a tree with a pointed element to suggest "thorn."

n–1028 **pig** A variant of PIG 279.

n–1032 **bone** A variant of VERTEBRA 474.

n–1036 **shears** From a pictograph of shears.

n–1039 **utensil** From a pictograph of a pair of hands holding up a kettle; came to mean "equipment."

n–1049 **follow** A very simiplified variant of CHASE 1172.

n–1058 **adze** From a pictograph of an adze.

n–1065 **exact** A variant of BLOCK 1089.

n–1096 **origin** As a stand-alone character, this has the readings *GEN, GAN, moto.*

n–1099 **mound** From a pictograph of mounds of earth.

n–1104 **hands** From a pictograph of two hands reaching to open the gate.

n–1110 **bar** Phonetic meaning.

n–1123 **walk** From an old character meaning "walk." Includes SLOW PROGRESS 1218.

n–1128 **fence** Phonetic meaning.

n–1131 **joined blocks** Symbolic meaning suggesting, acc. to Henshall, "connected rooms."

n–1133 **open up** Phonetic meaning.

n–1135 **arrow** The whole character comes from a pictograph of an arrow reaching its destination.

n–1150 **tower** From a pictograph of a tower.

n–1152 **castle** From a pictograph of a castle.

n–1158 **fast** Phonetic meaning.

n–1169 **multitude** As a stand-alone character, this has the reading *SHO.*

n–1175 **big** An inversion of BIG 913.

n–1220 **east** From a doubling of EAST 91.

n–1223 **bending person** From a pictograph of a person bending to greet someone.